OZ CLARKE'S

STORY OF WINE

OZ CLARKE'S

STORY OF WINE

8000 YEARS,
100 BOTTLES

PAVILION

First published in the United Kingdom in 2015 by Pavilion

This edition published in 2023 by Pavilion

An imprint of HarperCollins*Publishers* Ltd

1 London Bridge Street

London SE1 9GF

www.harpercollins.co.uk

HarperCollins*Publishers*

Macken House

39/40 Mayor Street Upper

Dublin 1

D01 C9W8

Ireland

10 9 8 7 6 5 4 3 2 1

First published in Great Britain as The History of Wine in 100 Bottles by Pavilion

An imprint of HarperCollins*Publishers* 2023

Copyright © Pavilion 2015, 2023

Text © Oz Clarke 2015, 2023

Oz Clarke asserts the moral rights to be identified as the author of this work.

A catalogue record for this book is available from the British Library.

ISBN 978-0-00-862149-0

This book is produced from independently certified FSC™ paper to ensure responsible forest management. For more information visit: www.harpercollins.co.uk/green

Publishing Director: Stephanie Milner

Commissioning Editor: Kiron Gill

Project Editor: Fiona Holman

Design Director: Laura Russell

Designer: James Boast

Senior Production Controller: Grace O'Byrne

Cover designer: Bess Daly

Printed and bound by PNB Print, Latvia

Follow Oz on Twitter @OzClarke

FOR SOPHIA, WITH LOVE.

HER FIRST BOOK.

CONTENTS

LE VIN

Phylloxera

Raisin

Panier de raisin

Hotte à raisin

Cannelle

Pièce de vin

Tire-bouchons

Panier de bouteilles

Foret

Verre

Carafe

Bouteille

INTRODUCTION

What should the story of wine be all about? The flavours of the wines? Of course. If we know what they're like, that is. Some of the flavours are brand new, some are old as time. Some we can experience tonight. Some haven't been experienced for a thousand years. But they're all relevant to our story. From the beginning of wine time to now, flavours have come, flavours have gone, some flavours have come again, and they're all part of this story.

And the bottle, the decanter, the glass? These are all part of wine's history. To begin with, they didn't exist. When wine began, glass didn't exist. So the invention of glass, the improvements made in glass, both as an artistic delight and as a reliable receptacle – these are crucial to our story. The bottle, which nowadays seems so integral to a part of wine, is really quite recent. Hollow glass vessels may have been crafted as long ago as 1500 BC. But bottles with necks and with corks to put in them only really became commonplace in the 17th century. They're both important to our story.

Since the 17th century, the bottle, stoppered with its cork, has almost been the visual definition of wine. Along with its label, of course. But labels didn't really figure until the 1860s, since when they rapidly became the most important way to declare what was in the bottle. They also became the most effective method of advertising and marketing. And this remains so to this day. The label is as important a part of our story as the flavour of the wine is.

And if the flavour, the bottle and the label are so important – what about more rarefied matters? The myths of wine, the legends of wine, the rituals of wine, the importance of wine in religious life, in political life, in trade – all of these are exciting parts of the story, and I talk about them all. I haven't even mentioned the vineyards, and with them the magic and the mystique of foreign lands and intriguing, seductive cultures whose images inhabit the dreams of so many wine lovers, especially those living in cold, northern climes, whose minds drift longingly towards the warm south in their drab winter months. The wines from these vineyards used to come from a mere handful of countries, mostly Western European. Not any more.

At the end of the 20th century, a worldwide wine revolution was led by so-called 'New World' producers. Some, like California and Australia, had been growing grapes and making wine since the early 19th century. Some, like South America and South Africa, had been at it for even longer. And some, like New Zealand's South Island, were starting from scratch. But they threw themselves into this crazy activity of trying to make wines whose whole objective was to give pleasure to the wine drinker.

Haven't wine producers always done that? No, they haven't. Sometimes because they didn't care to, but just as often because they didn't know how. The New World taught the Old World how. And then the Old World returned the compliment by slowly revealing the secrets that made their best wines the best wines in the world. These are wonderful stories, and I tell them all, right up to what is happening today.

What is happening today is very challenging. Climate change is shoving aside the old certainties of centuries. Wineries are being swept away by fire. Whole wine regions are being crippled by frost and hail, drought and flood. These stories must be told, but also the stories of hope. Of how climate change is encouraging people to grow vines in more and more extreme and unlikely places – further north, further south, higher, lower. Extreme parts of China, the chilly slopes of northern Japan, Tasmania in Australia, Patagonia in South America, states like Virginia and New York in the USA are all producing wines where the old timers said it wasn't possible.

And whole countries who never even took their own puny efforts seriously are now triumphantly proving that they can make wines that range from the interesting to the outstanding. The Low Countries and Scandinavia in Europe, Canada in the Americas, and, perhaps most of all, England in all its maritime glory, wedged between the Atlantic and the North Sea. All of these stories make up the thrilling history of wine.

And in between, there are fascinating oddball stories – of France's First World War 'Blood Vintages', of Nazi wine, of the birth of Liebfraumilch and Mateus Rose and Gallo's Hearty Burgundy – these are all important. Beaujolais Nouveau is important, White Zinfandel is important. Synthetic corks and screwcaps and bag-in-box are as important to many wine drinkers as the 1855 Classification of Bordeaux, the effect on wine's character of uber critic Robert Parker and uber consultant Michel Rolland, the births of Burgundy and Tokaji, Rioja, vintage port, sherry and champagne. I tell the story of them all.

If I count up the number of stories, going from 6000 BC and the probable birth of a wine culture in ancient Georgia, through the fact and fiction of Persia, Egypt, Greece and Rome and then on along the fascinating cluttered trail right up to the trends and tribulations of now – I tell, well, over a hundred stories, and woven into these tales are probably a hundred more. And I use endless illustrations to add colour and excitement to the stories, and to make your mouths water, and your eyes mist over with imagining – and your hand reach for the bottle – or the can, or the laminated pouch – of wine.

These stories are told to make wine more alive, to bring wine's wonders closer to you, and also to make you think, to ask you to ponder wine's past – where it comes from; wine's present – where it is now; and wine's future – where it is going. Wine's past was both good and bad. Wine's present is more good than bad. What will wine's future be?

The Georgians used to line their 9000-litre earthenware jars with beeswax, fill them with crushed grapes, bury them and leave them until ready. Traditionalists still use exactly the same methods.

6000 BC
WHERE DID IT ALL START?

It would be nice to be able to say where winemaking started, but it's a movable feast. For a long time, no one seemed to care too much about what happened before the Greeks and Romans, but in the last decade there has been a rising tide of interest in the Transcaucasus – in Georgia, Armenia and Azerbaijan – and also in Turkey's Southern Anatolia and the Zagros mountains of Iran.

So if I choose Georgia as my starting point, it's just that of all the potential candidates, Georgia has preserved and cherished a wine culture more closely linked to its past than any of the other countries. It certainly makes wines whose tastes are completely, utterly removed from the experience of any normal modern wine drinker. And it uses methods of winemaking that you couldn't invent in a modern world; you could only inherit them through the mists of time, maybe as far back as human records go. I've tasted a fair few now. Some have made me give thanks for the progress of science over the past 8000 years. But some have stopped me in my tracks, made me metaphorically throw down my notebook, scour my mind free of preconception, and wallow in amazement that after so many years of winetasting something entirely new and thrilling can still stun me. Here's just one example. It's a 2011 from the white Kisi grape. I'd never heard of it before. The wine – stems, skins, everything – spent six months in a submerged clay jar before emerging bright orange, smelling of chamomile, straw and peaches, tasting as chewy as any red; earthy, as though they should have washed the grapes first; bitter as tarpaulin, zesty as orange peel, rich as dried figs. And would I want a second glass? Absolutely, yes I would. Wouldn't you want a second glass of something as close to the wine style of 8000 years ago as you could get?

So what is this wine style? Well, firstly Georgia could be seen to be the crucible from which many of Europe's modern wine grape varieties emerged.

Certainly winemaking evidence has been found in Georgia dating way back into the sixth millennium BC. And how would they have made this wine? Georgians would hollow out a tree trunk, fill it with grapes, tread them, and then tip the juice, skins, pips and even stems into a big beeswax-lined clay jar called a *qvevri*. They would then seal it and leave the whole grape soup to ferment, for six months, or a year, before cracking it open and drinking it. Is that how they did it? That's how they do it *now*, in the villages and small towns of Georgia. And if they weren't the first to make wine, perhaps they were the first to give wine a name. The Georgians call wine *gvino* and the vintage month of October *Gvinobistve* – the month of wine. Where did the Greeks get *oenos* from? The Italians *vino*? The French *vin*? The English 'wine'?

The moment of truth. The lid's taken off the kvevri and in goes the ladle. Fill the decanter. Celebrate a tradition going back 8000 years.

C. 2350 BC
WINE IN LEGEND AND MYTH

Since drinkers love to spin tales, it's not surprising that there are a fair few legends about the discovery of wine and the planting of vineyards, which may – or may not – have an element of truth about them.

But they certainly have an element of plausibility, especially since the most ancient tales do imply that no one invented wine, it just happened one joyful day. After all, wild vines had been growing across great swathes of the world for millennia beyond count. Yeasts would have been sitting on their grape skins for at least as long. It was only a question of time before there was a lucky accident, and wine, as if by magic – or, if you wish, by divine intervention – occurred.

The most famous story comes from ancient Persia (Iran today) and concerns King Jamshid, one of the heroic figures of Persian mythology. Jamshid liked eating grapes throughout the year, and his servants would carefully store grapes in jars for him to eat out of season. Obviously one jar hadn't been packed carefully enough, because the grapes had split and out had seeped the juice, which then fermented.

Whoever opened that jar must have got a hell of a shock as the alcohol fumes and the sweet-sour pong of fermentation wafted up. Yuck. Probably poisonous, maybe some devious magical trick. Whatever. The jar was marked poison and put to one side. But a member of Jamshid's harem had noticed this jar of 'poison'. She was at her wit's end with 'nervous headaches', and decided to put an end to it by drinking the poison. The story goes that she was overcome and fell asleep, then awoke miraculously refreshed and cured of her headaches. I'd have thought she'd have a skull-splitter.

The story doesn't relate that the night before she got very high-spirited, starting singing lewd football songs, and had to be restrained from ripping her kit off and dancing on the kitchen table. But she obviously liked this 'poison' because she went back and finished off the jar. Attagirl!

After which Jamshid took over, ordered more grapes to be given the 'poison' treatment, and declared wine a sacred medicine. He presumably couldn't wait to give it a go himself. Well, this seems entirely likely to me. And it's actually possible that the wine tasted quite good because they might have dried the grapes into raisins to preserve them through the winter, and so the 'poison' could have been rather rich and exotic.

Now, Jamshid was Persian. A bit further south, in Mesopotamia, the Babylonian *Epic of Gilgamesh* has Enkidu, a 'wild man of the woods', being given his first glass of wine. 'He drank seven times. His thoughts wandered. He became hilarious. His heart was full of joy and his face shone.' Sounds pretty familiar to me.

We've all been there. It's possible this was date wine. But it could have been raisin wine. And the vines could have been wild. Or they could have been cultivated.

The Bible gives us the story of the first vineyard owner – Noah. In the Book of Genesis, pretty much the first thing Noah did after the great flood waters subsided, around 2350 BC, was to plant a vineyard. He also got drunk the first time he tried his wine – men never change. But the area where legend has it that Noah's ark finally came to rest is around Mount Ararat, in the Caucasus mountains, on the Turkish–Armenian border. Well, it's not just legend but sound archaeological evidence which tells us that either this region, or just a little further north, in Georgia, is where the first wineries probably were set up, and where mankind began to cultivate and civilise the wild vines whose grapes he might have been feasting off for a million years and more.

JAMSHEED

A fantastic Australian red wine named after the Persian king Jamshid (also called Jamsheed).

2000-146 BC
GREECE

It's not so much that we would swoon over the flavours of ancient Greek wine – there's every reason to believe that we wouldn't – but Greece is important partly because it's really the first society whose wine-drinking we can relate to. Even quite ordinary people sometimes got a slug of it, and Greek writers have been translated into readable English for centuries.

Greece is also the stepping-off point for the spread of wine and the vine through Europe. The Romans may be more famous for establishing vineyards in places like Spain, France, Germany and even England, but who got the Romans going? The Greeks. And they also had a wine god who sounded like a lot of fun, Dionysus. He didn't start out as a wine god – vegetation and fertility were his first responsibilities, but you can sort of see how that could eventually lead to wine: vegetation, the vine, grapes, wine, parties, loss of self-control, fertility issues. But, hang on. How did wine and divinity get tangled up? Well, the thing about wine was that no one knew how or why fermentation happened. Magic? Divine intervention? And if you drank the wine, your spirits were transformed, your inhibitions vanished. Was that the effect of the divine creation of wine? Or was the god of wine actually *in* the wine? Were we drinking a god? To the ancient Greeks, perhaps we were.

It's an important point, because the Greeks were not, in general, heavy drinkers. And when they did drink, they often diluted their wine significantly. The poet Hesiod drank his at three parts water, one part wine. Homer's tipple was 20 parts water to one of wine – keeping his head clear to finish the *Iliad* on time. Getting drunk was not a typical Greek activity. *Except* when they were involved in the quasi-religious business of worshipping Dionysus, God of Wine.

Understandably, Dionysus became one of the Greeks' most popular gods, and the regular Dionysian festivals became more and more rowdy, so the authorities nationalised them, thereby neutering their subversive nature. Politics 101.

Indeed, it was a Greek poet, Eubulus, who first set out a kind of drinkers' route map that still makes sense. He wrote: 'Three bowls do I mix for the temperate: one to health, which they empty first, the second to love and pleasure, the third to sleep. When this bowl is drunk up, wise guests go home. The fourth bowl is ours no longer, but belongs to violence, the fifth to uproar, the sixth to drunken revel, the seventh to black eyes, the eighth is the policeman's, the ninth belongs to biliousness, and the tenth to madness and hurling the furniture.' Ah yes, that brings my student Saturday nights right back.

Sweetness was the quality most sought after in ancient wines. Greek wines could be divided into two styles: early picked – thin, raw, quick to go sour – drunk by hoi polloi; and sweet wines made from fully ripe grapes that were laid on frames in the sun and covered with reeds until they shrivelled and intensified their sugar. They were then added to a clay jar of sweet grape juice for a week before being pressed and fermented.

The resulting wine was sweet and could age, but it was the Romans who took this concept to the next level.

And how did the Romans get the idea? Well, the Greeks settled in southern Italy, and brought their vines with them. The base of the Italian peninsula was called Greater Greece; and Syracuse in Sicily was at one time the biggest of all Greek cities. The Greeks also took wines and vines as far afield as southern France, North Africa and western Russia. But it was the Romans who did the hard yards of establishing Western Europe's vineyards.

1480–1300 BC
EGYPT

Tombs. They're not the first place you'd look to find out about a nation's drinking culture. But Egypt's tombs weren't your normal six-foot-under jobs. For kings and high officials, tombs were decorated with elaborate paintings and murals that are an archaeologist's dream.

The tombs were also filled with jars of wine. The most famous tomb of all is that of Tutankhamun (c. 1341–1323 BC), whose tomb held 36 jars of wine marked according to style, year, area of production and the name of the producer.

One example reads: 'Year Four. Wine of very good quality of the House of Aten on the Western River. Chief Vintner Kha'y.' That's fantastic – the vintage, the quality, which estate in which area, and the guy who made it. All we now need to know is what it tasted like, but we'd need a hotline to the afterlife to find out, because these jars of wine were never opened. Even so, this is the first example of a civilisation taking such pains about the provenance of a wine – you can almost feel the stirrings of an Appellation Contrôlée system on the Nile Delta.

Interestingly, it is the tombs of less exalted figures that give us the greatest insight into Egyptian wine, and they demonstrate that vineyard management and winery techniques were highly developed. Firstly, the western delta of the Nile was reckoned to be the best area for vines, with wine from Lake Mariout, hard by the Mediterranean, particularly praised. Most of the vines were grown on trellises, though later tombs show vines attached to poles or papyrus reeds for support. A mural in the tomb of Khaemwaset, from about 1480–1425 BC, has a particularly comprehensive view of the whole process. Grapes were grown on a high pergola – useful for providing shade and reducing evaporation in a hot country as well as making grape harvesting simple. Since the vines were growing in the silty delta, terraces of higher ground were built to provide less fertile, and less flood-prone, conditions.

The grapes were taken to the winery and put in a shallow trough and trodden. The treaders supported themselves with straps hanging from a pole – good thinking: it can get very slippery treading grapes.

The juice was then transferred to amphorae where it fermented, often quite furiously in the warm conditions, before the amphorae were sealed with clay, stamped with the details of the estate and the winemaker – and, in this case, transported down the Nile to what seems to be the guy's tomb. Other tomb murals show evidence of a wine press – the trodden grapes are put onto a big linen cloth hung like a hammock that is then literally wrung like a rudimentary mangle. This would also help filter the juice. There is also some evidence of wine being siphoned through pipes. And some pictures show vintners heating up the grape juice to boil into a very sweet grape syrup, a favourite activity of the Romans for sweetening wine. There are also pictures of women being sick and comatose men being carried out of feasts by their servants.

So, although wine-drinking was very much an upper-class activity in ancient Egypt – the everyday drink was beer – the Egyptians set down a lot of the principles that the Greeks and Romans followed. And of particular importance is their development of amphorae – the tall earthenware jars whose pointed bottoms could be buried in sand and so transported without breaking, and whose narrow necks were easily sealed to prevent air from attacking the wine.

In an attempt to solve the endless question of – yes, but what did it taste like? – an Egyptian called Nestor Gianaclis, in 1903, reckoned he'd found the old vineyard soils hidden under desert sands; they were chalky and seemed entirely suitable. He planted over 70 grape varieties over the next 30 years, but never came up with a wine that most self-respecting Pharaohs would want to take with them to the afterlife.

Above: The tomb of Khaemwaset, from about 1480–1425 BC, shows vine pergolas and wines fermenting in amphorae. Below: The tomb of Nakht (c. 1400 BC) shows a trough being used for treading grapes; the Romans adopted this method.

*A Phoenician amphora recovered from a shipwreck off the coast of Cyprus,
with the owner's and the wine inspector's names inscribed.*

PHOENICIA

The Phoenicians are best known for being the first of the nations whose objective in life was not to go round conquering people through rapine, pillage and slaughter, but rather to quietly offer the chance for peaceful, almost defiantly non-violent trading relationships.

One particular method of trade that they developed as they carefully picked their way along the north African coast was called 'dumb-trading'. The Phoenicians would land on a beach and leave a variety of goods that they wished to trade. Then they would retreat and wait. The local tribes be they Nubians, Berbers or whatever, would come down to the beach and place some gold by the goods. The Phoenicians would return, and if there was enough gold, they'd take it and head off. If there wasn't enough gold, they'd withdraw again and allow the locals to add a bit more. And they never got into fights, because they hardly ever came face to face with their trading partners. Non-violent trade at its most sublime.

The Phoenicians are also important because they, among one or two other candidates like the Syrians and the Egyptians, just might be credited with inventing the glass – the vessel from which to drink wine, though not, as yet, the bottle. There is some evidence of glass being made in the Bronze Age in Egypt and Mesopotamia, and certainly archaeologists think that hollow glass vessels were being made around 1500 BC, but the technique then got lost, only to re-emerge in the 8th century BC in the same region, as well as in nearby Phoenicia, situated mainly in what is now the small fertile enclave of Lebanon.

This wasn't a glass*blowing* technique – that came later. The Phoenician discovery, or rediscovery, entailed dipping a bag of sand into molten glass, moulding the shape of the glass by rolling it along a flat stone surface and then, when the glass had cooled, emptying out the sand – and you had a drinking vessel. The idea of blowing glass also originates in the area – maybe Syria, maybe Phoenicia – in about the 1st century BC, whence it took off, on the back of the Roman Empire's expansion, all over Europe.

By the 1st century BC, Phoenician power had faded away, but their influence is still with us, because they invented the written alphabet – as a writer it would be churlish of me not to say 'thank you' – then promptly gave it to the Greeks. But it is as traders and explorers that the Phoenicians are now largely remembered. If you look at their position on the Mediterranean coast, it's absolutely made for trading, situated between powerful civilisations to the south, east and north.

They established trading ports or colonies all around the Mediterranean, on the North African coast, and in southern Spain and Portugal, establishing the great city civilisation of Carthage (modern-day Tunis) as well as Cádiz at the mouth of Spain's Guadalquivir River. It is distinctly possible that it was Phoenician traders coming down from Ancient Persia with vine cuttings – the wine-producing city of Shiraz was one of their favourite sources – who introduced vine varieties to Europe, via Cyprus and Greece; varieties that are the forerunners of many modern white varieties in particular.

And they were also great vinegrowers and winemakers themselves. The wine of Byblos, a northern Phoenician town, was famous in Greece. The typical pattern of trade was to sell wine to the locals, get them fond of it, then establish vineyards to facilitate a cheaper and more profitable supply. The Romans were desperately jealous of their vineyard skills, causing Cato to demand, 'Carthage must be destroyed.' The Phoenicians famously didn't like to sail out of sight of land, and only hopped over to Spain and Portugal because of the narrowness of the Strait of Gibraltar. They pioneered right up the Douro and Tagus rivers in Portugal and the Guadalquivir and Ebro in Spain.

On the Ebro they got as far as Rioja, so when the Romans arrived there was a thriving little wine culture just waiting to be developed.

300 BC–AD 200
ROME

What have the Romans ever done for us? Well, by the time the Roman Empire collapsed in the 5th century AD, they'd pretty much set in place everything we now regard as normal for professional wine production.

Obviously they didn't have modern machinery, but as they were such prolific writers we can get a fair picture of what the world of wine was like in Roman times. They got the idea of wine from the Greeks, who had colonised the southern part of Italy to such an extent that it was called 'Greater Greece'. But Greece's last grand hurrah was in the 4th century BC when Alexander the Great created his vast empire. By the middle of the 1st century BC, Greek power was just a memory, and the new, hard-nosed Romans were taking their place.

And they did have an awful lot of wine writers. Everyone seemed to put their oar in – Cato, Horace, Virgil, Ovid, Pliny, Galen. They were all trying to tell us the best way to run a vineyard and make wine, and how to drink it. Horace tells us how wine improves with age; Virgil tells us about the virtues of late-harvesting the grapes and how to install drainage in damp vineyards. But it was Cato and a guy called Columella who really created primers for the winemaker. Cato set down the rules for efficient, large-scale wine estates, whereas Columella described methods of pruning and trellising, yield, harvesting dates and the like that still resonate today. His method of staked vines is still used in the northern Rhone and Mosel in Germany. Pliny actually classified the wines into different ranks, and he was also the first person to begin to categorise grape varieties. He reckoned there were 80 good varieties in Italy and some of them may still exist. Greco di Tufo is a wine made near Naples from the Greco grape that locals believe is one of the ancient Roman varieties. Fiano might be another, as might Piedirosso ('red-stalked'), which is still grown near Mount Vesuvius.

Modern dry table wines bear no resemblance to Roman wine, but some of the Romans' winemaking methods might have a few modern parallels. They used to seek a heavily oxidised, sweet style and achieved this in a similar way to traditional Vin Santo, still made in Tuscany. Amphorae of wine were left open to the air, mixed with boiled grape juice, then left to sit in the sun 'not more than four years'. The Romans also made use of the *fumarium*, a loft over a smoke room, so that the wine was heated, smoked, oxidised and pasteurised, all at once – just as Madeira is today. The most famous Roman wine, a Falernian wine from near Naples, made in 121 BC, is known as the Opimian vintage. It was still being drunk over 100 years later, but most tasting notes don't mention its flavour and are more concerned with the fact that it would burst into flames if you lit it.

These traditional styles were doomed by the Romans' empire-building. The armies took vines with them and established vineyards in Spain: in Catalonia, the Duero Valley and what is now Rioja. They established vines in the Danube, the Rhine and Mosel. But above all they established vines right across southern France, up the Rhône Valley, in Burgundy, in the Loire, in Champagne and in Bordeaux.

If you're wondering what the Romans ever did for us – apart from building roads that were straight – establishing the classic vineyards of Spain, Germany and France isn't a bad start.

A 3rd-century AD mosaic from Roman Spain showing vintagers treading grapes in a shallow trough or lagar. *Some Spanish vineyards still use them.*

AD 77-79
RESIN AND ALL THAT

If we're going to get lost in a dream world about what the Neolithic wines of Georgia and the Transcaucasus tasted like, if we fantasise about the heady beauty of the wines of ancient Greece, if we imagine ourselves supping nectar with the emperors of classical Rome, we're going to have to get used to one thing right away.

They probably all tasted of pine resin. Now, let me declare an interest. I like the taste of pine resin, and when I can find a good example of modern Greek retsina with the intoxicating resinous scent of pine, I'm thrilled. But I don't think there'd be an awful lot of similarity between modern retsina and the wines made in ancient times.

The thing is, nowadays we know how to keep wine fresh, to stop it turning to vinegar. In classical times, this was a major challenge. Wine will automatically start turning to vinegar unless you can find a way to protect it. Nowadays we use sulphur as an antioxidant, we use stainless steel tanks and glass bottles with hermetic seals. The ancients didn't enjoy any of these luxuries. What they *had* worked out was that the resin of the terebinth pine seemed to protect against disease. Doctors of that time used the resin to help heal human wounds, so it seemed to have antibacterial qualities. If you smeared the inside of your wine containers with resin, this might help the wine stave off its inevitable decline into vinegar, and, frankly, if the resulting drinks tasted strongly of pine resin, but not of vinegar, well, a chap could get used to it. And for hundreds of years, they did get used to it. Pliny was a particular 'resin snob'. He thought the best pitch (that's boiled resin) came from Calabria in southern Italy, while the best pure resin came from Cyprus. In his *Natural History* (AD 77–79), he described it as having the colour of honey with a fleshy consistency. He particularly liked the way little fragments of it stuck to his teeth 'with an agreeably tart taste'.

But Pliny was Roman. The Greeks came first. And despite Greek retsina being the only modern wine that is purposely flavoured with resin, the ancient Greeks weren't so keen. With the exception of the members of the Dionysian religious cult, they weren't even heavy drinkers and preferred their wine sweet if possible, and old if possible. Sweet, high-alcohol wines made from grapes picked late and then shrivelled and concentrated by laying them on mats under a blazing sky, have a natural protection – alcohol – against turning to vinegar. Even so, very few wines were drunk pure and unblended. Such additives as honey, powdered marble and potter's earth were commonly used to 'invigorate' the wine – though I'm not sure how. Salt water rather than sweet, fresh water was used to dilute the wine by as much as 20 times. As I said, most Greeks weren't heavy drinkers.

With the Romans, it was a bit different. For a start, they really liked the taste of resin added to their wine. That's if they could afford it. The basic drink of the Romans was *posca*, a mixture of thin sour wines – or vinegar, depending on how you looked at it. But mix this with three or four parts water and it could be passably refreshing. This was what Jesus was offered on the cross. The Roman soldiers were probably being kind. But sweetness was what the Roman epicures desired. The main wine drunk at banquets was called *mulsum* and was a mix of wine and honey.

Clearly the ancient Romans had a sweet tooth, and if you check out their cuisine – dominated by pungent, savoury flavours like fermented fish sauce and the nauseous asafoetida, which were sweetened up by fruits, honey and wine of every sort – you can see the need for a sweet accompaniment. They would pick their grapes as late as possible, and boil some of the grape juice to make it thick and intensely sweet to add to the basic wine. And they'd then add all kinds of extra flavours – saffron, pepper, violet, mint, rose petals, even the bitter herb wormwood. Just for the flavour? Well, partly, but partly as preservatives. And then they'd take some seawater, from well off shore and on a calm day – they weren't stupid – and dilute the concoction with that. Why? Tastes change. They used to eat dormice.

AD 79

POMPEII

When the top was blown off Mount Vesuvius by an almighty eruption on 24 August, AD 79, lava poured down towards the sea, ash clouds rose miles in the sky and then drifted downwards like a morbid cloak set on stifling life. Rocks and cinders showered the land for miles around and convulsions shook the earth.

Standing in the way of all this was Pompeii. The destruction of Pompeii and the consequent archaeological efforts that have revealed a town petrified in a moment in time are some of ancient Rome's most vivid images. Anything alive in the town was struck dead and the virtually mummified human remains do sometimes look as though a person was caught right in the middle of some mundane activity and, without time even to rub their eyes in disbelief, that final second of their life was caught for ever. But there is a further reason why we should be fascinated by Pompeii. It was Rome's main wine port. When Pompeii was destroyed, it was as if, in present time, Bordeaux had been obliterated by a massive earthquake – except that in Pompeii things weren't destroyed, they were preserved.

In wine terms, Pompeii was several things. It was a major port, specialising in profitably shipping the local wines of Campania, not only to Rome but also to other destinations as far away as Spain and even Bordeaux on France's Atlantic coast. Because of the mellow climate surrounding the bay, the slopes above Pompeii were dotted not only with working farms but also with villas where the wealthy wine people took their leisure.

This idea of a vineyard not run for profit and a villa to show off your wealth may have been a new idea in AD 79, but 17 or so centuries later, that is exactly what the grandees of Bordeaux were doing as they built their châteaux and spread their estates up the Medoc peninsula.

So Pompeii was about trade, about vineyard estates and ostentatious villas, and it was also about drinking. Around 120 bars

*A store of Pompeiian amphorae. These would
have been stacked behind the bar, full of wine.*

have been excavated and identified. And the Vesuvian eruption has frozen all these activities in time, giving us a fascinating insight into the bibulous habits of 1st-century Romans.

Firstly, the amphorae. These were used for export and for serving wine. Some of them were found behind bars, being used like a draught beer barrel might be today, and some of them were ready for export. Pompeiian merchants would put a stamp on the top of the amphora's handle and examples bearing identifiable Pompeii stamps have been found as far away as Spain and western France. These would have been loaded on ships, as many as two or three thousand at a time. It wasn't perfect. Amphorae are a bit fragile. An awful lot got broken. But they were fine in bars, usually stacked at the back, while fat jars called *dolia* were sunk into slabs of crazy paving serving as tables, and they'd be full of local wine and snacks like olives and pickled vegetables, or sometimes you'd find a stove beneath the jar to heat water – in winter the Romans were partial to wine mixed with hot water.

These bars were probably rowdy drinking joints. The villas in the hills had far more sophisticated outdoor dining rooms called *triclinia*, because Pompeii had pretty mild weather all year round. On three sides raised stone slabs sloped upwards to the centre, where food and drink was piled on a table; spare amphorae of wine would stand in the room's corner; and diners would literally lounge on cushions up towards the table, sprawled languidly and able to pick to their hearts' and stomachs' content from the goodies on offer. And the bars and dining rooms are so well preserved you can taste the wine, smell the food and hear the gossip even now.

AD 100
ROME PASSING THE BATON

As the Romans expanded their empire, they established vineyards wherever they could, laying down rules that are today accepted as absolutely classic.

Follow the river valleys. Find sheltered but open slopes. Don't plant too low down because of frost.

Don't plant too high because of wind and lack of heat. Choose the middle of the slopes, angled towards the morning or the evening sun. Don't plant on fertile soil – the vine will be too productive, and in any case you need fertile soil for food. Trellis and prune the vine to restrict its yield – the flavours will be much better, and, as you head north, it's only by restricting the yield that you will be able to ripen the grapes at all. And make sure you are close to transport – which, in the years of the 1st century AD, meant in almost every case a navigable river or a port. If you look at a map of the vineyards the Romans established at this time, they'd already chosen most of the best bits of the Rhône, of Burgundy, the Loire, Champagne, the Rhine and Mosel – and even southern England.

Yet if you look at a map of Roman Italy in the 1st century, virtually none of the vineyards regarded today as Italy's greatest sites are given much respect, if they're even marked. Nowadays it is the centre and north of Italy that are supposed to make the finest wines. When the Romans ruled, all the most revered vineyards were towards the south. The quality hotspot was south of Rome and especially around Naples, with some long-established stars in Sicily too. One reason is the oldest one in the book – vineyards are first planted next to the centres of population, even if the conditions are poor, because transportation is a nightmare. This would explain the cluster of vineyards on the Sicilian east coast next to the big cities of Syracuse, Catania and Messina. It would explain the vineyards of Naples – a big coastal city. It would explain the cluster around Rome, though opinion varied as to whether these wines were much good.

This 1st-century treasure is shown at almost twice its actual size. In fact, these glass amphoriskos *jugs were tiny – about 10 centimetres high and less than 5 centimetres across – hardly more than a big, thirsty mouthful.*

It was a mark of Roman society that no two writers seemed to be able to agree on what wines were best. The most fabled wines came from round Naples which was also fine – a big city, but also a coastal city, able to ship wines north to Rome with ease. But Florence, Bologna, Venice, Verona, Milan and Torino? These are all cities now served by famous vineyards and wine styles. Where were they then? It's probably to do with taste. At the end of the 1st century, we are on the cusp of a whole new style of wines taking over as the standard bearer of taste – lighter, thinner, less alcoholic, much more appetising, epitomised by the French classics.

With the collapse of the Roman Empire, and the ensuing Dark Ages, it is these new classics that managed to survive and re-emerge, while the classics of Rome and Naples and Sicily sank into mediocrity or oblivion, with just a few sparks of greatness kept alive around Naples. But remember the Roman lifestyle and cuisine – they needed their rich, spiced, frequently adulterated wines to cope with the amazingly powerful sweet-sour, fetid flavours of their favoured foods. Yet as cuisines developed in the far-off provinces, they used local provisions, local herbs and, if there were any, local traditions. And the wines developed in remarkable empathy with the dishes they accompanied. The great wine growths of Roman Italy were passing into folklore and history along with its startling cuisine, and the new leader of European wine was awakening just across the Alps and towards the Atlantic.

1100S-1200S
MONASTERIES - CLOS DE VOUGEOT

The easy way to look at the Dark Ages is to think of it as a period of unremitting gloom and slaughter and the loss of all the finer things in life, with the flickering flame of culture being kept alive in the silent halls of Europe's monasteries. And the preservation of a wine tradition brought to the rest of Europe by the Romans is central to this.

CLOS DE VOUGEOT
GRAND CRU
APPELLATION CLOS DE VOUGEOT GRAND CRU CONTRÔLÉE

MIS EN BOUTEILLE AU DOMAINE
CHATEAU DE MARSANNAY
PROPRIÉTAIRE, RÉCOLTANT À MARSANNAY, CÔTE D'OR, FRANCE

Well, there's no doubt that a mix of bishops and monasteries did play an important role in keeping wine going until the Middle Ages, but there's also quite serious evidence that the marauding tribes who kicked out the Romans were pretty keen on wine and were also keen to keep the supply of it healthy.

Burgundy is thought to be the birthplace of the great tradition tying wine to monasteries, but Germany got there first. The first monastery was probably founded in the 4th century at Trier, a city whose impressive, steeply angled vineyards had been established by the Romans in the 2nd century, high above the river Mosel. And the city's rulers, the Prince Bishops, supported vineyards and winemaking for the next few hundred years.

And this was not just through preservation of their own vineyards. The bishops had the power to promise salvation and eternal life. Lots of noblemen thought a gift of good vineyards would help towards this goal. And the view that the Church had to create and work its own vineyards to produce wine for the Eucharist is only partly true – tithes in wine were common, as were simple gifts.

The walled vineyard of Clos de Vougeot has more than 80 different proprietors, the result of the French inheritance laws set out in the Napoleonic Code. Since everything must be divided equally between heirs, some plots are now just a few rows of vines.

The importance of the monasteries stems from the Middle Ages. The Benedictines were the first great order to influence the world of wine. The Cistercians were the next. Both of them had their greatest abbeys in Burgundy: the Benedictines at Cluny in the hills behind Macon, and the Cistercian order at Cîteaux in the dark forests opposite Nuits-Saint-Georges. The Benedictines rather lost their reputation for austerity as they built up vineyards in Burgundy's Gevrey-Chambertin and Vosne-Romanée, but also in the Rhône, Champagne and the Loire. Many of these may have been donations, but the Benedictines were also planters. Since the 6th century they had been active in Germany, planting in the Mosel and Rhine valleys, and Franken, and also in Austria and Switzerland.

The Cistercians were founded in 1112 as an austere riposte to the indulgent Benedictines. But they too knew the value of vines and wine, to use for themselves, but also to trade. They developed vineyards in Champagne, the Loire, Provence and Germany – the great, gaunt Kloster Eberbach on the Rheingau was theirs.

But their biggest influence was in Burgundy. They may well have been helped by the fact that there were eight Crusades between 1097 and 1291, and knights would try to shore up their chances of eternal salvation with donations of land before they left. Their greatest legacy is the walled vineyard of Clos de Vougeot, which was fully enclosed by 1336. But all along Burgundy's Côte d'Or, or Golden Slope, they set to work to minutely understand and define every tiny parcel of vineyard land, painstakingly plotting the good and bad points of their geology and microclimate, and then comparing and defining their different flavours. Each plot was delineated, and the 'cru' system by which each batch of wine is kept separate and named separately – a fundamental part of how Burgundy is judged and appreciated – was started by the Cistercians at Vougeot.

1154-1453
THE BIRTH OF CLARET

So often in our history, it's politics, not taste, that decides what our favourite tipple is going to be. One of our lot marries the King of Spain's daughter, so suddenly we're all drinking sherry. A Dutch prince suddenly turns up on the English throne, so suddenly we're all drinking gin. And it's the same with Bordeaux and its wine, which for hundreds of years became known as the Englishman's drink – claret, or the light red wine of Bordeaux.

Bordeaux had been settled by the Romans, but not with the objective of planting vineyards. It was because the Gironde estuary with Bordeaux at its bend is the biggest natural harbour in western Europe. A perfect place for a trading post, because if you look at a map the best shortcut between the Mediterranean and the sea routes to the markets of northern Europe is across southwest France from Narbonne to Bordeaux. The Romans did plant vines – particularly around Blaye, Bourg and Saint-Émilion on the right side of the Gironde – but when their empire collapsed, Bordeaux's trade went with it. By the Middle Ages, the young port of La Rochelle to the north was far more prosperous, initially for its salt exports, but pretty quickly for its wine too. Again, it wasn't that the wine was good, but that the ships needed filling. Trade not taste.

In 1152, Henry Plantagenet, the future Henry II of England, married Eleanor of Aquitaine – and with her came the massive dowry of Aquitaine. The kingdom of France didn't cover all of modern France in those days, and Aquitaine was a powerful independent dukedom covering the whole of southwest France, including La Rochelle and Bordeaux. Aquitaine now became English. La Rochelle continued to prosper until the King of France attacked Aquitaine; La Rochelle surrendered, while Bordeaux pledged eternal loyalty to the English crown, and from then on a deep, special relationship developed between Bordeaux and England, with wine at its heart. To be honest, the local Bordeaux wines were a bit insipid and needed beefing up with wines from places like Cahors and Gaillac inland, but by the 14th century Bordeaux merchants – an increasing number of them British – were shipping casks equivalent to 110 million bottles of wine from the quays of Bordeaux each year.

Vines were planted all round the city walls and particularly in the Graves, though not in the Médoc to the north, which would eventually become Bordeaux's most famous region – but until the Dutch drained it in the 17th century it was a swamp. Great convoys of 200 or more ships at a time would arrive in Bordeaux each autumn and each spring to load up with Bordeaux 'claret' and head for English and Scottish ports such as Bristol, London, Leith and Dumbarton. By the 14th century some estimates reckon Bordeaux was sending Britain enough wine for every man, woman and child to have six bottles each. Bliss.

But it couldn't last. France wanted Aquitaine back. England wanted to keep it, and in 1337 the Hundred Years' War broke out. It ended in 1453 with Sir John Talbot of the English side being defeated at the Battle of Castillon. Some said he'd had too much to drink for lunch. No matter. The British taste for Bordeaux red wines was established, and remains to this day.

A very good Saint-Julien château, named after Sir John Talbot. I'm not sure why he deserved commemorating: he lost the Battle of Castillon, and with that Bordeaux ceased to be English. Ah – perhaps the owner was French.

1540
STEINWEIN

I've never tasted it, but I know a man who has. Hugh Johnson, the famous British wine writer, was one of a tiny group of people who gathered in the Mayfair shop of Rudi Nassauer in London in 1961.

Now, the bottle itself was probably something like 250 years old, because before the 1700s the cork required to stopper a bottle was still a lost item from Roman times waiting to be rediscovered. So for somewhere between 150 and 200 years, this wine had been sitting in a barrel. But between barrel and bottle, this 1540 Steinwein is presumably the oldest bottle of wine that has ever been drunk. 1540. Michelangelo was still at work in Rome; King Henry VIII had just married his fifth wife, Catherine Howard; Shakespeare wasn't even going to be born for another 24 years – and a group of guys in 1961 were sitting around in London tasting the fruits of the vintage, 1540.

There are several reasons why the world's oldest bottle of wine turns out to be German. The Riesling grape is one of them. During the 16th century the variety began to establish itself in German vineyards and the grape's ability to retain high acidity was immediately noted, because high acidity combats oxidation and is of immense value when you're trying to stop a wine decaying and turning to vinegar. Of course, high acidity without ripeness isn't any good, but the late 15th century and early 16th century saw a string of unusually warm vintages.

It didn't last long; it was a brief interlude in a mini ice-age that would cool European climates until the mid-19th century – but 1540 was the last great hurrah. The mighty Rhine River virtually dried up – you could splash across by foot. So, unprecedented ripeness allied to the Riesling grape gave a wine of immense vigour and depth. (By the way, we can't be sure it was the Riesling, but it's a fair guess that it was.) It came from the Würzburger Stein vineyards and the cask

This is the last remaining bottle, with its Steinwein label attached lopsidedly to the neck.

The Würzburg Bürgerspital cellar, where the last bottle of Steinwein 1540 has been stored since 1996. The famous bottle was given to the Bürgerspital by Henry G Simon, whose German ancestors acquired it at auction in the late 1800s.

was kept cool in the Prince-Bishops of Würzburg's cellars. The proficient use of sulphur as an antioxidant (sulphur had become a permitted additive to wine in 1487) and the financial means to build a big, strong, celebratory barrel for the wine – and judiciously top it up whenever the level of the liquid dropped – meant that we had to wait only for a decent cork and bottle to arrive in Würzburg. The bottled wine ended up in the cellars of King Ludwig of Bavaria, where it matured, cold and undisturbed for over two centuries, and at last a bunch of lucky gastronomes could have a sip of history in London. There is just one bottle left, preserved in the cellars of the Würzburg Bürgerspital: Steinwein 1540, the oldest bottle in the world.

So what was it like? Tell us, please. Hugh's words are the only ones I can use. 'Ancient Madeira, but less acid.' OK, that's the taste. But it's not just the taste you care about when you're sipping the oldest wine in the world.

Hugh said: 'Nothing has ever demonstrated to me so clearly that wine is indeed a living organism, and that this brown, Madeira-like fluid still held the active principles of the life that had been conceived in it by the sun of that distant summer.... For perhaps two mouthfuls we sipped a substance that had lived for over four centuries, before the exposure to air killed it. It gave up the ghost and became vinegar in our glasses.'

1571
TOKAJI

I've always presumed it was the gorgeous taste of Tokaji that first made it famous, or indeed its legendary restorative powers that had the great and good of Europe queuing round the block for their allocation. But perhaps it wasn't. Perhaps it was something altogether more compelling.

Sixteenth-century Europe was a melting pot of crazy ideas and fantastical propositions. And into this world of alchemy and intrigue strode Tokaji.

An Italian thinker called Marzio Galeotto spread the word that the wines of Tokaj contained gold. He'd visited Tokaj in Hungary and reported that there was golden ore in 'them thar' hills, that the sand in the vineyards' soils contained particles of gold, and that some of the vines even had golden shoots. That brought the most famous alchemist of the day, Paracelsus, to Tokaj and, not surprisingly, he failed to extract gold from the grapes or their wine, though he did make the rather baffling observation that sunshine 'like a thread of gold, passes through stock and root into the rock'. So this kept the Tokaji and gold legend bubbling away for quite a while yet.

Of course, imbibing gold flakes was supposed to be good for you, which might explain why the Tokaji wines were so popular with the potentates of the time. But I suspect the reason was simpler – the stuff tasted so scrumptious. Intense, succulent and sweet.

Nowadays, sweetness is everywhere in what we eat and drink, but it wasn't then. And any wine that could regularly come up with rich, sweet flavours was going to be clamoured for by the wealthy. And there's some evidence that the growers of Tokaj, in an obscure province in the east of Hungary, may have been the first to make naturally sweet wines on a regular basis.

This c. 1680 rarity is possibly the oldest unopened bottle of Tokaji.

To make a naturally sweet wine, it's not enough to simply have super-ripe grapes; they must be over-ripened to the point of shrivelling on the vine, or, ideally, attacked by a fungus called 'noble rot', which sucks out the moisture from a grape and concentrates the wine to the greatest extent physically possible. The Hungarians use the word *aszú* to describe shrivelled, desiccated grapes, and also to describe grapes whose sugar is concentrated by noble rot. The first mention of Aszú grape wine is in 1571, in a property deal clearly demonstrating that the Aszú grapes had been kept separate from the normal grapes in the vineyard of Mézes Mály. And this would at the very least imply that the producers of Tokaji were the first in the world to harvest shrivelled and nobly rotten grapes on purpose – the Germans on the Rhine didn't get the hang of purposefully nobly rotting their grapes until 1775.

The more commonly accepted legend is that a guy called Szepsi Laczkó Máté postponed the vintage at the great Oremus vineyard in 1630, fearing an attack by the Turks. Or was it 1633? Or was it 1650? That's the trouble with legends, who knows? Anyway, the Turks were certainly threatening – just over the Bodrog River (wonderful name) – and Oremus was the family estate of Prince Rákóczi, the most prominent local nobleman.

The date doesn't really matter, because the exceptional climatic conditions along the Bodrog River, with its morning mists and warm autumn days, would mean that grapes had been nobly rotting there on a regular basis for centuries. But it was the local Tokaji wine producers who first began to make one of the world's great wine styles – naturally sweet, luscious wine from nobly rotted grapes.

The Tokaj wine region, which has 5500 hectares of classified vineyards, was declared a National Heritage Site in 2002.

The Hungarians might have been the first wine growers to use grapes that had been nobly rotted. The result was Tokaji, a luscious, naturally sweet wine.

1587
SHERRY (SACK)

It's perfectly possible that the first wine to be fortified was at Montpellier in the south of France, but the first area to use fortification as an everyday technique was probably the southwest of Spain, in particular the area at the mouth of the Guadalquivir River that made the wine we now know as sherry.

Fortification involves adding strong alcoholic spirit to wine, principally to stop bacterial activity and to give it some muscle to survive the journey to distant markets. This was particularly relevant in southwest Spain, because this was where the Spanish fleets set off for their vast empire in the Americas, laden with wine. Dutch and British wine merchants had been increasingly active from the 14th century onwards. The British were looking for strength in their wine, and ideally some sweetness too. Their traditional source for sweet wine had been the eastern Mediterranean, with its various forms of rich Malmsey, but southwest Spain made much more sense as a trading partner. And there was a big plus point – the area was right next door to Moorish Spain, and the Muslim Moors were Europe's experts at distilling high-strength spirits, perfect for fortifying wine.

The English drank a wine called sack, usually sweet and always strong – 'hot', they called it. Sack could come from the Canary Islands, from Madeira or from Malaga in southeast Spain, but the most popular sack was 'Sherris sack' – named after the wine town of Jerez de la Fontera in the southwest. This is the wine Sir Francis Drake brought back when he 'singed the King of Spain's beard' in 1587. Sack was immortalised by Shakespeare's Falstaff, who downed it by the gallon, convinced it produced 'excellent wit' and 'warming of the blood'.

Because the best sweet Sherris sack would have been made from dried, raisined grapes, it wouldn't necessarily have been fortified, but as sack became all the rage in Elizabethan England, weaker examples needed fortification with spirit to survive shipment from southern Spain. By the 17th century, along with Madeira and port, sherry was a fortified wine ranging from very dry and pale to very sweet and dark.

Sherry has been in and out of fashion ever since. Halfway through the 19th century, 43 per cent of the wine drunk in Britain was sherry, but by the end of the century its reputation had been destroyed by counterfeit sherries, some made from potato spirit. Yet sherry hauled itself back. By the middle of the 20th century, Harvey's Bristol Cream Sherry was probably the most famous wine in Britain – even if most people drank it only once a year at Christmas. But then, in those days, most Britons drank wine of any sort only once a year – at Christmas.

Left: We drank so little wine in the 1950s that this 100 ml miniature bottle would probably have sufficed. In reality, the same 750 ml bottle often came out every year, getting a little emptier each Christmas – and a good deal less palatable. Right: One of sherry's most famous brands, playing on the fact that people thought it more sophisticated to say they liked 'dry' wines, yet actually preferred something a bit sweet. Since sack was usually sweet, calling the wine 'dry sack' would imply a medium wine – and that's exactly what it was – yet with the sophisticated word 'dry' in its title.

1632

THE NEW 'ENGLISH GLASS' BOTTLE

When people start talking about who invented champagne – how it became possible to bottle that foaming, lively liquid – they presume that the names will be French, led by the famous winemaker and cellar master of Hautvillers Abbey in Champagne – Dom Pérignon.

They don't generally reckon that equally important were Sir Robert Mansell, Lord John Scudamore, Sir Kenelm Digby or Captain Silas Taylor. These names don't have a very 'champagne' ring to them. They're as English as the oak tree, and their expertise was largely with cider and perry, not wine. But above all they were crucially involved in developing the new strong style of glass called *verre anglais* by the French, without which you would never be able to fashion a bottle strong enough to withstand the tremendous pressure – up to six atmospheres – that builds up when you create sparkling wine through second fermentation in the bottle.

But they were bottling cider from apples and perry from pears, not wine. Yet you might just about be able to suggest that the French were the cause of the invention of this tough new glass. In 1615, King James I had prohibited the chopping down of any more English forests to fuel the furnaces used to make glass, since England was running short of trees – especially fine English oaks, which were needed for their timber to build warships to fight the French. Luckily, alternative fuels had been used in Britain for some time: Newcastle was already famous for its coal, as was the Forest of Dean in Gloucestershire, and various other fuels like cliff coal and oil shale were in use. They all had the virtue of burning far hotter than any wood charcoal did, and consequently creating the opportunity for heavier, stronger glass to be smelted. Usually the heat was ferocious but also very dirty and smoky, giving a very dark colour to the glass, and the impurities in the various fuels – like manganese and iron – gave the glass extra strength.

A 1650s 'shaft and globe' bottle made of the thicker, darker glass typical of Sir Kenelm Digby's glassworks.

Sir Kenelm Digby had a glassworks at Newnham on Severn, hard by the Forest of Dean coalfield, and right next to the heartland of cider and perry production.

There is evidence that as early as 1632 he was making a new style of glass bottle here that was enthusiastically taken up by the leading cidermakers like Scudamore, who were already starting to experiment with sparkling cider. They would sometimes keep this cider for two to three years, and when sent in bottles to London, it was often lauded as the 'English champagne'. Digby made his glass even stronger by employing a wind tunnel to superheat his furnace. The colour of this new glass was dark, verging on black – quite different from the paler, more fragile glass made famous by the Venetians – and unwittingly this also led to the discovery that cider (and, later, wine) matures much better in a bottle of dark glass, protected from damage by light, especially sunshine.

And Kenelm Digby also worked on the shape. His new bottles were rounded like a giant onion in their lower body with a deep point or indentation on their base, making them stronger and more stable. And they had a long tapering neck with a pronounced collar called the 'string rim', which was there for securing the string used to tie down a glass stopper or a cork. Ah, the cork. Well, that's another big step forwards towards a world where wine could be aged and kept. But that's still in the future.

These bottles, made around 1660, are stamped with the names of their owners, rather than the name of the wine. They would be filled by a merchant or inn-keeper, emptied, washed and reused.

1662

CHRISTOPHER MERRET AND THE INVENTION OF SPARKLING WINE

You really can't go round saying that an Englishman invented champagne. Can you? Well, probably not. Can you say that an Englishman invented sparkling wine? Again, that would be tricky.

Wines were certainly prone to sparkle as long ago as Roman times – though probably not on purpose. Marc Antony was known to have served wines with *bullulae* – small bubbles, in Latin. And more recently, there is some evidence from Limoux in southwest France that they were producing sparkling wine as early as 1531, but probably simply because, after a cold winter, they bottled a wine that hadn't quite finished fermenting. Bottles were so fragile in those days, the wine can't have been more than barely prickly on the tongue. But we're talking about making wine sparkle on purpose by inducing a second fermentation inside the bottle, so that when you pull the cork out, the carbon dioxide reappears as a dancing cascade of foam and bubbles. Now, was it an Englishman who first did that, on purpose, not by accident? Perhaps it was.

England was a big market for wines and they would be shipped to a port like London in barrels. Usually the wines would have finished their fermentation, but the wines of Champagne were different. The Champagne region, northeast of Paris, is France's coolest and most northerly wine area. Frequently the autumns were cold and winter set in quickly. In which case, although a wine might start fermenting in the cellars, the yeasts wouldn't be able to operate as the temperature dropped, and the fermentation wouldn't finish. These wines were generally shipped to England in barrels at the end of winter with the fermentation still incomplete. Initially, the wines would simply be drawn from the barrel into a jug, and as the weather warmed up, the fermentation would continue – and for a few glorious days you'd have sparkling wine served in your tavern.

During the 17th century the English not only developed good, strong glass bottles, but they also rediscovered the use of cork as an effective bottle stopper. Now they could bottle the new champagne wine as soon as it arrived in England and hope that it would referment in the bottle as spring arrived, and they might have fizz all summer.

But it was still haphazard. Yet one section of British society had worked out how to create and control the second fermentation in bottle – the cidermakers of Hereford, Somerset and Gloucester. By the middle of the 17th century they were adding a little sugar to bottles of cider, then corking them up and letting them rest for two to three years to develop flavour and depth, but above all an irresistible foaming 'mousse' of bubbles through a second fermentation. That's what's called the 'champagne method'. Many in London called these bottle-fermented ciders 'English champagne'.

And it was from the cidermakers that Dr Christopher Merret learnt the methods of creating bubbles in wine by adding sugar and causing a second fermentation. He presented his findings in a paper to the Royal Society in London in 1662, more than 30 years before Dom Pérignon is supposed to have worked out how to make sparkling wine in Champagne.

Oh, there's one small point, though. Merret doesn't mention bottles, only barrels. Hmm. It doesn't mean an Englishman wasn't the first to create bubbles on purpose, but perhaps it's the cidermakers of the West Country we should be applauding. And it's cidermaker Silas Taylor who wrote my favourite description of a sparkling cider – though it could have been wine – that 'comes into the glass with a speedy vanishing nittiness which evaporates with a sparkling and whizzing noise'. Love it.

In the black part of the neck label, you can just decipher the word 'MERRET' (on either side of 'SR'). Merret is sometimes used by the wine company Ridgeview to denote 'English sparkling wine' made in the traditional, or champagne, method.

CHÂTEAU HAUT-BRION

Perhaps the greatest legacy left by the 17th-century landowner Arnaud de Pontac was that he foresaw a future where the red wines of Bordeaux would become items of luxury and status symbols for the wealthy.

Nowadays the great châteaux of Bordeaux sell their wine for ridiculous prices, but when de Pontac set out, there weren't even any châteaux to speak of, and wines from whatever estates there were never appeared under their own names – they were sold to merchants in Bordeaux city who blended them up without a thought for their provenance, and shipped them off in casks. The only names these wines would ever bear would be those of the Bordeaux merchant or of the importer.

That simply wasn't going to satisfy de Pontac. His family had acquired the estate of Haut-Brion just south of Bordeaux in 1525. Its land is described as 'white sand mixed in with a little gravel, which one would think would bear nothing'. Well, perhaps for a century it did bear little, but infertile land usually grows the best grapes – eventually. Yet the de Pontacs flourished, partly as merchants, but primarily as *parlementaires*. Whereas most of the power in French cities and provinces usually resided in aristocratic landowners or *noblesse de l'épée* – ex-soldiers grown rich through their exploits – the most powerful group in Bordeaux by the 17th century were lawyers and politicians. Arnaud de Pontac was as powerful as you could get: President of the Parlement. Yet he gained neither respect nor a decent price for his Haut-Brion wine. There are no records to show whether he employed better vineyard practices than his neighbours, whether he chose better grape varieties, harvested riper fruit or took more care in the winery. But we must assume that he felt his wine from that pale, infertile parcel of land was special, because he quite simply decided to charge so much more for it than the going rate that no one would dare blend it in with the rest. And he gave it the name of the estate – the first time this had been done in Bordeaux.

In 1663, Samuel Pepys was the pioneer of the modern tasting note when he wrote: 'Drank a sort of French wine, called Ho Bryan, that hath a good and most particular taste that ever I met with.' That was de Pontac's Haut-Brion. And it cost Pepys more than three times what a normal jug of claret would have cost.

De Pontac had started something. He also had some properties in the Médoc. These he labelled Pontac, and also sold for well above the going rate. The fact that he was in the Médoc is important. The Dutch had drained the Médoc early in the 17th century, revealing great gravel banks of marvellously infertile soil – just like at Haut-Brion. Within 50 years of Pepys's first accolade for Haut-Brion, auctions in London were offering Lafite, Margaux, Latour and others, by name. The hierarchy of great wines that would come to dominate Bordeaux by the 19th century was being established by canny parliamentarians in Bordeaux keen to set themselves up as landed gentry – in somewhere they could afford – the newly drained ex-swampland of the Médoc.

Samuel Pepys was an enthusiastic wine drinker. He also gave it up fairly regularly, but never for long. You can read the originals of his diaries and his report on 'Ho Bryan' at Magdalene College, Cambridge.

Haut-Brion has a differently shaped bottle from the other Bordeaux First Growths. It was redesigned by American owner Clarence Dillon and first used in 1960 on the 1958 vintage. The bottle closely resembles the shape used in 18th-century Bordeaux.

MADEIRA AND THE NEW WORLD

To understand why the wine of a little island off the coast of Africa should become world famous, you need to look at an old map. Preferably one from the age of sail.

The island of Madeira lies off the Moroccan coast. If you were an English merchant dealing with the exciting new markets of the West Indies or North America, you couldn't simply set sail from London, head directly west and hope for the best. The prevailing wind in the British Isles comes from the west and southwest; you'd be heading straight into it, and you'd never make it across the Atlantic. So you'd turn south past France, Spain and Portugal, and into African waters, waiting for that moment when a new wind tugged at your sails – a wind from the northeast, full of the vigour you needed to speed you across the Atlantic. And this change in the wind occurred near the isolated island of Madeira, 400 miles out to sea.

From there, you could run southwest across to the West Indies, or west, across to the great ports of the American South, Savannah, and Charleston.

The Portuguese had colonised what was an uninhabited island in 1420, and planted sugar and vines. By the late 16th century, vines had taken over and their rather light, acidic wine found a ready market, since virtually every ship heading across the Atlantic or to India would put in to Madeira to replenish water and take on stores – above all, casks of wine. Brandy was added to the barrels to try to give the wines a chance of surviving the long sea voyages. But the skippers began to notice that the wine underwent a remarkable transformation as the casks rolled around in the bowels of the ship. The wines became darker, richer, certainly much more mellow, and their disturbing rasping acidity transformed itself into a welcome piquancy, a streak of refreshing acid, which is the hallmark of Madeira, however sweet. Madeiras sold as 'Old East India' fetched several times the price of basic Madeira.

There are four main styles of Madeira, named after four different grape varieties: Sercial, the lightest and driest; then the fuller, sweetish Verdelho; then darker, denser Bual; and finally the deep, smoky, fascinating, unmatched richness of Malmsey. In general, the heavier styles were preferred in Indian army messes, and in the cold north of Europe. But the real connoisseurs of Madeira, until firstly the Civil War and then Prohibition put paid to such languid old-time pleasures, were the Americans, in particular those of grand old cities like Savannah and Charleston in the southern states, which were being established from the 1660s onwards. They preferred lighter styles and they became the world's greatest Madeira connoisseurs. So much so that they even differentiated between the casks from the different ships that carried the wine to the Americas. Wines were matched with the ship's name rather than the style, and it was easy to track how much travelling the barrels had done by checking the ship's log. Blind tasters were judged by their ability to guess which ship the wine had travelled on. And, interestingly, the wines weren't bottled on arrival in America, they were siphoned off into large five-gallon demijohns and put in bottles only when they were about to be drunk. And these demijohns weren't squirrelled away in a dark, damp cellar, but stored up in warm lofts and attics to continue their mellowing, begun under the blaze of the equatorial sun. The most famous Savannah merchant of the mid-1800s, William Habersham, built a solarium 'over his ballroom[!]' to really bake his wines.

One specialty of the Savannah merchants was a pale and delicate Madeira called Rainwater. Supposedly, some barrels of Verdelho had been left on the beach in Madeira with their bungs out, and overnight rain had slightly diluted the wine. Yet it proved wildly popular in America, and more was demanded of this wine – 'soft as rainwater'. The skipper, a Scot called Newton, was delighted. If it didn't rain, there were other ways of adding 'rainwater' to the barrel, and he regularly shipped batches of RWM – Rainwater Madeira. The accounts show that one important part of the blend was AP – *agua pura*, pure water. That's canny.

A pale 'soft as rainwater' style of Madeira, very popular amongst wine-drinkers in the American South.

1681
CORKSCREWS

Of course, you don't have to have a corkscrew if you want to remove a cork from a wine bottle, although that sort of depends on what you mean by 'remove'. If you've got a pair of red-hot tongs, you can very neatly snap the neck off the bottle. Or if you have a sabre, and have practised reasonably assiduously, you can sweep the top of a bottle off with a finely aimed swipe of the blade. All of which might explain why the corkscrew is the preferred device for getting corks out of bottles.

Cork has been used on and off for stoppering wine vessels since at least Ancient Greek times, and an Irish chap called Sedulius Scottus went on about his 'iron corkscrew' in the 9th century, but it is only in the later 17th century that we first hear of corkscrews – or 'bottlescrews' as they were initially known – being regularly talked about. By that time, bottles were being used to store wine and cider, not just to serve it, and a stopper was needed. Initially, the bottles were round-bellied – they weren't intended to be laid on their sides – and a tapered cork that was not completely driven in the bottle's mouth did perfectly well: you could use a claw or pincer to pull the cork out. The first printed reference to a 'steel worm' to extract corks was in 1681. It seems that these 'steel worms' had been used for most of the century for extracting bullets and wadding from guns when they had failed to fire.

Did someone make the connection with the firearms' 'steel worm' and transfer it to more peaceable use in wine bottles?

Well, by the 1740s straight-sided moulded bottles had become the normal shape for wine vessels, and with them had come the development of bins in cellars where these bottles were stacked horizontally to age. Corks were now rammed right into the bottle neck and the development of a reliable corkscrew to yank them out was becoming critical.

Early corkscrews were portable, and the worm either had a sheath, which could double as a handle, or had a bow shape and the worm

*An array of 18th- and 19th-century implements of greater and lesser
efficiency in cork-removal. In most cases, the simpler the better.*

folded into the bow. Initially the worm was a pretty feeble length of just one-and-a-half turns, but during the 18th century the worms got longer. Though portable corkscrews were still popular, more solid versions began to appear, notably ones with a barrel you placed on top of the bottle, into which you drew the cork.

The 19th century saw further refinements, and greater mechanisation of the simple concept of a handle and a steel worm. Most of these modifications were intended to reduce the effort required to extricate a stubborn cork. A British inventor called Charles Hull devised the 'bar corkscrew' in the 1860s – those fierce-looking cork extractors fixed to the counter, which simply require a swift down-up movement and the cork's out. Various concertina-like 'lazy tongs' appeared, which required very little effort on the part of the cork extractor. And in 1882, the Waiter's Friend was invented.

This is the most widely used corkscrew nowadays and allows you to use leverage to ease the cork out, rather than relying on brute force. In the 1970s, the Screwpull was invented, using flexible plastic to grip the bottle and with a high-quality Teflon-coated long steel worm. I can't see anything else beating them for efficiency and ease of use. Certainly not the compressed air device my Aunt Phyllis gave me, which removed the cork by pumping air through it into the bottle. It did work, but rather reduced my pleasure in opening bottles, since I was convinced that sooner or later one would blow up in my face.

The Waiter's Friend. I carry one of these with me wherever I go.
Except through airport X-ray machines. On one flight I lost three!

1685
CONSTANTIA

There's a well-known quotation attributed to Jan van Riebeeck, the first commander of the Dutch East India Company's settlement at the Cape of Good Hope. In 1659, he wrote, 'Today, praise be to God, wine was pressed for the first time from Cape grapes.'

Only three vines had actually ripened and given fruit, and these, he wrote, were 'French and Muscadel grapes'. This mattered because although no one has the slightest idea what the wine tasted like, you'd have expected van Riebeeck to have written some kind of tasting note, but since the meagre puddle of wine was probably fermented in a goatskin, perhaps words failed him. Then in 1685 a guy called Simon van der Stel – the first governor of the Cape – planted a vineyard in Constantia, on the slopes of the Table Mountain.

And he propagated his vines from what van Riebeeck had originally planted – above all, French Muscat, known as 'Frontignan,' or 'the little berry Muscat', the best, the most fragrant of all the Muscat family which can only have provided him with a bare handful of bottles. Within 20 years Constantia wine was being lauded back in Europe. The New World had begun to ship wine back to the Old World. This first flowering was brief, but by the end of the 18th century, Constantia was pretty much the most famous wine on the planet.

Constantia wine was legendary for its ability to age. This bottle from 1883 should still be in decent nick, if anyone wants to share it.

That's some claim, but it's true. The two wines that the high and mighty wanted were Hungarian Tokaji and Constantia.

Frederick the Great of Prussia drank Constantia, so did the Russian tsars and British monarchs, but none drank it as furiously as Napoleon. When he was exiled to St. Helena, he was drinking 30 bottles a month. Baudelaire was also keen on it, but, typically, was just a bit keener on his beloved's lips. He admits that only the lips of a lover surpass the wine in heavenly sweetness, but 'even more than Constantia… I prefer the elixir of your mouth where love performs its slow dance.' Well, there we are. Not a bad tasting note, but luckily there are some real tasting notes from the great Constantias of 1791 and 1809, which were discovered in abundance in the cellars of the Duke of Northumberland. Several wine buffs tasted them in the 1970s and 1980s and uniformly praised their extraordinary freshness, an almost orange-like acidity combining with the smoky, nutty richness of old Madeira. And that might have been it – a few remnants of a world-class wine from vineyards now extinct. Except the actual vineyards *weren't* extinct.

The Constantia Estate had been split up, but there were still vines and in 1980, Klein Constantia – little Constantia – was bought by Duggie Jooste, a guy determined to try to revive the long-lost Constantia wine. Jooste set out to discover everything he could about the original Constantia. Certainly, it was a sweet wine, and both red and white. But it was neither fortified, nor made sweet by noble rot attacking the grapes. Instead, the vinegrowers removed half the crop, removed all the leaves surrounding the remaining bunches, then snapped and twisted the wood holding the branches, so that the grapes shrivelled and concentrated in the sun. Then they fermented the juice until the yeasts died and a wine almost twice as sweet as port was left, which then lay in large oak barrels for four years. And Jooste did this with a clone of Muscat de Frontignan that almost certainly came from the original Constantia vineyards. The wine was released in 1986 as Vin de Constance, one of the very rare examples of an ancient wine style being raised from the dead. And as if to complete its resurrection, Nelson Mandela raised a glass of it in celebration after his release from prison in 1990.

Constantia is a truly beautiful corner of the Cape, and was understandably popular among the early grandees for establishing estates and vineyards.

A line-up of modern bottles, based on the old design. The wine, too, is as close an approximation to the original as possible.

Le Petit Journal

ADMINISTRATION
61, RUE LAFAYETTE, 61

Les manuscrits ne sont pas rendus

On s'abonne sans frais
dans tous les bureaux de poste

5 CENT.

25ᵐᵉ Année

SUPPLÉMENT ILLUSTRÉ

5 CENT.

Numéro 1.270

DIMANCHE 14 JUIN 1914

ABONNEMENTS

SIX MOIS   UN AN

SEINE et SEINE-ET-OISE.. 2 fr.   3 fr. 50
DÉPARTEMENTS............ 2 fr.   4 fr. »
ÉTRANGER .... 2 50   5 fr. »

UN BICENTENAIRE

Il y a exactement deux cents ans que Dom Pérignon, moine bénédictin de Hautvillers, découvrit l'art de faire mousser le vin de Champagne

Nice idea, Dom old chap, but entirely fanciful. Dom Pérignon spent most of his career trying to keep the bubbles out of champagne, rather than trying to create them.

DOM PÉRIGNON

Every record that you read gives a slightly different view of what exactly Dom Pérignon did. But one thing is certain. He did not invent champagne. Indeed, he spent most of his career trying to keep bubbles *out* of his wine.

Vineyards had been established around the Valley of the Marne and the Mountain of Reims since at least the 5th century AD. Probably because they were so close to Paris, just to the west along the Marne River, they achieved a fair amount of fame. By the time that Louis XIV ruled during the 17th century, they were some of France's most famous.

But the wines didn't sparkle – at least, they weren't supposed to, and the king didn't like it if they did. Generally, they were a vague pinkish colour from the Pinot Noir grape. And when the sun didn't shine – which was the case two years in three in Champagne – the wine was pale, thin, sour and all too likely to fizz sullenly when drawn from the barrel.

The reason for this was that, being so far north in France, the autumns were frequently cold. The wine might start off fermenting, but then the cellars would get so chilly the fermentation would stop until the warmth of spring started it off again, and you were left with a thin, reedy, murky pinkish wine full of bubbles that no one wanted – particularly at the very conservative court of Louis XIV.

Dom Pérignon was appointed cellarmaster of the Abbey of Hautvillers just outside Épernay in 1668. The Abbey's wines were already well known, but Dom Pérignon was a man on a mission to transform them – and in doing so he transformed all the wines of Champagne. His first two tasks were to find a way of making clear, still white wines from the red grapes of the region, and when possible making serious red wines too. He admitted that making red wine of true quality couldn't be done every year, but by using only the fruit of old Pinot Noir vines whose grapes were always riper and deeper coloured, by removing any less ripe grapes from the bunch, and by instituting fermentation and maceration of the juice on the grape skins, he did manage proper reds. And he realised that in every vintage, different areas and different vineyards will produce different qualities. Champagne is now celebrated as a 'blended' wine. It was Dom Pérignon who realised that the sum was greater than the parts in champagne, and each year he could produce a cuvée, or blend, of something fine by close attention to the climatic conditions of the vineyards; the age, health and vigour of the vines; and ripeness at harvest. And, of course, he seems to have had a fantastic palate.

But what about bubbles? Well, by the end of the 17th century, sparkling wines had become the rage, so, against his better judgment, he had to try to perfect their production at Hautvillers. In the 1690s he brought in strong 'English glass' bottles – French glass was too fragile to cope with the pressure in the bottle – and reintroduced the use of cork as a closure, which hadn't been used in France for many centuries. Dom Pérignon understood that if you wanted a consistent, predictable bubble in your wine, you needed a cool cellar to allow the bottles to rest, so he dug caves into the soft chalk hills behind the Abbey. Luckily, there's loads of chalk in Champagne, and all the greatest champagne cellars are now in chalk caves.

Dom Pérignon, commemorating the monk and his achievements, is now the best-known luxury champagne in the world.

1716
CHIANTI

Chianti, as a wine, has been trying to organise and define itself for a very long time, but has been successful as a serious red wine only since the end of the 20th century.

Given that what we call the Chianti area is spread across the region between Siena and Florence, you'd expect it to have rapidly gained a reputation for its wine. Presumably the powerful and sophisticated local nobles and merchants during medieval and Renaissance periods – and afterwards too – wanted something decent to drink, and, if necessary, trade. Maybe strife between the Florentines and Sienese prevented ambitious vineyard projects in these disputed hills, because although the Lega del Chianti was formed in the 13th century, it was concerned only with protecting property, not promoting or defining wine. Indeed the first time the word 'Chianti' is applied to wine, right after the end of the 14th century, it was described as a white wine.

As it happened, there was red Chianti wine, but it was called Vino Vermiglio during the Renaissance, or plain 'Florence' when exported to London, but no one seems to have liked it that much. Maybe this is because the famous Chianti flask was being employed – exports of wine were sent as uncorked flasks, sealed with olive oil and rags, then packed into chests. I shouldn't have thought the success rate was that high.

It took the Medicis to do something about it – what a surprise. In 1716, Cosimo de Medici issued an edict defining the boundaries of Chianti, Pomino, Carmignano and Val d'Arno di Sopra. Pomino and Carmignano are still there, Val d'Arno forms part of the Chianti Colli Fiorentini – but, most importantly, those original Chianti vineyards are bang in the middle of what is Chianti Classico today.

But that still didn't seem to make Chianti a particularly thrilling drink. Maybe some of this was due to the fact that most of the land was held by sharecroppers who gave half their crop to the landlord rather than there being big estates cultivated assiduously by the owners themselves. Things took a turn for the better when Baron Bettino Ricasoli committed himself to running his estate at Castello di Brolio, and laid down the formula that many modern winemakers now think of as the classic Chianti mix – Sangiovese and Canaiolo for ageworthy reds, and these two black grapes plus the white Malvasia for early drinkers. He wasn't exactly without distractions – 1848 was the Year of Revolutions. The push for Italian Unification eventually led to nationhood in 1861, and Ricasoli, heavily involved all the way, became Italy's second prime minister. But by 1872, he was finally putting his formula for Chianti into effect.

And the flask, so distinctive, so Tuscan in everyone's mind, did not prove to be a symbol of quality abroad.

The bulbous flask had been blown from glass since at least the 12th century. But the glass was thin and fragile in those days. That's why a straw covering was introduced in the 15th century – and remained the symbol of Chianti until the end of the 20th century. By then, however, there was a massive renaissance at work in Tuscan wine which disdained the flask, and the straw-covered *fiasco* became more of a street-corner trattoria joke than a symbol of any kind of particular flavour or personality in the wine. You can still find a few being used as candleholders in the homes of people of a certain age.

Ah, this brings back memories of dingy trattorias, spaghetti
bolognese and a date who didn't think you were quite as cool
as you thought you were. Tempus fugit.

1727
RÜDESHEIMER APOSTELWEIN

I'm not an envious sort of chap, but whenever I read the tasting notes of the late great Michael Broadbent I do suffer a bit of a twinge. He had drunk so much old and great wine. And by 'old' I don't just mean 20 or 30 years – they're delicious and I've had my fair share of those. No. I mean 50 years old, 100 years old, 200 years old, 256 years old, 314 years old. This was all in a day's work for Michael – the world's greatest expert on ancient wines.

Now, quite a few of these venerable bottles were German. Even if German wines are not much thought of today as long-distance runners, they are probably the original wines – if we except a few remarkable freaks from Greece and Rome – that were expected to age, and were treated to make them age-worthy. One of the reasons this was possible is that Germany is the home of the Riesling grape, which always gives wines with a high level of acidity – even in warm, ripe years – and acidity is one of nature's great antidotes to oxidation and decay in wine. So, long before the arrival of the bottle and the cork had made it possible to age most other wines for anything more than a few months before the whole lot turned to vinegar, Germany found that its best wines positively demanded ageing. But in what type of container? Well, the top German estates were owned either by wealthy noblemen or by long-established monasteries. When the vintages were good, it was almost a matter of pride to build a mighty barrel to contain the wine – and these estates had the money to construct them.

The bigger the barrel, the less the wine will come into contact with the air and the slower will be its development and, eventually, decline. Riesling wine's acidity and the use of sulphur as a further antioxidant – the Germans had been using sulphur since at least 1487 – meant you could keep the wine for years, decades even. Thomas Jefferson, one of America's Founding Fathers, visited the Rhine in the 1780s, and his hotel had barrels of wine going all the way back to 1726. Now, these wines were not entirely made up of

A rare bottle of the 1727 Rüdesheimer Apostelwein, drawn from a 'mother cask' in the Bremer Ratskeller.

the named vintage. The Germans used a sort of 'solera' system of topping up the vast barrels with younger wine whenever they were broached, rather as they do nowadays when making sherry in the cellars of Jerez in Spain. And there's one place where they still have an array of these mighty casks – the Ratskeller ('city hall cellar') in the City of Bremen, at one time a great wine trading centre. They've actually got some 1653, but their most famous wine is the 1727 Rüdesheimer Apostelwein. And Michael Broadbent drank it six times. He said it tasted of some ethereal hinterland suspended between ancient sherry and Madeira. And as always, Michael being the God of the good and ancient, I believe him.

The restaurant at the Bremer Ratskeller is lined with huge painted wine casks from the 17th and 18th centuries. Wines have been stored in its cellars since the town hall was erected in 1405.

1740s

AIRTIGHT CORKS

There's not an awful lot of point in perfecting a really good glass bottle ideal for maturing wine if you don't have some highly efficient and consistent method of stoppering the bottle.

For at least 2000 years, before a decent wine bottle was invented, there had been infrequent attempts to age wine – and there was indeed some understanding that exposure to air seemed to hasten a wine's relentless progression to vinegar. But although the bark of the cork oak tree was known about, neither the Romans nor the Greeks seemed to make the leap of faith required to see that it is nature's supreme bottle stopper. They generally used a film of oil to keep out the air or a stopper of pitch or plaster.

And as the Roman Empire collapsed, the use of corks seemed to have been forgotten. If a plug were needed for a jug or early bottle, it might be simply a twist of cloth; it might be a wad of paper or rags; it might be leather, perhaps covered with sealing wax; and during the 17th century when Dom Pérignon was wrestling with the problems of how to contain the bubbles in champagne, the stoppers he had to rely on were usually made of wood wrapped in oil-soaked hemp. One thing's for certain: they weren't airtight.

And yet the Romans and Greeks so nearly hit upon the perfect closure. The cork oak grows in a number of places all round the Mediterranean. Its cultivation is most intense in southern Portugal and southwestern Spain. It's a remarkable tree. If you strip it of its bark, it doesn't die; it simply grows a new coat of bark. And it's a thick coat, of a uniquely light, spongy, elastic consistency. You can squeeze the cork into half its natural mass and it will bounce back as if nothing has happened. The bark's microstructure is made up of very small, tightly packed, 14-sided cells – there are 200 million cells per square inch – which as well as being remarkably elastic, are pretty impermeable to liquids and gases and are usually neutral to taste. If you take a sheet of cork bark, dry it, boil it to sterilise it, and then cut out a rounded oblong at right angles to the surface, you've got the basis for the perfect bottle stopper. A simple hand-

corking machine would squeeze the cork and ram it into the mouth
of the bottle, where it would immediately expand and effortlessly
fill the space, stopping wine leaking out and air creeping in.

And it seems as if it was the English who 'rediscovered' the use
of cork as the perfect bottle stopper. Certainly cork was being
mentioned in England – and not anywhere else – by the 16th century.

Shakespeare has Rosalind say, 'I pray thee take the cork out of thy
mouth' in *As You Like It* in 1599. And it was soon afterwards that
James I, in 1615, forbade the cutting down of forests to fuel glass
furnaces. This led to the development of coal as a far more effective
fuel than wood, and the creation of the dark, strong bottles known
as 'English glass' – the first bottles that might realistically be able
to be stored for maturing wine, and consequently the first bottles
that absolutely demanded a decent stopper. But even then, corks
were more likely to be used as temporary stoppers. It was only
when straight-sided bottles started to be produced from moulds
in the 1740s that an airtight cork had to surface. Cork had been
waiting for 2000 years. And, frankly, so had decent wine.

Foresters harvesting the cork bark from their trees.
Methods haven't changed much to this day.

THE MODERN WINE BOTTLE

The invention of *verre anglais* **– tough, heavy, dark English glass created by the use of coal-fired rather than wood-fired furnaces – was a massive step forward for wine.**

The rediscovery of cork – light, elastic, flexible, able to be squeezed into the neck of a bottle, creating an airtight closure – was another leap forward. Yet the cork dries out and loses its seal over time. Laying a bottle on its side would keep the cork moist and effective, but the round, chubby, onion-shaped bottles of the 17th century were not intended for laying on their sides.

To be honest, it didn't greatly matter in the 17th century. Wines were drunk young. The bottle's main purpose was to carry wine from the taverner's cask to the table. Once empty, bottles would be sent back to be refilled. Regular wine drinkers had their own bottles made by glass blowers, complete with a glass seal attached to the side that displayed the owner's name, initials or heraldic device. There was no statutory shape or size; whimsy and personal taste won the day. Even the newly invented 'champagnes' needed to be kept only long enough for the bubbles to be created, and that was a case of months, not years. But long ago, in Roman times, people had sometimes aged wines, and there's an example of a 4th-century Roman bottle with a cork in the Speyer Museum in Germany. But more significant is the fact that this ancient bottle had straight sides, so it could be laid down and matured.

Both the use of cork and the desire – or indeed, ability – to lay down wines to age seems to have been lost with the fall of the Roman Empire. But by the beginning of the 18th century, winemaking had advanced sufficiently that wines stable enough to age were becoming more common. The shape of the wine bottle began to change – the body of the bottle became thinner and taller, especially in Britain, where connoisseurship was far ahead of elsewhere in Europe. Two types of wines were increasingly drunk. Port was the dominant style, accounting for as much as three-quarters of British consumption at times during the 18th century. Initially it was drunk black and fierce and drawn straight from the cask. But the new connoisseurs bought port by the 'pipe' – a cask containing 600 bottles' worth of wine – which would then be bottled and stored in their cellars. They quickly became aware that a bit of ageing softened up this firewater no end. Red Bordeaux was the other most popular style, especially in Scotland, and, once again, it became clear that aged wines were more mellow and therefore more enjoyable.

Experiments were made with keeping the bulbous bottles on their sides in beds of sand, but the glass manufacturers saw the need for narrower and straighter bottles; by the middle of the 18th century they had developed reliable moulds for making bottles. At the same time, country house cellars were all being equipped with 'bins' – side cellars or vaults – generally capable of each maturing 300 bottles of wine all laid on their sides and piled on top of each other, so long as the sides of the bottles were straight. By the end of the century they were very close to the shape of the modern wine bottle that we still find today in Oporto – for port – and Bordeaux.

| 1714 | 1725 | 1741 | 1768 | 1780 | 1793 |

A gradual progression from the bottle simply being a serving vessel (filled from the cask and taken to the table), to its modern, straight-sided manfestation (suitable for ageing and laying on its side).

The evolution of the early straight-sided bottle: the bottle on the left is from the 1760s, the one on the right is from the 1810s. The seals denote the owners' names, not that of the wine.

DECANTERS

**Jugs of various sorts have been used to bring wine to the table
since the earliest times. If wine was being stored in a goatskin, an
amphora, a vat or a barrel, you needed to transfer the liquid to a
smaller vessel so that you could easily serve it. And certainly since
Roman times these jugs may have been of glass. So a wine jug was
simply a thing of necessity.**

Things began to change dramatically in the late 17th century, and,
particularly, in the 18th century, when more wines were being
bottled and corked so that they might be able to mature. Especially
since about the 1740s when straight-sided moulded bottles became
common, the wine jug lost its role as a simple dispenser of wine,
and assumed a far more glamorous role as an indulgence, a
decoration to the table. Designs became less juglike – the handle
on the neck, which was common in the 17th century, largely
disappeared except for the occasional 'retro' claret jug – and the
term *decanter* was now generally accepted instead of *jug*.

Although decanters became highly decorative, there were practical
reasons for using them from the 18th century onwards, in
particular for those British favourites – Bordeaux and port. These
wines were now being made darker and denser, and their ability
to age was increasingly appreciated. However, as they aged they
threw sediment and the act of decanting the wine from the bottle
to the decanter was the obvious way to separate the clear wine
from the sludgy deposit. It also became obvious that many wines
softened and improved with exposure to air.

Prior to the 18th century, with irregular-shaped bottles and
ineffectual stoppers, all contact with air was thought to be
detrimental to the wine, hastening it on its downward spiral to
vinegarhood. Now, with good bottles and sound cork stoppers,
wine was largely protected from air while being stored, and good
Bordeaux and port clearly softened and developed scents and
flavours if poured into a decanter for an hour or two. For this
reason most decanters held about one litre of liquid, so a 750 ml
bottle of wine could aerate easily in it.

A beautiful example of a George Ravenscroft decanter from the late 1670s.
This is the classic 'shaft-and-globe' shape, but in an extravagant mood.

Venetian glass had dominated the glass business since the 16th century, and Murano in particular produced large amounts of brilliant glassware that must have thrilled those who could afford this new, glittering material. However, by the 1670s, George Ravenscroft in England was the first to use lead in his production method, facilitating the creation of clear but strong glass that could be used for both utilitarian and fashionable objects – decanters being a prime example.

The preferred shapes of decanters changed throughout the 18th century. The Victorians created beautiful ovoid and pear-shaped decanters but were likely to decorate them to within an inch of their lives.

Modern decanters are more likely to be plain, but the sheer joy of seeing good red – or white – wine in something like a classic 'shaft and globe' shape is one of the quiet delights of relaxed dining. Claret jugs, by the way, are still designed and used. Not least by golfers. Very good golfers. The claret jug is the trophy for The Open, the oldest golf tournament in the world. In 2014 it was won by Irishman Rory McIlroy, who promptly celebrated by filling the venerable jug with Jägermeister.

1756
DELIMITATION OF THE DOURO

We've got an earthquake to thank for the first ever legal delimitation of a wine area, the first appellation, the first cast-iron attempt to lay down laws – not just suggestions – as to what constituted a vineyard area.

It was 1755, and one of Europe's worst ever earthquakes hit Lisbon, Portugal's capital. Forty thousand people were killed. The country slumped into chaos, with a weak king desperate for guidance and leadership. He got it. In spades. His chief minister was Sebastião de Carvalho – later Marquês de Pombal. He quickly established monopolistic government power over a variety of Portuguese activities, but the act that changed the world of wine for good was his creation of the Real Companhia das Vinhas do Alto Douro – the Douro Wine Company, as it soon came to be known.

Let's go back a bit. Britain had signed the Methuen Treaty with Portugal in 1703, slashing duty on Portuguese wine. As usual in those days Britain and France were at odds, so it could be seen to be as much anti-French as pro-Portuguese. The English had already established numerous shipping companies in Oporto to service a triangular trade of cloth from England, wine from Portugal and cod from Newfoundland (dried cod, *bacalhau*, is Portugal's national dish, not sure why). Indeed the English merchants were a powerful and probably locally resented bunch in Oporto, but they rarely ventured up the Douro River to find out where their wines (increasingly called 'port' after Oporto) actually came from. The 18th century started out fairly well for everybody – the quality of port wine coming from the Upper Douro was good, growers and shippers prospered. But the rising demand couldn't be met by true Douro wine and the shippers were growing greedy. From 1700 to 1750, the price the shippers were prepared to pay the growers for a barrel of wine dropped by 90 per cent. To keep the merchants supplied, adulteration became the norm – either with wines from other parts of northern Portugal, or with Spanish wines – 'bullock's blood' they called it; raisin wines or cheap malt-based spirits bolstered the volume. But most notorious of all were the additions of dried hot peppers and elderberries to provide fire and colour to the increasingly lifeless brew.

So the Marquês de Pombal had two objectives in 1756. First to wrest back power from the mainly English merchants, and second to restore pride and financial security to the Portuguese growers of the Upper Douro. His new Douro Wine Company had control over all port shipments, and even those of the English companies could go ahead only after they had passed a 'tasting' by the company. He ordered all the elderberry trees to be uprooted and every vineyard registered.

And, most importantly, he designated the vineyards on schist soil – a black, crumbly rock soil set between big granite outcrops – as being solely for the production of *vinho de feitoria* (wines for export, superior wines).

He guaranteed high prices for these grapes as against grapes grown on soil only suitable for *ramo* – home consumption and export to Brazil. The best vineyards were staked out with granite posts, of which a few remain there even today. And over 250 years later, these schist soils are accepted as the core of port production, and evidence of the first time laws were put in place to delimit a vineyard area.

An elegant barco rabelo, *the vessel used to transport wine down the Douro before the mighty river was dammed.*

1775

SCHLOSS JOHANNISBERG'S SPÄTLESE WINE

Wherever sweet wines are reckoned to be a region's greatest achievement, you'll find legends relating to delays, misunderstandings, sieges and the like, all of which stopped the grapes being picked until they'd rotted in the vineyards.

The ugly, mushy mess is then picked by an estate manager who confidently expects to be taken to the gallows for having mucked up a whole year's harvest – yet, as if by magic, the wines turn out to be magnificent and he's a hero. You'll find these tales in France, Austria and Hungary, and in Germany you will find them at Schloss Johannisberg on the awesome 19-mile long, south-facing slope of Riesling vines that is the Rheingau, one of Europe's greatest vineyard sites.

Sweet wines had definitely been made on the Rheingau before 1775, but the legend states 1775, so we'll go with it. The site had been picked out by Charlemagne as long ago as the 8th century and was already well known by AD 850. Then the Benedictines arrived and led the way in establishing the Rheingau as a great wine producer. The Thirty Years' War, ending in 1648, brought chaos to Germany. The vineyards were in a rotten state in 1716 when the Prince-Bishop of Fulda bought the monastery at Johannisberg and set about reviving the estate and building himself an imposing schloss, or castle.

Let's look at 1775. Fulda was seven days' ride from Johannisberg. So the vineyard manager sent a courier off to Fulda asking for permission to pick the grapes. I don't know what the courier got up to on the journey to Fulda, but he certainly wasn't back in 14 days. When the

A modern version of the original Johannisberger Spätlese. This wine will have a fair amunt of residual sweetness.

courier finally got back the vineyards were a sorry sight, the grapes all shrivelled with rot, and all the neighbouring estates had long finished their harvests.

They picked the grapes anyway and made the wine without any great hopes. Yet the next February it finally stopped fermenting and was rich and sweet – by April, when outsiders were allowed to taste the 1775 Schloss Johannisberger, the verdict was 'this is unlike anything we've ever tasted before'. The idea of 'late harvesting' – Spätlese in German – was conceived. In other words, you delay the harvest to let the grapes fully ripen, then over-ripen, and, if the weather allows it, nobly rot with the objective of obtaining the sweetest juice possible. This was the complete opposite of the view held by winemakers up until then. Grapes were only left hanging on the vine in poor years, in the hope that they might eventually ripen, and if they didn't the vintage was a write-off. Good years, when the sun shone, were picked early. In the outstanding vintages of 1727 and 1728, Schloss Johannisberg picked early – on 25 September and 4 October – delighted to have got in a healthy crop of grapes so early, not realising that leaving the grapes out in the sunny autumn weather would have made far finer wine.

So this 1775 Spätlese Johannisberger wine set in motion what was eventually established in German wine law – that the quality of the wine depends on how much sugar the grapes contained at harvest time and, until modern times, how much was left as sweetness in the wine.

The imposing Schloss Johannisberg, above the sweep of vines down to the Rhine – a site that Charlemagne spotted as early as the 8th century.

EARLY 1800s
BOTTLE SHAPES

Bottle shapes for most of the last 1000 or so years have been severely restricted by the knowledge and skills of the bottlemakers. The Phoenicians, Syrians and Egyptians did use glass, and the Romans became quite expert at manufacturing glass vessels.

But the rudimentary methods they used didn't allow for much choice when it came to shape, although the Romans do seem to have had a go at straight-sided bottles if an exhibit from the 4th century at the Speyer Museum in Southern Germany is anything to go by.

In general, bottles were used rather as jugs or decanters, to be filled with wine, and pretty much straight away emptied again at the table. With the fall of Rome there wasn't any development of glass-making techniques until the rise of the great Venetian glass foundries in the 16th century. The products of Murano especially thrilled Europe, but Venetian vessels were still used for serving rather than storing wine, since one of the great creative skills of the Venetians was their ability to blow incredibly thin glass – beautiful, but fragile. It was the invention of darker, stronger 'English' glass in the 1630s that began the change in bottle shapes. Initially the demand came from cidermakers and champagne importers, who wanted to make a sparkling drink available all year round. They weren't interested in long-term storage – the shape of the bottles showed that. They started out in the beautiful 'shaft and globe' style – a round chubby belly and a long neck – then became more and more bulbous and onion-shaped.

In the 18th century they dramatically thinned, first to a mallet shape with reasonably straight sides, and

Three typical modern examples of classic bottle shapes: the cylindrical Bordeaux shape for a Pauillac, the sloping Burgundy shape for a Meursault, and the elegant German shape for an Austrian Riesling.

by the 1740s to something more cylindrical, resembling our modern wine bottle with its straight sides and higher shoulders.

These bottles were used by merchants or private clients, and increasingly were stored on their sides. But the bottling was done by the importers. Bottling of wine at source and the development of bottle shapes unique to different areas took place gradually during the 19th century; the shapes have since become important tools by which regions and wine styles can differentiate themselves. The most important shapes are the high-shouldered, cylindrical Bordeaux bottle; the more gently sloping Burgundy bottle; and the tall, thin German bottle. In general, in the New World, wines based on the Bordeaux grapes will use the Bordeaux shape, wines based on the Burgundy or Rhône grapes will use the Burgundy bottle; and wines from Germanic grapes like Riesling or Gewürztraminer will use the German bottle.

There are other bottle shapes particular to certain wines, but not much copied. These include the 620 ml 'Clavelin' for Jura's Vin Jaune, the Tokaji 500 ml bottle and the Vin de Constance bottle in South Africa. But in general the three main bottle styles are followed, sometimes with slight variations. Champagne bottles are of the Burgundy shape but thicker, and Châteauneuf-du-Pape uses Burgundy-style bottles with an embossed crest. Rioja uses mostly Bordeaux bottles with a few Burgundies, as does Tuscany in Italy, whereas Piedmont is more likely to use Burgundy bottles. And so it goes on.

The colour of glass is also important, because it protects wine against damage from ultraviolet light. Really dark glass like that used for vintage port would be best, but then you can't see the colour at all, so some compromise is usual. Bordeaux is usually dark green, though Sauternes and the sweet whites are in clear glass. White Burgundy is in pale olive leaf green glass called 'dead leaf'. German Rhine wine is usually in brown glass, as is sherry, whereas Mosel wine and French Alsace wine is usually in a tall green flute. Oddballs like the Mateus Rosé bottle and the German Bocksbeutel are actually based on old traditional shapes, as are the straw-covered Chianti flasks.

1801
CHAPTAL'S TRAITÉ

I knew the name of Jean-Antoine Chaptal really early on in my wine life. 'Yuck, the wine's been chaptalised,' the experts would cry as yet another pale, flabby yet strangely alcoholic wine with a surprisingly smart Burgundy label was laid before them.

Or when a Bordeaux from a frankly execrable vintage would appear to be quite rich and almost sweet until the tug-of-war acidity threatened to part your gums from their teeth.

What had happened to these is that they had been sugared. That is, they'd had mounds of sugar added to the juice before fermentation started, and this greatly increased the alcoholic strength of the wine. Because alcohol is rather soft and mellow in the mouth, the wines assumed a texture that was indeed much rounder, more syrupy even, than the grape juice ever would have been able to achieve by itself. But the sugar gave no flavour – it was all eaten up in the process of fermentation, and you were left with a fairly miserable base wine botoxed up and fattened for the slaughter.

Well, this showed how far Chaptal's reputation had fallen, but this isn't fair. He didn't invent the idea of adding sugar to increase the strength of wine; ever since the 1700s, when sugarcane became a staple in Europe and scientists had established the link between sugar sweetness and ripeness, people had been messing about with it. The thing is, Chaptal became Napoleon's interior minister. He already knew the terrible state of France's vineyards, devastated by neglect, bad weather, overproduction and revolution. He also knew how important the supply of wine was in keeping France going at all, but that most of it tasted like vinegar. Crucially, he was a chemist. He was sure that if winemakers could understand the chemistry of wine, the laws of fermentation, the effects of climate, soil, aspect and wine cultivation; if, in effect, they could take control and apply a scientific mind to what was a process that needed science to explain it – then the terrible quality of French wine could be improved.

And one of the ways to provide stability in wine was to give it a reasonable alcohol level. Not only would wine taste better straight off, get you a bit more lit up – naturally – but it would also last better, and the struggle to stop wine turning to vinegar within weeks or months, frequently before it could be got to market, was one of the biggest challenges. Adding sugar to the grape juice before fermentation was in Chaptal's mind a step toward better quality and stability. Unfortunately, the majority of winegrowers, especially in France, saw it as a way to legitimise overproduction and show contempt for quality. Nowadays, 'chaptalisation' is still used, but generally only when the weather has really let the grape grower down.

What we should remember M Chaptal for is his *Traité théorique et pratique sur la Culture de la Vigne*, which first appeared in 1801, and which put science, chemistry, the need to control the nature of vinegrowing, and winemaking itself at the heart of understanding wine. There had been many books on wine before, all talking of ancient precedence and personal experience. Chaptal put science and reason at the heart of his book. And although his name is honoured for the promotion of sugaring wine to increase its strength, his actual principles should be more respected as laying a scientific groundwork for the greater understanding of that French wine ideal above all others – terroir, whose integrity is compromised by excessive 'chaptalisation'.

A wine from the South of France incorporating Chaptal's name, but these sun-drenched vineyards are the last place you would need any help to increase alcohol from his 'sugaring' methods.

45 CHAPTAL

Chaptal is primarily known for promoting the use of sugar in fermentation to increase alcoholic strength, but he was a highly influential and effective scientist in all matters to do with wine – and he had a nice taste in stockings.

1840s
DOCTORS & GERMANS

There must be something in the water in Australia. No other country in the world has thrown up so many doctors determined to change the world of wine. In recent times you had doctors Cullity, Pannell and Cullen establishing the Margaret River wine region in Western Australia in the 1960s, and Dr Max Lake certainly believed that he revived New South Wales' Hunter Valley virtually single-handedly at about the same time.

But the real influence of the medics was right back at the start of the Australian wine industry.

Henry Lindeman and Christopher Penfold came to Australia as physicians, yet ended up by creating two of Australia's most famous wine companies. Dr Lindeman settled in the Hunter Valley in 1841; Dr Penfold in Adelaide in South Australia in 1844. If you look in the annals of the old wine companies, there were quite a few more doctors involved; some, like Angove, whose names live on in their wine companies. Lindeman took all of two years to establish his vines at Cawarra in 1843, whereas Penfold had actually brought vine cuttings with him on the boat from Europe, and was planting a vineyard at what is now Magill Estate as fast as he was establishing a medical practice.

Their motives were very similar. They came to a society that was rough, violent and drunken. Rum was so much in demand that it was used as a kind of currency. They knew that wine not only had numerous medicinal qualities which would make up for the almost complete lack of more sophisticated medicines, but they also followed Thomas Jefferson, the third president of the newly formed United States of America, in believing 'no nation is drunken where wine is cheap… it is, in truth, the only antidote to the bane of whiskey', or, in their case, rum. It took more than a century for Australia to become a wine-drinking nation – rum was followed by beer as the national tipple – but by then, the vineyards Lindeman and Penfold had established in the 1840s had been transformed into Australia's two most famous wine companies: Lindeman's and Penfolds.

*Left: This Lindeman's bottle is now simply a large-volume blend of a grape variety –
Merlot – that didn't appear in Australia until long after Dr Lindeman's arrival. Right:
The Penfold bottle however, is a high-quality special bottling from ancient Shiraz
vines on one of the original Barossa plantations – the great Kalimna Vineyard.*

At the same time as the doctors were establishing their vines, another group of immigrants were making their mark equally indelibly on the new wine culture of Australia. Three boatloads of German Silesians arrived in South Australia in 1842; religious refugees fleeing from the excesses of the King of Prussia to a place where they'd heard there was religious freedom, where there was land available for them to farm and around which to rebuild their communities – and where the weather was doubtless much better than in Silesia.

The first families settled in a place called Bethany in the Barossa Valley, north of Adelaide – and immediately began to plant vineyards. To this day, most of the gnarled old grape growers in Barossa are direct descendants of those first settlers, and much of the Barossa seems like a German time warp, with German place names more common than English. But many of those old vines are still there, because South Australia never got attacked by the phylloxera aphid, and the ancient Shiraz vines now make some of the most treasured red wines in the world.

Is it just me, or does he have a twinkle in his eye? Dr Lindeman in his maturity. Note how he's left a gap in his whiskers for the wineglass to reach his mouth.

1843
BAROLO

For most of the last 100 years, Barolo has been talked of as Italy's leading wine. Brunello di Montalcino (currently very trendy in Italy) takes a tilt at it now and then, but while Brunello might be likened to some other wines, nothing is likened to Barolo.

Any attempt to say that Barolo resembles Burgundy founder as soon as you put two glasses side by side. They're both light in colour, they are increasingly offered as the produce of single vineyards, and they're expensive, but they are not alike. They don't smell alike, they don't taste alike, and Barolo – with its hallmark smack of tannic grip – doesn't feel like Burgundy either.

So is it an ancient wine? No, not really; it's a modern invention, though the Nebbiolo grape is certainly as old as the 13th century. Some people think Pliny the Elder wrote about it, while others contend that its DNA threads all the way to the ancient wines of Georgia, thousands of years back. If so, it wasn't exactly doing its pedigree proud by the time a 19th-century politician took an interest in trying to improve the quality of the wine. His name was Cavour, the great patriot who led the surge towards Italian Unification and, interestingly, he wasn't convinced by Nebbiolo. He planted five hectares of Pinot Noir to see if he could make something a bit like the Burgundies he'd tasted at the court of Savoy in Turin. He couldn't. That's the key. Unlike most Italians, he had tasted fine French wines, so saw the enormous improvements that his local Italian wineries would need to make. And he was lucky to have another local landowner desperate for change. The Marchesa di Barolo had enjoyed French wines while in France as a young woman. She got back home and found the wines of Barolo tart yet sweetish and frequently fizzy.

Nothing like Burgundy or Bordeaux. Nothing like the Barolo of today.

Barolo from the successors to the Marchesa di Barolo, who began the modernisation of the area in 1843.

The stroke of genius came from Cavour, who hired a French winemaker to come and sort things out – Louis Oudart, from Champagne admittedly, but with a passion for the thrilling reds of Bordeaux. In 1843, the Marchesa also employed him. What Oudart found in Barolo was that the Nebbiolo was allowed to crop very heavily, that it ripened only at the end of October or even into November, and then it was picked and bundled into dirty, unhygienic cellars. There, an erratic fermentation took place that was usually halted by the icy grip of winter well before all the sugar was fermented out. And you were left with a souring, sugary, prickly pale red. Oudart cut the yields, ensured his grapes were picked ripe, cleaned up the cellars, bought in new equipment, and heated the fermentation areas so that he could produce a full-flavoured, balanced and *dry* red wine.

He had the great red wines of Bordeaux in mind. I'm sure his wines didn't resemble them one bit, but it was his vision of their flavours, his knowledge of their techniques, that allowed him to literally invent what is now Italy's greatest red wine.

The King of Wines, the Wine of Kings, they called Barolo. King Carlo Alberto of Savoy liked the Marchesa's new wine so much he ordered a barrel for every day of the year (excluding Lent, of course). King Victor Emmanuel, first king of the unified Italy, was equally keen. They both planted Barolo vineyards – not a bad start for the red that was to become Italy's finest.

Barolo wines are increasingly bottled according to the villages or even single vineyards their grapes come from. La Morra is an outstanding village producing some of Barolo's most scented and approachable reds.

1845

HOCK

If you're wondering where the name *hock* **– a generic term for most German wine – comes from, well, it has to come from the village of Hochheim, an important producer of high-quality wine in Germany's Rheingau region for centuries.**

But when did hock become the catch-all name for German wine? And why? After all, in the Middle Ages you were far more likely to come across the term *Rhenish* – from the Rhine. But that didn't necessarily mean the wine itself came from the banks of the Rhine River. Wine was often named after its point of export, or, in this case, after the Rhine, which was one of the main transport arteries of northern Europe. An awful lot of wine was trundled across to ports on the Rhine from other parts of Germany, but also from other parts of Europe, and barged up to the Rhine's mouth and transshipped to markets simply labelled 'Rhenish'.

During the 18th century, as the estates of the Rheingau revolutionised their vineyard and winemaking methods, and began to produce what were clearly some of Germany's finest wines, the term *hock* gradually replaced Rhenish. During the 17th century, an English playwright was already able to describe 'the best old Hock' as being a fine mid-morning pick-me-up. Old Brown Hock was sold in England at the end of the 17th century, though sometimes it was offered 'with sugar', which implies it was a pretty tart drink in need of sweetening.

Hochheim is actually a village just off the Rhine itself, a mile or two up the River Main tributary near Mainz. But it has always been thought of as part of the Rheingau, and initially may have been thought of as the best. Hochheim generally managed to grow grapes with the highest sugar levels in the Rheingau, yet the grapes retained excellent acidity. This is because they were Riesling. During the 18th century, Hochheim was the first German wine village to become 100 per cent Riesling. When Schloss Johannisberg decided to go 100 per cent Riesling, they got their vine plants from Flörsheim, Hochheim's neighbour. So it stands to reason, shippers wanted to call their wine *Hochheimer* – it would sell for more money – and the English first garbled the name into *hockamore* and then, simply, *hock*.

But hock came into its own when Queen Victoria ascended the throne in 1837. Accompanied by her beloved German husband Albert, she stopped off in a Hochheim vineyard for a picnic in 1845. The vineyard's owner asked if he might call the site 'Hochheimer Königin Victoria Berg' (Queen Victoria's Hill). She said yes, and over the next 50 years the reputation of Germany's wines soared in Britain. At the same time the growing British middle class adopted hock as a favourite drink, especially as it was preferred by Queen Victoria herself.

Prices for the top German wines were often above those of Burgundy and Bordeaux. An 1896 list from London's long-established merchants Berry Brothers & Rudd showed, for instance, two hocks – a Rüdesheimer and a Marcobrunn from 1862 (34 years old!) – selling for 200 shillings (£10) a dozen. The most expensive Bordeaux was Château Lafite 1870 – a famous wine – offered for 144 shillings (£7.20) a dozen. Ah, how are the mighty fallen. Two World Wars involving Germany and Britain wrecked the close relationship these countries' wine businesses used to enjoy. Hock is now a term usually seen only on the cheapest own-label German wines on a supermarket shelf.

Here's the Queen Victoria's Hill wine. The owner is still successfully playing on the grand old Queen's name.

Nowadays we drink our Rhine wines fairly young, but in the 18th century anything that aged was much revered, and hock, because of its high acidity, was able to age better than most wines. How long it would last in a decanter is another matter.

LARGE-FORMAT BOTTLES

The drinking excesses of the 18th century are usually thought to be the fault of gin. Hogarth's 1751 print *Gin Lane* gives a fairly graphic demonstration of a society disintegrating under the weight of outrageous gin consumption.

Well, I don't think the wine drinkers ought to be all that smug. This was the age of the four-bottle man, the five-bottle man, even the six-bottle man. That's bottles per day. Dr Samuel Johnson was a three bottles of port man, Boswell's uncle was a five bottles of claret man, a chap called Mytton drank four to six bottles of port a day, and, good grief, a French general called Bisson drank eight bottles of wine for *dinner*. Every day! It's simply not possible for us to comprehend how people could function – or even stay alive – on such vast amounts of booze. I wondered whether the bottles were significantly smaller in the 18th century. But the Ashmolean Museum at Oxford has a wide collection of bottles, and just looking at the results between 1660 and 1817, the typical wine bottle is bigger than today's 750 ml, sometimes by as much as 25 per cent. I don't know how they did it.

There have been numerous attempts to standardise measures for beer and wine vessels, in part to make taxation easier, but also to stop people being cheated. Some measurements are implausibly precise, given how artisanal the methods of production would have been. Medieval Venice, for instance, was able to stipulate that an amphora should hold precisely 518.5 litres of wine. Yet in Tuscany, where they were starting to use barrels, the Florence barrel was 45.5 litres, and the Pisa one was 68 litres. Even in relatively recent times France's different wine regions had different barrel sizes, though almost every winemaker in France now uses the 225-litre Bordeaux barrel.

As for bottles, these have pretty much been standardised by the EU into multiples of 250 ml, the normal bottle being 750 ml.

The range of Champagne bottles, from quarter up to 20-bottle Nebuchadnezzar. There are in theory two even bigger sizes – Melchior and Sovereign. The four-bottle Jeroboam dates back to 1725, but most of these large-scale bottles appeared in the promotion-mad 1800s or the Jazz Age 1920s.

An imposing array of Bordeaux reds. Collectors pay big money for large-format bottles, but the best size for maturing wine is probably the two-bottle magnum (third from the right).

Supposedly there is a 100-ml size permitted, but I'm glad to say I've never seen it. Quarter bottles of 187.5 ml on the other hand are served all over the place. A quarter of champagne is supposedly called a Piccolo – that makes sense, a little one. A 250-ml Bordeaux is a Chopine, while you may get bemused looks if you call a half bottle a Fillette.

Nice name, though. Things get more interesting with the bigger bottles. We used to have Imperial pints in Britain – but they weren't very metric, so disappeared after we joined the European Common Market in 1972. A Magnum is two bottles, and often thought to be the best size if you're interested in ageing wines.

Then it gets more complicated. Bordeaux has a three-bottle size (the Marie-Jeanne), a four-bottle Double Magnum and a six-bottle Jeroboam. But Champagne and Burgundy call the four-bottle size a Jeroboam, and the six-bottle size a Rehoboam. And we're not done. Bordeaux strikes back with an eight-bottle Imperial, while Champagne and Burgundy call their eight-bottle a Methuselah. And it now gets more and more biblical. Burgundy and Champagne do a 12-bottle Salmanazar, but Bordeaux doesn't bite at 12 bottles at all. Sixteen, though – they all do a Balthazar; 20 is a Nebuchadnezzar, 24 a Melchior and someone, somewhere, supposedly has a 34-bottle Sovereign. In theory, eight bottles is as big as a Bordeaux goes, and most of the other giants will be promotional tricks for champagne houses. It's worth remembering, if someone offers you a monster bottle of champagne, that anything more than a Magnum will have been created by refilling the big beast with wine from smaller bottles. That can't do the flavour any good.

And as to why these biblical figures have had their names appropriated? No one really seems to know. Methuselah was Noah's dad and lived to 969, and Nebuchadnezzar built the Hanging Gardens of Babylon, but then he went mad and ate nothing but grass. Which doesn't really help, does it?

1855
BORDEAUX CLASSIFICATION

It wasn't about how good the wines tasted. It was about how much they cost. When Prince Napoléon-Jérôme, who was in charge of the Universal Exposition being held in Paris in 1855, decided to have a display of Bordeaux's wines at the show, he clearly wanted the best to impress the visiting dignitaries.

Now, you might have thought that the Bordeaux wine trade would have held a general tasting to judge which wines *were* the best. But that's not how Bordeaux worked. Bordeaux has always been about money. Fame and prestige built on the bricks and mortar of trade and hard cash. Prince Napoléon wanted a display, and a classification of the best – well, they had just such a thing at their fingertips, because the merchants had been unofficially classifying properties in Bordeaux since the 17th century.

Bordeaux's wine development was built on trade. Sure, the locals needed something to drink, but because of its situation at the base of the Gironde estuary, one of Europe's most effective natural harbours ever since Roman times, Bordeaux was dominated by trade. From 1154 to 1453, Bordeaux was English and wine was its most important commodity. The Dutch also traded Bordeaux wines enthusiastically, and so it's obvious that some hierarchy of what was best would develop, if only because some wines regularly cost more than others.

Well, that is *exactly* how the hierarchy developed. The first sort of classification occurred in 1647, influenced by Dutch traders, and the sweet white wines of Sauternes were put at the top because they achieved the highest prices. During the rest of the 17th century, the red wines of the Graves area south of Bordeaux were becoming important, and Château Haut-Brion became the first property to sell wine under its own name. At the same time, there was enormous expansion of wine properties in the Médoc to the north of Bordeaux, as the *nouveaux riches* of the city discovered there were many outcrops of gravelly soil, similar to that found in Graves, where they could develop estates – thanks to the Dutch draining the surrounding marshes during the 17th century.

By the 19th century, the gravel outcrops in the Médoc that grew the best grapes had been planted, and their wines traded for a century or more. But they were rarely sold direct; the traders in Bordeaux exercised tight control and gradually classified the estates according to price. To a large extent you could also say 'according to quality', because the best sites, especially those near Bordeaux, were developed first and established high prices first. Classifications were made in 1816, 1824, 1828 and 1848, and they mostly confirmed the traders' view of quality. And were the growers consulted? No. Bordeaux's Chamber of Commerce and its wine brokers made the decisions.

So when Napoléon's call came in 1855, Bordeaux's business community had a long-established hierarchy of five price or quality levels not decided on the spur of the moment, but based on generations of experience, and records of the prices the different properties achieved. Sauternes still gained the highest prices for its sweet wines, and Château d'Yquem was accorded the top title 'Superior First Growth'. Sauternes had 11 First Growths as against only four First Growths among the red wines. Why?

Price. Second Growths were shared between Sauternes and the Médoc but the Third, Fourth and Fifth levels were all Médoc red wines. This classification was not meant to be set in stone; it would naturally have continued to evolve, according to price. But, interestingly, in 1862, when London's Great Exhibition wanted to exhibit Bordeaux wines, the same list was sent. And to this day the only changes have been the addition of Château Cantemerle as an afterthought in 1855, and the promotion of Mouton Rothschild to First Growth in 1973. The members of this elite are understandably unwilling to disturb their profitable equilibrium.

Château Haut-Brion is the only wine from the historic Graves area classified in 1855. Lafite Rothschild, Margaux and Latour are the three Médoc properties that had developed the highest reputation and price by then. Mouton Rothschild became a First Growth in 1973.

1855-1870s
THE CONCEPT OF CHÂTEAU

A direct translation of the word 'château' is castle. Very grand. Very imposing. Often fairly ancient. And there are a few properties in Bordeaux that match this description. But these were mostly built in the 18th and 19th centuries to give the impression of nobility and aristocratic tradition, where in fact none existed.

Although some of the fine estate houses in the Graves area south of Bordeaux can claim reasonable longevity, the biggest concentration of these 'châteaux' edifices lies in the Médoc, to the north of Bordeaux, an area that was basically lawless, savage marshland until drained by Dutch engineers during the 17th century. It wasn't until the 18th century that Bordeaux's wealthy businessmen and parliamentarians began to develop estates and build grand houses there, and indeed the grandest – like Château Pichon Longueville and Château Margaux – weren't built until the 19th century. Partly this was simply to do with showing off. But there was often a deeper motive. These newly wealthy estate owners were desperate for legitimacy. Bordeaux had a long wine tradition, but their estates didn't. Building a château in 'faux-classic' or some other grandiose style could buy their wines a venerable tradition they didn't actually possess.

*Château Margaux – a Palladian masterpiece,
but completed only in 1816.*

Left: Pichon Lalande (it is usually known by its shorter name) was made famous by this wine – the great, lush, sensuous 1982 vintage. Middle: Most châteaux develop a 'second label' for batches of their wine that don't quite make the top blend. This one from Pichon Longueville is as good as many other châteaux's top wines. Right: Château Léoville Barton doesn't actually have a château – its wines are made at Château Langoa Barton, which is depicted on the label.

As it happens, their wines so quickly became recognised for their quality during the 19th century that they might not have needed this veneer of tradition in what was, after all, the century of massive industrial and political change. But the idea caught on. In the Classification of Bordeaux wines in 1855, only five estates called themselves 'Château'. By 1874, Bordeaux boasted 700 châteaux, 1300 by 1893, and nowadays there are thousands of estates called 'Château this or that', even if the property is barely more than a cottage at the corner of a field of vines. Call your wine 'Château' and you immediately improve your chances of selling it for a higher price.

So a château wine is, simply, the wine of an estate. But this estate can expand or shrink, and the 'Château' name remains the same. Many estates have increased in size, often by up to ten times, in the last century. If the original owner had established a reputation for a wine from the original vineyard, this might now comprise only a tiny part of the total. Indeed, a 'classified' château can buy vineyards that were not included in the famous 1855 classification and these are immediately accorded 'Classified Growth' status. However, if a 'classified' château sells some vines to a non-classified property, those vines lose their Classified status. So what does 'Château' stand for? A brand, maybe. A wine probably based on one particular patch of vines, but not necessarily so. An estate, definitely, and a marketing tool par excellence. 'Château.' Sounds very impressive. Just don't pry too much into the details.

Just about as space age as you can get. The Norman Foster-designed winery of Le Dôme – a Saint-Emilion 'garage' wine created by Englishman Jonathan Maltus.

1857

AGOSTON HARASZTHY'S BUENA VISTA WINERY

Buena Vista was pretty much the first wine estate established in California. There'd been vineyards earlier – those established by Spanish missionaries, some by Mexicans and several by French and German settlers – but the first really grandiose, 'look at me, ye mighty, and despair' operation in California was Buena Vista near the town of Sonoma.

The Buena Vista winery has now moved a few miles, though the original cellars are still left as a kind of museum. But it's not so much Buena Vista that's important, it's the guy who created it: Agoston Haraszthy.

Trying to pin down exactly who, what, why, when, where Haraszthy was is virtually impossible. Every source you check gives you different details. His reputation was as the man who invented the California wine industry. I suspect that's how he saw it, because he was without doubt the first massive personality of California wine – but how much of it was bluster? What did he really achieve? Has he really got a legacy at all?

Well. He called himself either 'Count' or 'Colonel' – both seemingly without foundation: he did come from some sort of vaguely noble family in Hungary, and he had certainly been a soldier, but had he been in the Imperial Bodyguard? In his early life had he already been a grape grower, a silkworm farmer and a member of the Hungarian parliament, all before he upped and fled to America as a political fugitive in 1840?

Maybe, maybe. Because he had untold energy. He arrived in Wisconsin, founded a town called Haraszthy – well, you would, wouldn't you? – and started a vineyard. In Wisconsin. Yup, you got it. The vines all froze. But then, fortune intervened. The California Gold Rush. And off he scarpered to the West Coast.

The thing is, I expect you're getting the message by now. He was an adventurer at heart, with all the charm, enthusiasm and energy that required, yet with the fatal flaw of never quite following things through. But California and the Gold Rush were made for him. He started a vineyard in San Diego. Didn't like it. Moved on. He planted his next vineyard in what is now the heart of San Francisco. Pity Mark Twain wasn't around to remind him that the worst winter he ever spent was summer in San Francisco. And then, finally, he got to Sonoma, north of San Francisco Bay, and planted Buena Vista.

And this is where his fame comes from. He was a relentless promoter of California as a viticultural paradise. He was the first – but not the last – Californian to realise that if you make enough noise, it eventually works. And one of the great needs of California, as vineyards expanded like mad with the Gold Rush, was decent grape varieties to replace the rather feeble Mission variety. Now, for a long time, abetted by his son Arpad (he had another: Attila the Hungarian), he was known as the man who introduced Zinfandel to California. But he didn't. He is supposed to have brought it back from a vine-gathering trip to Europe in 1862. But it had been growing on Long Island in New York as early as the 1820s and probably got to California before Haraszthy himself did. Fair enough.

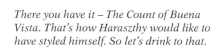

There you have it – The Count of Buena Vista. That's how Haraszthy would like to have styled himself. So let's drink to that.

The 'Buena Vista Ranche' from Agoston Haraszthy's 1862 book, Grape Culture, Wines, and Wine-Making. *I presume those are vines around the house. They look more like Christmas trees to me.*

He's also known as the guy who improved all the other European varieties that California so desperately needed. He did indeed bring back 100,000 vines of 300 different varieties, but he wasn't the first to bring in European wines. A French guy called Vignes (yes, really), some Germans called Kohler and Frohling, and then a whole array of French and Germans had been importing European wines since the 1830s.

But none of them made so much noise as Haraszthy. None of them had so much energy and self-belief. None of them were heroes. Haraszthy was. Flawed, yes. Tragic, really. Giving up Buena Vista, he went to Nicaragua and got eaten by an alligator. Or did he?

1860
WINE LABELS

A label on a bottle of wine, telling us all we need to know about it, is such a commonplace for us nowadays that it's difficult to remind ourselves that this is a modern phenomenon.

With a few exceptions during the ancient Egyptian and Roman periods, when individual vineyards *were* noted on amphorae (not bottles), wine was generally offered for sale in extremely generic terms – Rhenish, sack, claret, champagne – without any reference to the vineyard or the proprietor. This is because wine wasn't shipped or sold in bottles. Indeed, in England it was illegal to sell single bottles of wine from 1636 until the Grocers' Licensing Act of 1860 opened up a mass market. Wine would be shipped in barrels, and served from the barrel in taverns, inns and private houses. The barrel would have no precise name – you either trusted the merchant or you didn't.

Things began to change in the early 18th century as the fashion for laying down bottled wines in your cellar took hold. But the bottles still weren't labelled.

A 'bin' in the cellar might hold hundreds of bottles lain horizontally and there would be a coathanger-shaped pottery or slate label with stencilled information that was hung over each bin so that you knew which wine was which. Of course you would have to know what you were serving. Consequently, the 'bottle ticket' – or what we would call a neck label on a chain – was developed to hang on the neck of the bottle (or, more likely, the decanter) served at table. But the information was still purely generic – port, Madeira, claret and so on. The host might know which property the wine came from, but, far more likely, he knew only the name of his merchant.

But things were changing; the top Bordeaux properties were becoming better known, for instance, yet they were more likely to be identified by branded corks than by a label applied to the bottle. Burgundy was starting to be shipped under the name of the village

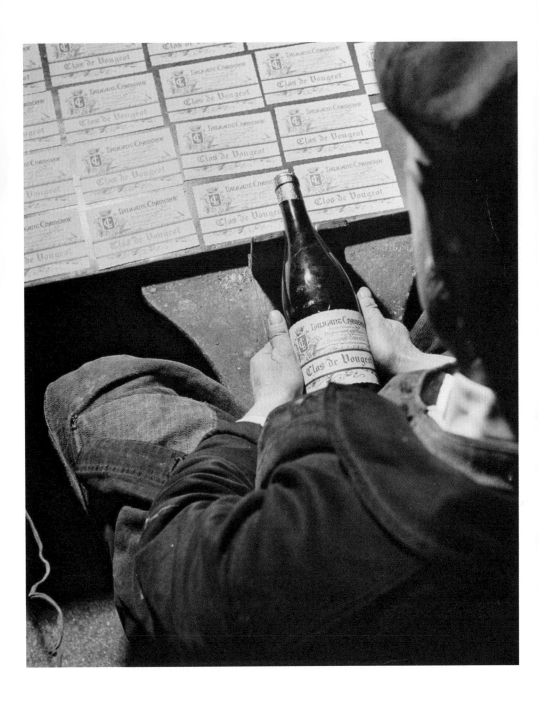

Hand labelling of Laligant Chameroy Clos de Vougeot in 1946.

at very least, but even so the earlier Burgundy labels are simply slips of white paper with the name of a village – Nuits, Volnay, etc. – stamped on it. Then came The Grocer's Licensing Act in 1860. Bottles could now be sold in shops, individually. The wines had to be identifiable. Merchants could merely put their own name on the label – and many did – but glues were now available that could stick to glass, and the paper label became commonplace. From then onwards the progression goes from bare bones information to simple information about the vintage, the region and maybe the property, to the beginnings of the label being used as a marketing tool – not merely as a provider of simple information. Bordeaux and Germany led the way in designing labels that promoted their superiority and individuality. Obviously, champagne leapt at the chance, but since champagne was usually served from an ice bucket, the glues had to be very strong. And of course, the labels didn't have to tell the truth. The phylloxera crisis (a devastating insect infestation) in Europe, starting in the 1860s, led to fraud and counterfeiting on an unprecedented scale. You could get lots of information off a 19th-century label, but it wouldn't be until well into the 20th century that you could be sure the information was accurate.

Many wines this old would have been stored without labels. These fabled vintages of Château Margaux have proper labels but are now covered in dust and mould.

1860
MURRIETA & RISCAL

It shouldn't be that difficult to agree on who was responsible for creating the modern style of Rioja – it was either Marqués de Murrieta or Marqués de Riscal. But it's not quite as clear-cut as you might want.

Murrieta made his first Rioja vintage in 1852 – but it wasn't at his bodega. Riscal started building his bodega in 1850, but he didn't make his first vintage until 1860. Which was the year that Murrieta established his own bodega. Both of them imported Bordeaux ideas, especially concerning oak barrels, how to make them and how to use them. Both began by planting Bordeaux grape varieties like Cabernet Sauvignon, partly because no one really had the slightest idea what was growing in Rioja or what it was called. But whereas Murrieta now concentrates on nurturing the traditional, Riscal still makes a big deal of its Cabernet Sauvignon. Murrieta taught himself how to make wine in Bordeaux, whereas Riscal hired a French winemaker. Murrieta exported under the estate name of Ygay, whereas Riscal sold his as Médoc Alavesa. But Riscal invented the wire mesh as a precaution against fraud, and this came to be a trademark of Rioja bottles.

I could throw in another name: a priest called Quintano from Labastida in Rioja Alavesa. He started visiting Bordeaux in 1780, did the vintage there in 1786, came back to Rioja with knowledge of Bordeaux techniques and a cartload of Bordeaux barrels, and exported ten barrels of reputedly excellent 'modern' wine to Cuba in 1795 – 60 years before Murrieta. But since no one has ever had a bottle of Quintano wine, I'll vouch for Murrieta and Riscal as joint 'first moderns'.

Why does it matter? Well, Spain as a wine country was vast but antediluvian. Whereas France had developed sophisticated export markets in northern Europe and North America, which demanded high quality and encouraged experimentation and improvement, Spain relied on a famously undemanding Spanish-speaking ex-empire and an undemanding local population. But Rioja should

No, your eyes do not deceive you. This is the new Frank O. Gehry-designed Riscal hotel and winery complex. As described by the architect, 'It is a marvellous creature, with its hair flying in all directions, launching itself over the vineyards.'

The two twins at the birth of modern Rioja – and by definition,
modern Spanish wine – are still both highly successful today.

be different. Wine was being made here by Celtic tribes when the Romans arrived in about 100 BC and rumour has it that they were even using barrels. That skill got lost for a very long time in a welter of clay pots, pigskins and unwieldy wooden butts, all used to clumsily convey their wine about the place.

Spain needed a kick in the backside to enter the modern world, and Murrieta and Riscal provided it. They brought Bordeaux ideas of improved vineyard practice (planting specific varieties in specific plots of land, limiting yields and picking ripe grapes); improved winery practice (keeping your winery clean, using sulphur to sterilise your fermentation and storage vessels); and using the barrel to age your wine – properly coopered barrels, watertight and clean, imparting a delightful spicy richness of newly toasted wood to the liquid it held.

Bordeaux was widely regarded as the world's best red wine in the 19th century. Suddenly here was another example, perhaps even a little spicier, perhaps with slightly riper fruit, being made only a couple of hundred miles south of Bordeaux. When the phylloxera aphid devastated Bordeaux in the 1870s, Rioja, led by Murrieta and Riscal, was ready to offer the world an equally delicious barrel-aged alternative.

LOUIS PASTEUR

Every time we pick up a pint of milk in a supermarket, we are reminded of Louis Pasteur. Pasteurised milk is now so completely accepted as the norm that unpasteurised milk is regarded as weird, if not positively dangerous.

Pasteurisation is indeed a wonderful invention – it's a process whereby you can kill virtually all bugs and microorganisms by heating, rendering them sterilised. In the mid-19th century, spoilage of liquids and foods was a massive social problem, and Pasteur's work in inventing sterilisation by heating can't be overestimated. But his most far-reaching discovery came in 1860, when he described the process of fermentation. Wine had been fermenting for at least 8000 years, but no one knew what was happening as sweet, gooey grape juice foamed and frothed, got hot and bothered and very lively, then finally calmed down to reveal a dry, sugarless liquid, tasting totally unlike grape juice. When you slurped it back, it made you bright and witty, flirtatious, playful, poetic, emotional, all-conquering, unsteady, cross-eyed, unintelligible, comatose, and, when you woke, very thick-headed. All down to the effects of alcohol. But what was alcohol? How on earth did it create itself?

Though the existence of yeasts had been known for some time, it was Pasteur who showed that fermentation was not some strange spontaneous activity, but an entirely predictable process whereby yeasts eat the sugar available in a liquid and create a precise amount of alcohol and carbon dioxide according to how much sugar was available to consume. Once this was understood, the first step had been taken towards the complete control that many modern wineries exert over a wine's fermentation, and the manipulation of flavour that today's winemakers can achieve through the choice of specific yeasts and regulation of the speed, the temperature and the length of their fermentations.

But of more immediate urgency in the France of the 1860s was the way wine turned sour so quickly. Why? Well, Pasteur came from

This 1885 painting by Finnish artist Albert Edelfelt makes Pasteur look like an amateur scientist popping by his chemistry set after dinner to do a quick experiment before joining the gentlemen for port. Artistic licence, I suspect, because Pasteur was one of the 19th-century's great scientists.

the Jura mountains in eastern France, where he had a vineyard. Spoiled wine was commonplace in the Jura, so Pasteur collected numerous samples of wines with all the different faults – like sourness, sliminess, sludginess, opacity – put samples of them all under his microscope and saw that each defect was being caused by a completely different microorganism. The more bacteria in the wine, the quicker it sickens. But the bacteria needed oxygen, he discovered. The more oxygen they had, the faster they multiplied. A jug of wine open to the air quickly sours. A half-full bottle with a cork in it sours much more slowly. Wine sealed in a test tube without any air didn't decay at all.

Now, at last, scientists and winemakers could begin to tackle the problem of wine inevitably turning to vinegar. And by so doing the creation of fine wine specifically meant for ageing could flourish. And after all this, Pasteur went off and invented a vaccine for rabies. Clever guy.

Until Pasteur, the prevailing view in France was that fermentation came about through spontaneous generation. Using this swan-neck bottle, Pasteur proved that grape juice sterilised and protected from the air could not ferment: the necessary yeasts were either airborne or resident in the grape skins.

1863
PHYLLOXERA

The phylloxera aphid did untold harm to the world's vineyards – and, indeed, is still seeking out and destroying vines in many parts of the world – but it also unwittingly did much good in fundamentally changing the way the world's vines are grown, and where they are grown. But the catastrophe had to be got through first. In 1863, vines began dying for no apparent reason, near Arles, in southern France.

Each year further patches of vines became sick, failed to produce proper leaves and shoots, couldn't ripen an increasingly meagre crop, and then died. By 1868 local scientists had discovered a tiny yellow aphid that clustered round the roots of the vine, sucking the sap and poisoning its root system. The rest of France took no notice. Plagues had occurred before.

In Roman times, Pliny the Elder advocated placing a live toad under sick vines to draw the poison. The Burgundians in 1540 had a plague of beetles. So they excommunicated the beetles. That'll teach 'em. Well, as usual, these kinds of remedies cropped up again, but then it all began to get a bit serious. The infestation started advancing up the Rhône Valley in 1867. It arrived in Bordeaux in 1869, was in Burgundy by the 1870s, and looked as though it might destroy all the vines in France., region by region And if France, what about all the other vineyards of Europe? Or, as it turned out, the world?

There were two major issues. How did the aphid spread? It became clear it both crawled through the earth and flew. It could be blown by the wind. And much later people realised it could be carried on boots, clothing or machinery, and especially on cuttings of vines. Secondly, could you kill it? Well, just about.

They developed a lethal mixture called carbon bisulphide which, if you injected it into the soil, would kill the aphid – but it could easily kill everything else as well, including your vines and, because it was very flammable, you.

The other method of dealing with it was worked out when the experts realised that phylloxera was indigenous to northeast America, and it didn't harm their native vines there, which were quite different from the European wine vine species. Indeed, the pest had probably arrived in Europe on a shipment of ornamental vines. Experiments of grafting French vines onto a rootstock of American species showed that the phylloxera didn't kill the American rootstock – and the French vines (Cabernet, Chardonnay and the rest) could continue to produce wine that was in effect indistinguishable from the produce of ungrafted vines. There was a massive resistance to allowing grafting with American rootstock, but as the plague spread, so resistance dropped, and grafting became commonplace.

With tiny local exceptions, phylloxera has spread right through Europe and the rest of the world. Phylloxera hit California in a big way in the 1980s due to a non-resistant rootstock being used. Most of the States' vineyards had to be replanted on resistant rootstocks and the old vines were simply ripped out and burned.

Somehow Chile and South Australia are phylloxera-free, and don't have to graft their vines. But the development of the science of grafting has actually allowed vineyards to manipulate a vine's productivity, disease resistance and ripening efficiency. Many marginal areas of vines were pulled out and never replanted. Other areas of the world – Rioja being a prime example – filled a vacuum for fine wine and created their reputations. After phylloxera, grape-growing is more expensive, and more complicated, but the results are probably better, not worse.

1889
CHAMPAGNE MARKETING

A lot of people say they don't like the taste of champagne. But they drink it all the same. Why? Because they want to be part of all it stands for. They want to belong to the gaiety, the laughter, the thrilling chance of romance, the celebration, the whole damned fun of it.

Champagne, for as long as it has foamed and sparkled from the bottle to the glass, promises the drinker that fun is within reach, that gaiety and laughter are there to be purchased – that for the price of a bottle of champagne it can be yours.

But it's not just fun and flirtatiousness and laughter.

No other wine has ever managed to symbolise a culture of excess, extravagance and luxury like champagne. It became known for its bubbles only in the latter part of the 17th century. Its dash to fame began with the famously debauched Restoration court in England as the nation put Puritanism behind itself and hedonism in front. France followed in the early 18th century with an even more debauched period during the Regency of Louis XV. The Duke of Orleans ran the country on a tide of champagne until Louis XV took over – and frankly he was pretty keen on it too, as was Louis XVI, who knocked off a bottle before they took him to the guillotine in the French Revolution.

And so it went. Napoleon was bosom pals with M Moët (who ran Moët & Chandon) and during the Napoleonic Wars champagne salesmen followed the troops wherever they went – all the way to Moscow if necessary. Napoleon may have lost at Waterloo in 1815, but champagne was established as the only wine for celebration in half of Europe. Who could resist the cascade of bubbles, the light-headedness, the explosion of delight? Certainly not the roués, the rakes, the relentless partygoers – the celebrities of their time, their antics drooled over by the common horde. Did anyone approve of the stars' behaviour? No. No more than we do today. But they were obsessed by it, and longed to get just a little taste of what that world was like.

Champagne offered that chance. Throughout the 19th century it became more and more widely available. And this meant it became more and more relentlessly marketed and advertised. And this took different forms. For the 1889 Universal Exposition in Paris, Mercier built the largest barrel in the world – it took 20 years to construct. It could hold 200,000 bottles of wine, and was drawn through Paris by 24 white oxen. Mercier also made the world's first advertising film – about champagne, of course – and had a giant advertising hot air balloon that inevitably broke loose and ended up in Austria.

In England, music-hall stars belted out songs proclaiming the superiority of one champagne or another. Two singers – the Great Vance (promoting Veuve Clicquot) and George Leybourne, known as Champagne Charlie (promoting Moët & Chandon) – held a singing duel from either side of a London stage. Mumm became the champagne of jazz in the United States and fought over the market with Piper-Heidsieck and Moët. Up into the Belle Époque, the Fin de Siècle and the Edwardian age, the party spiralled on. Two world wars and the Great Depression rather put a damper on things, but Prohibition, with its speakeasies and frantic pleasure-seeking, kept champagne flowing as the only nightclub wine.

And then came Hollywood. The stars again. They didn't just drink champagne. Marilyn Monroe ordered 150 bottles at a time so that she could bathe in it, and said she went to bed every night with Chanel No 5 behind each ear and woke up every morning with a glass of Piper-Heidsieck. And as for James Bond, well, no one sold the image of champagne better than 007, who used his knowledge of the vintage of Dom Pérignon or Bollinger to confound the lack of breeding in his villainous rivals or, more likely, to give his free arm something to do while the other one was dealing with a succession of the most beautiful women in the world. And the message hasn't changed: 'For the price of a bottle of champagne, you can get a tiny taste of what my life is like.'

1914-1915
CHAMPAGNE - THE BLOOD VINTAGES

The fiercest and bloodiest battle in the history of mankind was fought just to the east of the city of Reims in AD 451when Attila the Hun was finally pushed back from Europe and 200,000 men died in a single day's battle. You would have thought that in 1914 they would again defend this great city in whose cathedral 29 kings of France were crowned. But they didn't. As the German troops to the north were rattling their sabres, the locals were more worried about their upcoming vintage, which was looking very promising.

But the Germans swept in on 3 September, and by 6 September they'd gone round and over the Mountain of Reims to reach Épernay. The Seine River was only 30 miles away, the gateway to Paris; they thought they'd be dancing up the Champs-Élysées by October. But the Germans never got to Paris in World War I. In the First Battle of the Marne they were squeezed back out of Épernay with the help of the famous 'Taxis de la Marne' reinforcements from Paris, then ejected from Reims on 13 September, and it looked as though the Champagne region would be free after the briefest of occupations. A cruel delusion.

Reims was, technically, free, in that the Germans had gone. But they hadn't gone far. They were still dug in on the slopes of the Mountain of Reims, where much of Champagne's finest Pinot Noir was grown. The front line ran right through some of the best vineyards. Trenches criss-crossed these precious slopes and shells thudded into the earth between the rows of vines. And yet the harvest was brought in. At a cost. No one's quite sure how many adults died in the harvest, since so many men were being killed on all sides, but 20 children died in the

This 1914 Pol Roger champagne is one of the very rare 'blood vintages', which were harvested under the fury of German guns. It was sold in 2014, at Bonhams in London, for £5640.

These deep cellars in Reims protected precious stores of champagne perfectly from the shelling as well as providing shelter for up to 50,000 soldiers.

Harvesting the grapes for this 1914 Moët & Chandon would have been a heroic act, as shells rained down into the vineyards.

vineyard bringing in those 1914 grapes. Many more died in 1915, in particular two little girls of 12 and 15, as another spectacular vintage was somehow harvested under the rage of the German guns. The 'blood vintages', 1914 and 1915 are called. They say the blood of France runs through them, and very occasionally an old bottle is brought out and drunk in a solemn mood of respect quite unlike the gay high spirits that usually accompany champagne.

If harvesting the grapes was heroic, so was making the wine. The Germans began bombarding Reims on 14 September, only a day after they had been forced to retreat, and they continued the bombardment for 1051 days. The great cathedral was gutted and not one single home escaped damage. Almost the entire population of the city was evacuated, so that by the end of the war only 100 civilians out of a prewar population of 120,000 were left.

Yet in the first couple years of war, the citizens had survived by simply going subterranean. The vast chalk cellars that had first been dug by the Romans provided perfect shelter from the bombs – they say that not a single bottle of champagne in these vast cellars was broken by shelling during the war. And not only did the wine continue to be made there, but the life of the city continued in the safety of the caves, with thousands of citizens in effect living underground. And the French army took note. They cut connecting passageways between the cellars of rival companies – Veuve Clicquot, Pommery, Mumm and Ruinart were just some of the companies whose cellars were joined up; soldiers jostled with the millions of bottles of young champagne slumbering fitfully amid the chaos. By March 1916, this network of caves was big enough to hold 50,000 soldiers.

The years 1914 and 1915 were great vintages; and 1917 was also very fine. I'm sure they tasted wonderful. But I hope that those who drank them could taste the sacrifice and the pain as well as the kindly warmth of the September sun.

1915

VEGA SICILIA

The telephone rings. 'Hallo, Vega Sicilia.' 'Good afternoon. I'd like to order a case of your wine, please.' 'Have to wait your turn, sir. There's a waiting list.' 'Have you any idea who I am? I'm the King of Spain.' 'That's as may be, sir. Have to wait your turn, sir, like everybody else.'

That may not be an exact transcript of the phone conversation, but it's certainly one of the tales they tell at Vega Sicilia: that when King Juan Carlos of Spain rang up and asked for some wine, he was told he'd have to wait his turn. And I suspect it's true. Vega Sicilia has always played on its unavailability, its exclusivity and the need to know someone to get hold of a few bottles of this mysterious nectar, and for generations it was thought of as Spain's finest red wine.

But calling it nectar might have been stretching things a bit. Since Vega Sicilia never turned up at tastings it wasn't until the late 1980s, in Stockholm, that I finally got a taste. It was the legendary 1968, and well, it was certainly different. Intriguing, dark flavours of black fruit and wild scent, all carried along on a wave of high acidity that frankly verged on the volatile. And yet, this didn't seem to matter. This shimmering rapier of acid had pierced the fine gauze of fruit and aroma and carried it aloft, tangled and helpless so that the wine simply refused to disappear, long after the glass was drained. Memorable stuff.

Quite different from anything else I knew, Vega Sicilia was called Spain's only First Growth, the first table wine in Spain to be whispered of in the same breath as the great reds of Bordeaux.

The Bordeaux comparison is certainly valid because the owner of Vega Sicilia – which was then an isolated farm on the Duero River north of Madrid – went to Bordeaux

The legendary 1968. 'Unico' is the top selection of Vega Sicilia – the fine estate wine. Lesser parcels of wine are sold under the Valbuena label.

in 1864 and bought 18,000 vines: Cabernet Sauvignon, Merlot, Malbec, Carmenère and, somehow, the Burgundian Pinot Noir, which the Spanish authorities called 'exotic plants of recognised usefulness'. By doing this he was following the pattern set by Murrieta and Riscal in Rioja, but his wines didn't seem to make much impact – indeed, any fame the estate gained was for brandy and fruit eaux-de-vie. And it was only when the famous red-wine area of Rioja, to the northeast, was attacked by the vine-destroying phylloxera aphid in the 1890s that Vega Sicilia's red wine assumed some importance – the company of Cosme Palacio used to ship the estate's red to its cellars in Rioja where, one may suppose, it was magically transformed into Rioja and sold as such.

In 1915, the first Vega Sicilia red wine was released – the owner simply gave the bottles to his friends, most of whom seemed to be at the peak of Spanish aristocratic society. And so the legend grew. Only the grandest people drank Vega Sicilia, and you would never taste it because it was never offered for sale. If this doesn't sound like a great business strategy, well, it wasn't. Mostly the estate limped along. But it did make Vega Sicilia a magnet if someone very rich wanted to buy 'prestige'. This happened in 1982 when the wealthy Alvarez family bought the estate; since then they have assiduously cultivated the wine's mystique and exclusivity while gently modernising its style. But only up to a point.

This remarkable mix of Tempranillo (here called Tinto Fino) and Bordeaux varieties (usually Cabernet Sauvignon) still spends as much as six to seven years in wood, followed by several years in bottle – *musculación* and *educación*, the winemaker calls it – but they take much more care to express their 'terroir' and 'sense of place' nowadays. They have 19 different soil types in the estate and vinify up to 64 parcels of vines separately. And the dark sweet fruits, the same haunting scent wrapped round the javelin of acidity are still there, as ever. As the winemaker says, 'In Vega Sicilia our acidity is our passport to eternity.' And the King of Spain did get his allocation. Although Great Britain's Queen Elizabeth may not have been so lucky. When she visited Madrid in 1988, the ambassador wanted to serve Vega Sicilia but, well, he had to wait his turn, just like everybody else.

PROHIBITION

They called Prohibition the 'Noble Experiment'. But the effort between 1920 and 1933 to make the United States an 'alcohol-free zone' was anything but noble.

America has always had an ambivalent relationship with booze – not surprising when you realise that many of the Founding Fathers were Puritan. Indeed, the 'dry' lobby had been at work in the States almost from the start, and began to gain momentum during the 19th century. The target was strong liquor, not wine, but eventually all alcohol got swept up in a national fervour for prohibition. The first state to go dry was Maine in 1851. By the time World War I started in 1914, 33 states were dry. The Wartime Prohibition Act was passed on 18 November 1918 – even though the Armistice had been signed a week earlier – and the infamous Volstead Act, or Eighteenth Amendment, came into force on 17 January 1920 and lasted until 5 December 1933. During which time winemaking in the States increased by 50 per cent.

Sorry? Winemaking increased during Prohibition? Sure. Not winemaking by professional wine companies – that dwindled away – but winemaking by people in their homes, by entrepreneurs, by bootleggers. And most of this activity was legal! The Volstead Act firstly was woolly about whether actual consumption was illegal, and secondly left a crucial loophole in the amendment. It banned 'the manufacture, sale or transportation of intoxicating liquors', yet allowed a person to manufacture 'non-intoxicating cider and fruit juices exclusively for use in his home'. What constituted non-intoxicating was never defined. You could crush 200 gallons of grape juice a year for your family. But what if it started fermenting? Ah, what indeed!

Vineyards boomed. Plantings went crazy. Grape prices leapt from $10–$20 a ton to $100–$150 a ton. But not all grape prices. You couldn't sell Pinot Noir or Riesling for these prices, because they were fragile, had thin skins and couldn't be shoved into boxcars at the railway depot and trundled all the way across the continent to

New York, Boston and Philadelphia, where queues of people were waiting to buy them and take them home to crush. No – the grapes that sold best were thick-skinned, dark-coloured, coarse grapes, and none was more popular than Alicante Bouschet, whose skin was tough as leather and whose juice was black as sin.

By adding water and sugar to the Alicante, bootleggers could squeeze out four times as much hooch as from a typical wine grape. It became the number one grape variety used for 'non-intoxicating' wine all over the nation, and within a couple of years more homemade wine was being produced annually than all the commercial wineries had produced before the ban.

And there was some great ingenuity. Wine was still legal for religious use. Catholic congregations soared, and Jewish synagogues sprang up everywhere, because the Jewish faith requires wine in its rituals. But you could get registered as a rabbi just by presenting a list of your congregation. The phone book was useful for that. Doctors could write a prescription for liquor if a patient suffered from 'some known ailment'. Does thirst count? Paul Masson's 'medicinal champagne' boomed right through Prohibition. Virginia Dare, America's best-known wine before Prohibition, became Virginia Dare Wine Tonic and continued to flourish. And as for grape concentrate… 'grape bricks' and kegs of juice were sold with a yeast pill attached, which you were exhorted not to use 'because if you do, this will turn into wine, which would be illegal'. It was all so blatant. None more so than Vine-Glo concentrate, which offered home delivery of a 5- or 10-gallon keg. A deliveryman would start the fermentation off and return 60 days later bearing boxes full of empty bottles, which he'd happily fill up with your 'non-intoxicating' wine. He'd then leave you another keg of juice to start the whole process off again. It must have been popular: Al Capone banned it in Chicago on pain of death. It all seems like a bad joke now, and the wine side of flaunting Prohibition may not have done much harm. The story of hard liquor, bootlegging and gang warfare is much less light-hearted.

This scene was repeated all over the States – excise men raiding illegal stores, breweries and warehouses and destroying the liquor. It made no difference. The liquor kept coming, the gangsters kept getting richer – and more alcohol was being drunk at the end of Prohibition than at the beginning.

In very small letters this label tells you the wine is 'non-intoxicating' – a successful attempt to keep alive the Virginia Dare brand during Prohibition. The grapes pictured are Muscadines from the Deep South, whose musky flavour gave Virginia Dare its personality.

1924
MOUTON ROTHSCHILD – CHÂTEAU BOTTLING

The red wines of Bordeaux had been blended with darker, richer, sturdier wines from elsewhere virtually from the first day a ship left its quays for northern Europe 2000 years ago.

It was regarded as perfectly normal to 'improve' the rather light wines that Bordeaux naturally produced – the 'claret' as the English called it, meaning a light red or dark pink wine. Sometimes this blending was a good idea – at the end of the 18th century they used to mix Hermitage from the Rhône Valley with Bordeaux's top reds, and these 'improved' wines got the best prices. But more often, adulteration was carried out for baser motives. Thick Spanish reds – especially from Alicante – were routinely mixed with even respectable estate wines, and in the late 19th century, after the phylloxera scourge had devastated French vineyards, you could find so-called single estate wines containing nothing but North African hooch, maybe brightened up a bit with some elderberry juice, some blackberries or some floral concoction from the countryside. It was this sort of situation that the 20-year-old Baron Philippe de Rothschild discovered when he took over the family property, Château Mouton Rothschild, in 1922.

One thing particularly struck him. The wine that was to be sold to the wide world was carted off to the city of Bordeaux in barrels as soon as it had finished fermenting. No one knew what the merchants did to it in their cellars. It might be recognisable, or it might not, if the estate owner chanced a bottle later on. Yet the wine that the estate was keeping for its own use was cosseted and cared for day and night until it was bottled off by hand. It always tasted completely, integrally of its place – the vineyard, the vintage, the experts who had made it. How could you promote your wine as special unless you had total control over its authenticity and quality? Baron Philippe decided the wine of Mouton must from

The artists get paid in wine for their illustrations. Chagall with his powerful 1970 was a good deal luckier than Miró and Kandinsky, whose fees were the comparatively feeble wines from the 1969 and 1971 vintages.

then on be bottled at the property, the château, so that the ones who prepared it, then guaranteed its provenance and quality, were those who cared about it most.

This seems perfectly normal nowadays, but when Baron Philippe persuaded the four other top estates in Bordeaux – the First Growths of the 1855 classification – to join him in offering for sale only their wine bottled at the château, it threw the Bordeaux trade into turmoil as their whole integrity was, quite rightly, questioned. It took until 1971 for it to be mandatory for all the Bordeaux 'Classed Growths' to bottle their wine at the château itself. It's fitting that the flamboyant Philippe de Rothschild set this movement going. He could see Bordeaux was old and stuffy in the 1920s and needed a good shake. He provided it in 1924 when his first 'château-bottled' label was illustrated by an electrifying Cubist masterpiece from Carlu.

From the 1945 vintage, Mouton Rothschild has commissioned a new artist every year to design the label for its top wine or *grand vin*. Many others worldwide have followed but none do it with the flair of Mouton Rothschild.

The first Château Mouton Rothschild label from 1924. Jean Carlu's thrilling design is one of the greatest examples of Cubism in commercial art.

1931
QUINTA DO NOVAL NACIONAL

Have I ever tasted the world's rarest port, Quinta do Noval Nacional 1931? Tasted it? I've drunk it, old boy. Knocked it back. Straight from the bottle. Set me up nicely for a jug of Pimm's.

Port lovers go pale when I tell this tale; they break out in sweat and shakily reach for the balustrade to avoid collapsing in a heap of sputtering outrage. Shameful. Sacrilege. It can't be true. But it is. I was at a very poor college in a very rich university. We probably struggled to pay the electricity bill, let alone go around constructing new libraries and science wings. But there was one thing we had more of than anyone else. And I mean anyone else in the world – Quinta do Noval 1931. There were stacks of it in the cellar. So one summer's evening my friend Andrew said, 'Come to a drinks party.' I'd been playing cricket, but thought I'd go because Andrew always seemed to have a bevy of attractive girls fluttering round him. I turned up, a bit sweaty, and thirsty. 'Here's your drink, old boy.' He called me 'old boy' – he did! – and handed me a half bottle of wine. No glass. Just the wine. Quinta do Noval 1931. His roof terrace was full of attractive girls, all right. All holding half bottles of Noval 1931. I'm not sure some of them didn't also have straws.

Well, I drank it. In amazement, frankly, because even then I'd heard of its legendary quality and exalted price. I reckon we drank the college out of half a new library building that evening. And I didn't even take notes. But why is it so rare, so expensive – and so good? OK. Most great vintage ports are made from blending together the wines of various *quintas* or farms. Of the top producers, only Quinta do Noval is an estate wine. Traditionally port shippers, rather like champagne producers, would say, 'Oh, the blend is always better, the sum is better than the parts.' We don't believe that any longer in Champagne, nor in the Douro Valley, home of port.

Not only has Quinta do Noval always come from this one unbelievably beautiful, steeply terraced property high above the river valley, but on the property there are a few rows of vines that were never killed by the phylloxera aphid that destroyed Europe's vineyards in the 19th and early 20th centuries. Just 2.5 hectares.

Although this tiny patch was replanted with Touriga Nacional vines in 1925, the vines were on their own rootstocks, ungrafted, and have always given barely half the crop common on the rest of the estate – a crop of tiny, intensely sweet grapes. So the vines were only six years old in 1931 and young vines are not supposed to give great red wine. I can only say that in Bordeaux, 1961 was possibly the greatest vintage of the 20th century, and many of the vines were only five years old after a catastrophic frost in 1956.

And then there's rarity. In 1931, the world was in the grip of the Great Depression. Before things had got really bad, there had been a large and superb quality port vintage in 1927. Britain was the most important export market, and they bought heavily of these wines. Then the Bad Times really hit. No business was being done and the merchants' cellars were bulging with unsold 1927 port, as most people decided that whatever money they had was certainly not going on port. So when the whisper went out that 1931 was as good as 1927, might be even better, the wine trade didn't want to know.

Shipping of vintage port was largely a British activity, and they simply turned their backs on 1931. Yet funnily enough it was a solitary English merchant who took the risk on 1931. His name was Butler. He tasted the 1931 wine and was bowled over. He thought it might be the greatest vintage ever made, yet everyone was blending their 1931s away. Except one property: Quinta do Noval. Butler begged them to make the vintage wine, and he said he'd buy most of it if they did. He kept his word.

Noval made about 6000 dozen of Vintage 1931, and just a couple of hundred dozen of 1931 Nacional – only from that tiny plot of ungrafted vines. Which did I drink? Not all the Nacional was branded as such. Could it be…? And anyway, why did my college have such a store? Well, the price being asked was just 30 pence a bottle. Much cheaper than the 1927. They were probably just trying to stock up on the cheap. Bless them.

This might be the most famous port ever, but they didn't muck around with fancy presentation in those days. Actually, the fact it had a paper label at all was pretty good going. The wine still tastes wonderful – and my college still hasn't got a new library.

1935
APPELLATION CONTRÔLÉE

It's only when the cheating and the counterfeiting and the fraud get unbearable that someone steps in and says, 'Enough! We simply have to try to regulate.' And nowhere was the cheating and the counterfeiting and the fraud getting worse than in the French wine industry as the 20th century dawned.

Cheating has been around for a long time in wine – you only have to read English writers going back to the times of Pepys, Shakespeare and Chaucer to know that recipes for producing fake Bordeaux, Burgundy, champagne, port, sherry or sack abounded. Taverns were full of drinks purporting to be something smart but likely to have been brewed up down by the docks a mere couple of weeks previously.

But in the early 20th century there were more pressing social forces than before. The scourge of the phylloxera aphid had wiped out many of France's vineyards, and was in the process of wiping out the remainder and then proceeding on through the rest of Europe. Real wine was at such a premium that a million tons a year of raisins were being imported into southern France to boil up into a form of wine. The port of Sète became the main point for imports from Spain, Italy and Algeria which would exit the port northwards labelled as anything from First Growth Bordeaux to Burgundy or Hermitage. Riots took place from southern France to northern Champagne against the counterfeiters. And at last the politicians took action. Local laws, then national decrees, appeared, sometimes simply stating for the first time that wine must be made 'exclusively from the alcoholic fermentation of fresh grapes or fresh grape juice'. That was a start. The next move was to delimit areas of vineyard that could use a title like Chablis or Bordeaux. Politics entered in, because who decides where the boundary is drawn? Being in or out would make a big difference to your income.

Left: Château Fortia is the estate of Baron Le Roy, who got the ball rolling for Appellation Contrôlée in 1923. Is this the real thing? It might be. But I can't be certain. It was bottled in Luton. Right: A typical bottle of Nuit-Saint-Georges on the British market, before membership of the EU in 1973 forced them to obey Appellation Contrôlée laws. You won't find the words Appellation Contrôlée on the label. Not surprising. Most of the Nuits-Saint-Georges in Britain in the 1960s was blended and bottled in Ipswich. Actually, this one was bottled in France, and was delicious.

Roquefort cheese posed, then answered, the next question. The cheese had been granted a delimited area of production – that's wonderfully French, the cheese's origin is just as important as the wine's – but the decree didn't mention that it must be made out of ewe's milk. They soon put that right. A man called Capus seized on this for wine, adding another decree saying different wines could use only 'grape varieties hallowed by local, loyal and established customs'. The framework of the French Appellation Contrôlée, or Controlled Appellation, system was in place.

In 1923, Baron Le Roy in Châteauneuf-du-Pape produced further refinements demanding that only suitable land inside a delimited area should be allowed to use the local name; and in 1935, the French set up the Comité National des Appellations Contrôlées – now the Institut National de l'Origine et de la Qualité. Though it is easy to see this system of Controlled Appellation as a brake on ingenuity and innovation – which is probably true – much more important is the way in which it set out rules to try to guarantee authenticity of origin and ingredients as well as such things as maximum yields, pruning methods, alcoholic strength and winemaking procedures.

All round the world, when authorities try to set up a system of controlled appellation, it's to the French and this system that they look first.

A remarkable old bottle of Château Margaux, before Appellation Contrôlée kicked in. No vintage – but I was told it was 1900. No Appellation. And it was bottled in Bradford by a family company more famous for silk manufacture. But the bottle does have the most humungous punt – that's the indentation at the bottom of the bottle.

1935

PRESTIGE CUVÉES

Prestige Cuvée champagnes don't get a massively good rap among normal wine drinkers. They're fiendishly expensive and they often seem to be drunk only by celebs and Eurotrash who've definitely got more money than sense.

If you let the whole glitzy nonsense get to you, you could become pretty irritated at the amount of this supposedly gorgeous foaming nectar that is swilled down the gormless throats of the glitterati. So are Prestige Cuvées the pinnacle of the winemakers' art, or are they an awful lot of style and not a lot of substance? Or can they be fantastically beautiful wines despite being dolled up in courtesan's glad rags? Well, some of these bottles have a very long heritage. Indeed the rather beautiful pear-shaped and narrow-necked bottle that has its most striking manifestation in the simple elegance of Dom Pérignon – Moët & Chandon's Prestige Cuvée – dates right back to 1735, when a Royal Decree standardised the size and glass quality of the champagne bottle. Exactly 200 years later, in 1935, Moët & Chandon produced a couple of hundred bottles very similar in design to the originals as a defiant blow against the ravages of the Great Depression – Dom Pérignon, the first unashamed luxury brand. They make an awful lot more Dom Pérignon nowadays, and it can almost be accused of being too successful a brand to be exclusive any more. Until you taste a perfectly matured bottle, and understand what all the fuss is about.

Roederer Cristal is another wildly successful Prestige Cuvée which genuinely did seem to be exclusive, until 'Cris' became all the rage on the New York music scene. It comes in a clear glass bottle wrapped in orange cellophane. Just a gambit? No, there's a good reason for it. Although

This must be one of the most beautiful and elegant of Prestige bottles – Perrier-Jouet's Belle Epoque with its alluring, dreamy presentation.

the first commercial release of Roederer Cristal was in 1945, its popularity in Russia began in the mid-1800s. Part of the reason for this was because Roederer played mercilessly on Tsar Alexander II's sweet tooth. Not only did they add 20 per cent of sweet liqueur to their wine for the Russian court, but for good measure they threw in a dollop of yellow Chartreuse as well. To distinguish the wine at the Tsar's table from the stuff his subjects drank, Roederer came up with the see-through bottle – just for the Tsar. The others got green bottles. Nowadays, a glass of properly matured Cristal is beautiful wine – and regally dry in style.

Of course these Prestige Cuvées are drunk by the rich and famous, and of course the companies will charge as much money as they can get away with. And they'll take advantage of the worlds of music, film and fashion as much as they can. Piper-Heidsieck launched a super-cuvée in 1999 'dressed' by Jean Paul Gaultier. But for all the surface froth, most of the Prestige Cuvées from serious producers really are their most rigorous selection from their very best vineyards, in the finest vintage years. And for that, you'll pay.

Left: Roederer Cristal was Tsar Alexander II's favourite. The orange cellophane is to protect the clear glass bottle against sunlight – not a common commodity in Tsarist Russia. Right: Piper-Heidsieck gets the Jean Paul Gaultier treatment.

BEAULIEU CABERNET SAUVIGNON

Nowadays the words Cabernet Sauvignon and Napa Valley are so closely linked you would think they'd been partners from the moment the first vine was planted in the valley.

In fact, Cabernet was a slow starter – vines like Zinfandel, Cinsault, Chasselas and Mission dominated early plantings. Around 1880, a guy called Crabb probably planted Napa's first Cabernet in Oakville at what is now one of the valley's famous Cabernet sites – the To-Kalon vineyard, source of Mondavi's top Cab. During the 1880s, the Bordeaux varieties still accounted for less than 5 per cent of the total. By the 1890s, the phylloxera aphid was ravaging the vineyards, and Prohibition didn't exactly help – vineyards, paradoxically, flourished to supply the 'home-winemaking' market, but this required thick-skinned, hardy varieties like Alicante Bouschet and Carignan, not Cabernet or Merlot.

But there was one ray of light. A Frenchman named Georges de Latour had planted an estate called Beaulieu at the end of the 19th century, and in 1909 began producing wines, in particular Cabernet Sauvignons, which rapidly became famous. He survived Prohibition because he gained the approval of the Archbishop of San Francisco to supply altar wines – one of the numerous loopholes in the Prohibition framework – and Beaulieu went on providing altar wine until 1978!

So when Prohibition ended in 1933, Beaulieu was one of the only Napa wineries in operational order and with a mature vineyard of Cabernet Sauvignon vines. But most of Beaulieu's wines were being made in pretty decrepit conditions and sold off in bulk. Just one small batch of Cabernet Sauvignon was kept back each year in small barrels. This was the tinder for the flame that became Napa's crowning glory. And the appointment of a Russian emigré named André Tchelistcheff as winemaker provided the spark. He came from France in 1938, well-trained in the latest French techniques.

Above: One of California's historic bottles. I had a bottle in a neighbouring vineyard after a hard day's filming, and at 40 years old it was in spectacular nick – much more vibrant than much younger wines. Facing page: Tchelistcheff sorts his Cabernet Sauvignon at Beaulieu.

In Napa Valley Tchelistcheff found ill-kempt vineyards and worn-out, rusting wineries and even basic requirements like temperature control weren't being – or, indeed, couldn't be – fulfilled. There was no equipment. Tchelistcheff had to throw in blocks of ice to cool his first vintages' fermentations. And no one had the slightest clue as to how important cleanliness was. At Beaulieu, Louis Pasteur's work had never penetrated the vinegary confines of the old winery. Except in the little room full of oak barrels maturing the 1936 Cabernet Sauvignon wine. And here he saw what the future could hold. Tchelistcheff tried to persuade Beaulieu to concentrate solely on Cabernet; they wouldn't, but he set out to prove that Cabernet Sauvignon from the vineyards of two tiny villages in Napa Valley (Rutherford and Oakville) could be world class. Starting with the 1936 vintage, he named his top Cabernet Georges de Latour Private Reserve, in honour of the founder of Beaulieu, and over the next 35 years he consistently produced profound, memorable Cabernets that set the standard for Napa vintners to follow. And he helped them. Appalled by the lack of technological know-how, he established in 1947 the Napa Valley Wine Technical Group, which gave technical advice to over 80 wineries. He also acted as consultant to wineries in Sonoma, Paso Robles, Santa Barbara and elsewhere in California, always beating the drum for quality. And when he heard the rumours of wineries being established in Oregon and Washington he went up there to help them too. Georges de Latour Private Reserve was the first great wine of Napa's modern era, but André Tchelistcheff was the inspiration and guide for, quite literally, hundreds of the great wines that followed.

1942
MATEUS

I can't be absolutely sure that this is true. No, that's not right. It is true. It has to be true. My mum told me. Admittedly, she was a great believer in never letting the facts get in the way of a good story, but there are no other witnesses, so here goes.

When my dad demobbed after World War II, my parents went to a basement club called the Bag O'Nails, near Piccadilly in London – supposedly a fairly swish place. With his new bride and a small wodge of money, my dad decided to splash out. He called over the maître d' and ordered a bottle of champagne. 'Ah, sir,' said this august subterranean, 'I *could* give you champagne, but the new fashion is for something far superior. Pink sparkling wine from Portugal. Mateus Rosé.' My dad had been in the jungle for five years, so maybe his bullshit detector wasn't working too well. So he ordered the Mateus.

I never got a tasting note, but my mum swears it was more expensive than the champagne. I bet it was.

Mateus, more fashionable than champagne, more expensive than champagne! How could this be? Well, it was certainly new. When my dad left these shores for the East, it hadn't even been thought of. Indeed, pink wine in Portugal was pretty much unheard of, and pink sparkling wine decidedly so. But in the depths of wartime, despite Portugal being neutral, you can come up with some desperate schemes to make a buck. And the wine business in Oporto was in trouble. Oporto is the centre of the port trade, but with war cutting off most of the traditional markets like Britain and northern Europe, port shipments had dropped to their lowest levels ever recorded. This meant there was a great deal of red wine hanging about going to waste, and a big surplus of grapes with no market.

Thirty business friends founded a new company to export wine to one of the few markets they could get to – Portuguese-speaking Brazil, directly across the Atlantic, and away from the depredations

This is the bottle that launched a million romances – my mother's included – and later doubled as a candleholder for those same millions embedded in marital bliss.

of the U-boats. They hired a rundown co-operative at Vila Real, north of the Douro River, to make their wine, which was initially red and white. Fernando Van Zeller Guedes thought they were missing a trick. The spritzy, light, Vinho Verde wines were very popular in Brazil. Surely one of the ways to soak up the surplus of black grapes would be to make a slightly fizzy pink wine in the style of Vinho Verde. Easier said than done. With no tradition of pink winemaking in Portugal, they were unsuccessful until they hired a French winemaker – who they nicknamed 'little de Gaulle' – and he showed them how to make fresh, slightly fizzy, not quite dry, rosé wine.

So they had the wine. Now they needed the bottle and a name. The bottle they chose was based on the traditional slightly flattened Portuguese water flask that soldiers used to carry in World War I. The label featured a beautiful 18th-century baroque palace, which just happened to be situated close to the winery, and just happened to be called Mateus. Guedes offered the owners 50 cents a bottle royalty for the use of their name and label, or a single down payment. No, you don't want to know which the owners chose. OK. They picked the single payment. Following its launch in 1942, and hundreds of millions of bottles of Mateus later, it's still not a subject to be brought up in conversation.

The elegant baroque beauty of the Mateus Estate. What you can't see is the owners inside, gnashing their teeth and crying, 'Why didn't we take a royalty payment per bottle?'

1945
NAZI WINE

For anyone who loves culture, art and the good things of life, there are many tales of wreckage and destruction from World War II that are still harrowing all these years later.

For those of us living in a Western civilisation during the 21st century it is almost impossible to realise how brutal, how eviscerating, military defeat in a war can be. You no longer own your country, your possessions, your career, and often your life. The conqueror struts through your streets, casually taking what he will, cuffing aside any resistance, your life no more important to him than that of a stray mutt. And so it was with France after Germany literally strode into that country in 1940.

France suffered the typical humiliation, and occupying forces quickly identified and commandeered as much gold, jewellery, fine art, sculpture – even luxury cars – as they could. But there was something that set France apart from any other nation in the world. It made the world's greatest wines. The Germans knew this. And they wanted them.

Well, up to a point, they got them. Large amounts of France's greatest Bordeaux, Burgundy and champagne were shipped off to Germany. How much? Gobsmacking amounts. Field Marshal Göring – you could tell he was a bon viveur by how he was always busting out of his uniform – was, unfortunately for the French, a genuine connoisseur of wine, and so were Goebbels and Ribbentrop. Hitler wasn't. He didn't like the taste. Of wine, that is. But he did like the taste of victory and subjugation. He may not have been interested in drinking the spoils of victory, but he still wanted to establish the greatest wine cellar in history. And he did. In the Eagle's Nest, the Alpine retreat where he hatched his plans for the Thousand Year Reich,

Hitler gave these bottles of Führerwein to his generals on his birthday in 1943.

he scooped up enough plunder from the great French vineyards to stock a cellar full of half a million bottles of France's finest wine.

There were some in Germany's high command who wanted to tread cautiously as regards pillaging France. Not so Göring. 'I intend to plunder, and plunder copiously,' he said. His boss Hitler had a similar opinion. 'We will give back nothing, and we will take everything,' was his view. And the crème de la crème of French wine ended up here, in the Eagle's Nest. Vintages going back to the 19th century of Romanée Conti, Mouton Rothschild, Lafite Rothschild, Latour and d'Yquem. And for the young sergeant from Champagne who first forced open the doors of the cellar in May 1945, case upon case of Salon 1928. Salon, the most exclusive label in champagne; 1928, the vintage of the century. Luckily, Hitler had had neither the time nor the inclination to drink it, and all these precious bottles, the jewels of France (well, minus a few, of course – the liberators were a thirsty bunch and deserved a bit of refreshment) made their way back to Champagne, back to where they really belonged.

The thirsty conquerors. Soldiers of the 3rd US Infantry
relax over a few bottles of Hitler's hooch.

Wartime vintages of Bordeaux and Burgundy. The wine in these bottles may have been genuine, but the French were masters at passing off gut rot in correctly labelled bottles – and Hitler, for one, wouldn't have been able to tell the difference.

1949
ÉMILE PEYNAUD

They really should erect a statue at Château Duplessis-Hauchecorne. This was the first property to employ Professor Émile Peynaud, in 1949, and so, you could say, the property that ushered in the modern age of wine in Bordeaux.

We take so many things for granted nowadays in wine: ripeness of fruit in the vineyard, lack of disease in the grapes, clean balanced flavours in the wine, the gentle kiss of oak, and even the certainty that the wine won't start fermenting again in the bottle. In Bordeaux all of these things are now a foregone conclusion. But they weren't. Not before Professor Peynaud arrived on the scene.

So what are we talking about? Well, firstly Peynaud was pretty dismissive about how great wines had come about during the previous 200 years. In fact, he said they hadn't been made, they had occurred. In other words, good luck was more of a factor than skill in the vineyard or winery. He said that in fine vintages you might find a fair number of superb wines because the grapes were healthy and ripe when picked, and they had sufficient tannin, acid structure and sugar richness not to be destroyed by the hopelessly hit-and-miss winemaking practised in the cellar. And in less good years, far fewer decent wines had been made, and in some cases, none at all. Peynaud was certain that he could transform affairs by applying basic good science to the production of wine, eliminating the haphazard by relentlessly emphasising the logical.

He could obviously preach this gospel from the pulpit of Bordeaux University, where he taught. But he knew that most winegrowers had no time for attending academic lectures when there was work

Mas de Daumas Gassac, near Montpellier in southern France, was described as the First Growth of the Midi after Peynaud showed them how to handle the Bordeaux vines – Cabernet Sauvignon in particular – and how to make wine in his Bordeaux way.

Émile Peynaud, 'the forefather of modern oenology'. His research and coaxing and cajoling of the winegrowers transformed Bordeaux wine.

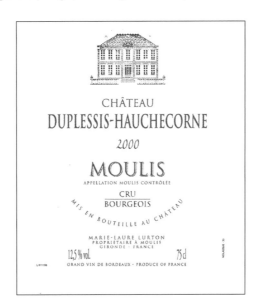

This Bordeaux château is now called simply Duplessis, but it's the same place where Peynaud was first employed to consult.

to be done in the vineyards. And though he wrote some seminal books, which I have read with great pleasure, he knew that most of the estate owners had better things to do than sit down by the fire with a cup of cocoa of an evening and thumb through his musings. So he got on his bike and visited the properties, one by one. He clocked up hundreds of consultancies and his objective was to visit them, again and again, to explain face to face what he wanted the producers to do in the vineyard and winery.

In the vineyard he insisted that rotten grapes be discarded – they hadn't been before – and that growers should relentlessly assess the ripening of their grapes, and pick only when ripe. Again, most growers left the grapes on the vine into autumn only in bad years, to achieve some sort of ripeness; in good years, they too often picked as early as they could to guarantee a crop, but thereby wasted weeks of autumn sun. And he persuaded them to ferment different varieties and ripeness levels separately.

In the winery he preached cleanliness – kick out the dirty old bacteria-infested vats and barrels and replace them with stainless steel vats and new oak barrels. He also realised that lack of temperature control was a nightmare, since out-of-control fermentations could easily stall and turn to vinegar, and in any case bacteria multiply far faster in warm conditions – so cool cellars were crucial, and temperature-controlled tanks were an expensive necessity.

And he figured out malolactic fermentation – the bacterial action that turns harsh malic acid into soft lactic acid. Vintners had often noted what seemed to be a second fermentation in their vats, or sometimes in their bottles, but hadn't known what it was. Peynaud showed it was a crucial phase in the softening of a red wine, but that it must be – and could be – controlled.

This softness, allied to the gentle spicy warmth of new oak barrels, created an entirely new, mellower type of red Bordeaux. His insistence on strict selection of the best barrels in the winery, and the creation of second labels for those not up to the mark, created a new depth and intensity in Bordeaux during the 1970s and 1980s. Modern Bordeaux was ushered in by Professor Peynaud.

1951
GRANGE HERMITAGE

If you're going to make great wine, the first thing you must have is imagination. You can find the grapes, you can buy the barrels and you can design the label – but if you don't have a vision of flavour, a vision of greatness bubbling away in your brain, you'll never make great wine.

Well, Max Schubert must have had some imagination. There he was in 1950, prowling around a sherry cellar in Spain, the air filled with the sweet-sour fumes of fermenting sherry – and his mind was racing with the vision of a great *red* wine that he suddenly knew he could make. Because he wasn't smelling sherry. He was smelling wood – the sweet, spicy, smoky pungency of new American oak.

He'd never smelled that exotic marriage of wine and new oak before. He smelled it again in Bordeaux a few weeks later, tasting the results of the super-ripe Cabernet and Merlot grapes of the 1949 vintage aged in new barrels. Combine all this with numerous old bottles of Bordeaux – his favourite was a 1916 Château Léoville-Poyferré – which his hosts opened for him to show how elegantly a structured oaky red wine could age, and he headed back to Australia, to his employers, Penfolds, with the dream of making a great Australian red.

Except that Australia had no small new oak barrels, precious little Cabernet, and no Merlot. So he'd do it the Australian way: he'd use the best Shiraz he could find, there was loads of that – and he chose two old vineyards in cool sites near Adelaide. Then he'd beg or borrow any sort of new barrel he could locate – he finally found five fairly small American oak barrels. So here he was, with a vision based on Bordeaux that he was going to have to execute in a uniquely Australian way. And he'd call it Grange Hermitage – Grange was the name of the original Dr Penfold's house and Hermitage was the most famous Shiraz vineyard in France. The first Grange was made in 1951, but it wasn't until 1960 that the wine began to throw off its dark tannins and brooding personality and exhibit its thrilling mixture of cedar and blackcurrant, tar and smoke, beef blood, leather and liquorice – and poignant, memorable balance – which can remind you of the great wines of Bordeaux and Burgundy and the Rhône all thrown together, just for a moment, before you realise you don't need any comparisons with the great wines of France.

This is a true original. A wine as good as anything from Europe and uniquely Australian.

We almost didn't have any Grange. Because it tasted tough and impenetrable when it was young – just like any great Pauillac or Hermitage – Penfolds ordered Max to stop making it in 1957. But Max was a gritty bugger and kept on making it in the dark reaches of the cellar where management never went, knowing that time to mature was all that his masterpiece needed. And in 1960 he could finally show his bosses the 1951 in all its glory – one man's vision that would not be denied. It swept away generations of cultural cringe and inferiority complex, and ushered in the modern wine age for Australia; now, perhaps, the most self-confident wine nation in the world.

The mighty nose which started the red wine revolution in Australia at work.
Max Schubert checking out the aroma of his beloved Grange.

Left: Wonderfully understated, the rudimentary label that ushered in the modern era of great Australian wine. It doesn't even say it's an Australian wine. Right: The label of this modern Grange is still reassuringly unflashy. And I like the homage to Max Schubert in the top left-hand corner.

1952
BARCA VELHA

The history of the Douro region of Portugal as the producer of some of Europe's most exquisite table wines, both red and white – but overwhelmingly red – is extremely recent. Indeed, it's virtually a 21st-century phenomenon. But it began in 1952.

It always amazed me how poor Douro red wine was. It was offered to you almost apologetically if you dined with port shippers in Oporto. After they'd enthusiastically plied you with slugs of icy white port, a barely digestible drink of which they seemed inordinately proud, they would then ladle out a dark, chewy, baked red wine simply because the main course required it, but all their attention was on the sweet fortified red port wine that would be lingered over until the night was old. If you were dining up the Douro Valley with the shippers, the white port routine was similar, but it tasted more refreshing on a verandah gazing out over the river valley. The dense, chewy red was dismissed as the house plonk. And, of course, the vintage ports tasted wonderful, and inspired scholarly comparison of their qualities, witty conversation and impenetrable slumber in about equal measure. A British consul in Oporto had written in 1880 that Douro table wine was a 'strong, rough and comparatively flavourless wine. If a man were to add six drops of ink to a glass of very common red burgundy he would get something exceedingly like unfortified port.' From some of my experiences, he was being kind.

The thing is that Douro wine used to be shipped to England unfortified and dry, and the English drank it because it was cheap and French wines were unavailable because of war. They called it blackstrap. Once sweet fortified port caught on during the 18th century, all the best grapes from all the best vineyards were used for that. Grapes that were unripe, or, more likely, overripe and raisined were used for table wine. Yet sweet port had all that sugar to disguise any roughness and nastiness. Dry table wine displayed all its faults, especially when the grapes had been given the crude handling common in port production until quite recently. Indeed, the leading vintage port houses used to make the most cloddish

*Barca Velha – the first great Douro table wine. This bottle was
the tenth release from Barca Velha since its first vintage of 1952.*

table wine and it is significant that it was Ferreira, one of the greatest producers of delicate tawny ports, who decided there had to be a way to make decent dry red wine in the Douro. In 1950, they sent their technical director, Fernando Nicolau de Almeida, to Bordeaux to learn how they made red wines that were so refined and balanced.

He came back knowing that he had a battle on his hands. Bordeaux was a temperate maritime area, with a couple of centuries' experience in making the world's best red wines out of Cabernet and Merlot grapes.

His chosen spot was high up the Douro Valley near the Spanish border, where the conditions were torrid, there was no Cabernet or Merlot, and his winery was antediluvian. He didn't have modern presses, he didn't have barrels. He didn't even have electricity to cool his fermentation; he had blocks of ice coated in sawdust and brought upriver from Oporto on the local train, and he passed the fermenting juice over them to try to stop it from boiling over. But somehow, by 1952, he'd produced the first Barca Velha, which is now regarded as the first great Douro table wine since, well, no one knew when. No one had ever waxed remotely lyrical about great dry wine from the Douro. Perhaps there had never been any. There's an awful lot now. But progress was painfully slow at first. In the first 40 years, up to 1991, there were only 12 releases of Barca Velha. But that in itself gave the wine a legendary status as Portugal's only First Growth red wine.

And as demand for sweet port has waned, more and more producers – usually those without a reputation for great port, and consequently with an open mind as to how to grow their grapes and make their wine – are turning out a string of superb Douro reds: scented, complex, original, excitingly different from any other European reds. Many of these now outshine Barca Velha. But without the pioneering of Ferreira and Sr de Almeida in 1952, they'd have had nothing to outshine.

1950s-1960s
THE BORDEAUX EFFECT

Bordeaux has had more impact on the way wines are made around the world than any other region. And it is not simply the ubiquity of the Cabernet Sauvignon grape and its magnetic effect on global winemakers trying to hit the big time.

There are other Bordeaux grapes that have been taken up, to a greater or lesser extent, by winemakers around the world. There are the styles of Bordeaux wine – red, white, sweet and dry. And there are the methods of creating this wine in the first place.

The methods that Bordeaux spread round the world are based on practice in the vineyards and in the cellar.

Since most of the new wine areas are warmer and drier than Bordeaux, a precise copy of what works in Bordeaux may not suffice, but the objectives are relevant – limiting yields to achieve ripeness, sampling of grapes, rejection of rotten fruit, picking and vinifying each variety separately, and separating inferior fruit straight away to be sold under a second label. In the winery, a fuller understanding of 'malolactic' fermentation – the second fermentation that in many areas didn't happen at all or happened in the bottle – contributed massively to softer, more consistent wines. Temperature control and cleanliness are thought of as the gifts of the New World to Europe, but Bordeaux vintners were working hard on them by the 1960s. And the *barrique bordelaise*, the Bordeaux barrel of 225 litres, became adopted around the world in regions where most wooden vessels had been big, old and dirty, piled into hot warehouses that were simply guaranteed to spoil most of the wines. All of these elements made up the Bordeaux Effect.

The style of wine that was initially imitated and emulated was the dark, strong, age-worthy style of the Cabernet Sauvignon–dominated wines of villages like Pauillac and Saint-Julien, and

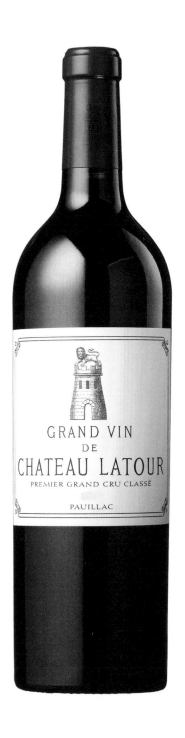

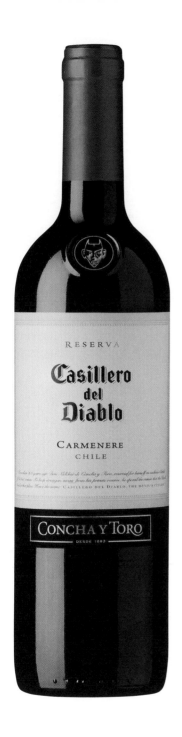

Latour is the most powerful statesman of the Cabernet-dominated Bordeaux style in the world. La Conseillante is altogether gentler and mellower, reflecting its Merlot base. The Bordeaux effect is truly global – here's a Carmenère from Chile and a Merlot from California.

properties like Latour and Lafite Rothschild. But the softer red styles of Saint-Émilion and Pomerol, based on the Merlot grape, have had an equal impact in the last 20 years. Barrel-fermenting and blending Semillon and Sauvignon Blanc has created a classic dry white style much emulated in South Africa, Australia and New Zealand.

And the great sweet wines of Sauternes have influenced dessert winemakers in these countries and in North and South America.

Apart from Cabernet Sauvignon, the Merlot grape has made an enormous impact because of its easy, lush style, not only on the wines of California, Washington and Chile, but also all over Europe and the Far East. But it's not such an adaptable grape as Cabernet Sauvignon. It ripens quickly, and yields prodigiously. In some parts of Europe it has fuelled a wine revival, but too often it has merely produced oceans of easygoing forgettable red grog.

Cabernet Franc is an under-respected grape in Bordeaux but is showing that in some areas it is the best of the Bordeaux reds – close to home in the Loire Valley just north of Bordeaux, but also in places like Virginia, Uruguay, Brazil and Canada, as well as with the bigger boys like Argentina, Chile and New Zealand. Petit Verdot is also showing how good it can be as a dark, scented, late ripener, ideal in the cooler parts of Argentina and Chile and the warmer parts of Australia, as well as in havens like Virginia. Malbec has made Argentina its new home, and Carmenère, the great Bordeaux grape lost in the phylloxera crisis, has triumphantly reappeared in Chile and more circumspectly in China.

1960
J BOLLINGER V COSTA BRAVA WINE COMPANY

Michael Grylls was just a student coming home from a lovely, lazy summer holiday on the Costa Brava in Spain, having thought up a brilliant wheeze. I don't think he expected to be standing in the dock of the notorious No 1 Court at the Old Bailey in London a few years later, having his precious wheeze ripped apart by the cream of Britain's legal eagles.

A precedent was being set that has dramatically influenced not only British wine practice regarding truthfulness in the naming of a wine, but wine practice worldwide.

Grylls had tasted some very pleasant sparkling wine called Perelada while on holiday on the Costa Brava; in 1958 he founded the Costa Brava Wine Company to import the Perelada fizz, which he called Perelada 'Spanish Champagne'. He probably thought he was on pretty firm ground here. Britain had been importing Spanish Burgundy, Spanish Graves, Spanish Sauternes for generations. A significant number of important British wine merchants did most of their business with these Spanish knock-offs. And it went to the heart of how the British saw wine. Did wine really come from a particular place? Was Sauternes just a generic term for sweet; did Burgundy just mean a rich, beefy red; and did champagne just mean a wine with bubbles in it, not a wine specifically from the delimited and legally protected Champagne region to the northeast of Paris? So if a Spanish wine called itself 'champagne', was this firstly a lie, and secondly a case of 'passing off'?

Unlike Costa Brava's Spanish 'champagne', this bottle of Perelada clearly labels itself as Cava.

Nowadays, we'd probably say, 'Both.' But it wasn't so clear then. The champagne producers seemed like a bunch of well-heeled Continental bullies victimising a blameless young English entrepreneur, and sure enough the English jury found the Costa Brava Wine Company not guilty, and the popular British press cheered. Not so the French. And not so the more thoughtful among the British wine world. Authenticity was what was being brought into question. France had made good progress in enforcing its laws about Appellations of Origin.

To them it really mattered – not only in France, but worldwide. No one in Britain had yet degraded the term 'champagne' by applying it to wines of a completely alien geographical provenance. They wanted to stop the rot before it started. And since Champagne relied so heavily on exports for its profits, they wanted a legal precedent with which to fight against producers in other countries who used the term 'champagne' for their domestic fizz.

So in 1960 the champagne exporters, led by Bollinger, brought a new action to try to establish that they collectively and exclusively owned the right to the name 'champagne'. A pamphlet issued by the Costa Brava Wine Company called 'Giving a champagne party' and clearly designed to tempt retailers to sell the Spanish Perelada as champagne, finally swayed the judge. He ordered the Costa Brava Wine Company to stop selling their Perelada under any name that included the word 'champagne'. And from that moment onwards the Champagne producers have been most energetic in prosecuting anyone outside the Champagne region making and selling sparkling wine and selling it as champagne. The United States still holds out, but none of its good fizzes call themselves champagne – paradoxically only the cheapest bubbles do. I can't disapprove of any of this. But the Champenois have become relentless in their defence of the word 'champagne'. A 'champagne' shampoo in Germany and a 'champagne' deodorant in Austria, even a 'champagne' perfume by Yves Saint Laurent in France, were taken to court. And Thorncroft, a little English company making traditional 'Elderflower Champagne', was taken to court accused of 'passing off' this old countryside drink as champagne. No one with one tenth of a palate could not tell the difference. That's when the word 'bully' does come to mind.

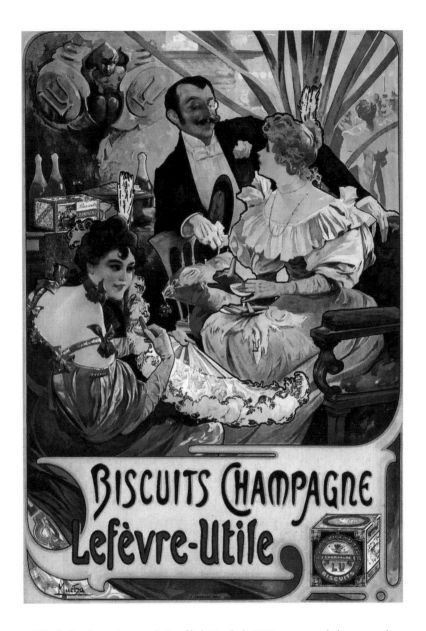

Way before lawsuits were being filed, Mucha's 1896 poster used champagne's association with high society and glamour to sell these dainty biscuits.

1961
KONSTANTIN FRANK

You don't really think of the Dutch as great vineyard planters, but they were the first ones to try to establish a New York wine industry between 1647 and 1664.

Then the English had a go. Their efforts failed too, as did everyone's along America's East Coast for the best part of the next 300 years – primarily because of the phylloxera aphid. Lethal to European vines, though not to local vine species, the pest is native to the Northeast. And in New York State, there was an extra problem: cold; winters so cold that they routinely destroyed European *Vitis vinifera* vines. The problem had been partially solved by Philip Wagner, a grape grower in Maryland who pioneered hybridised crossings of European and local vines. Then in 1952, a man named Konstantin Frank took the bus up from New York City to Geneva, in the heart of New York's main wine region, the Finger Lakes – a group of deep glacial lakes just south of Lake Ontario, whose relatively warm waters allow vineyards to be planted on their shores. He was determined to prove that the classic grape varieties of Europe could work in New York State.

And he wasn't just Konstantin Frank. He was *Dr* Konstantin Frank, and he was headed for the New York State Agricultural Experiment Station in Geneva to try to get a job working on vine research. He should have been the perfect candidate. He had a doctorate from Odessa University in Ukraine, and his thesis had been on growing high-quality *Vitis vinifera* grapes in cold climates. And by cold, he meant cold. He'd grown *vinifera* in Russia, where the temperature went to 40 below, 'where we had to bury the entire vine in winter, where when we spit it froze before it hit the ground.' He didn't get the job, though; they put him to work hoeing blueberries. Maybe the fact he could hardly speak English didn't count in his favour. But word of this crazy Ukranian guy got to Charles Fournier, boss of a wine company called Gold Seal. Fournier had been chief winemaker at Veuve Clicquot champagne in France and had come to Gold Seal to make 'champagne'. He was eager to plant *vinifera* grapes, but didn't know how to deal with the intense winter cold.

Frank persuaded Fournier that in areas where the ground froze the secret was to find supremely hardy roots onto which you could graft the sensitive *vinifera* vines. Together they set off to comb the American Northeast, and in a convent in Quebec, Canada, they got lucky.

With a winter climate even worse than that of New York, the convent produced wine from Pinot Noir vines one year in three. Back at Gold Seal they grafted vines onto the Canadian roots – mostly Riesling and Chardonnay because they had hardier, cold-resistant wood, but also Gewürztraminer and Cabernet Sauvignon. In 1957, temperatures dropped to –25°C. Even many of the native vines were killed. But the Riesling and Chardonnay on the Canadian rootstocks showed less than 10 per cent damage, and at vintage time produced a healthy crop of three to four tons an acre. Frank's biggest triumph came when his 1961 Riesling Trockenbeerenauslese sweet wine was served at the White House.

And the vines that are now making world-class wines in these lakeside vineyards are Rieslings on some of Dr Frank's super-cold climate rootstocks, just as he had predicted.

New York's Finger Lakes now make some of the world's most delicate, delicious Riesling. Konstantin Frank's pioneering work made it possbile. His winery on the western banks of Keuka Lake enjoys balmy and tranquil summers but the winters can be particularly vicious with great swthes of vines killed in 1980, 2003, 2014 and 2021.

1963
A FUTURE WITHOUT GLASS

I've been seeing the future for quite a while when it comes to alternative packaging for wine. On one of my first wine trips to Spain I was seriously impressed by a Tetra Brik packaging line in the middle of La Mancha: the wines in these little wine bricks were far fresher than their brethren in bottles.

I've made the same kind of discoveries in Chile and Argentina, where they don't want you to taste the wines that the locals drink, but they can't exactly say 'no' when you see a Tetra Brik machine at full tilt, and you say, 'Ooh, can I try that?' Again, much fresher than the equivalent wine in a bottle. But then I've also tried wine enthusiastically offered to me at wine trade fairs in what seemed to be orange juice cartons. I've been offered wine in tin cans – red, white, pink, sweet and dry, still or fizzy – and all tasting more of tin than wine, and then suddenly you stumble across a Pinot Noir in a tin can that tastes delightful.

Funnily enough, the fact that none of these products look remotely like a wine bottle probably works in their favour in the long run. They're making no attempt to be a glass bottle. They're saying, 'Forget all that old-fashioned stuff. This is progress. This is ecologically sound, this takes a hatchet to your carbon miles.' Which of course is what the 'paper bottle', which I saw at a wine fair back in 2012, does too. This weighs only 55 grams versus 500 grams for a glass bottle, transport is cheaper, and the carbon footprint is only 10 per cent of a glass bottle. It's biodegradable – important when you consider that some experts thought the UK, for example, would run out of landfill space by 2018. But I still thought it looked like a papier-mâché mock-up that somehow had ink spilled all over it. If I'm going for alternative packaging, I'm happy for it to look futuristic and totally non-bottleish.

Well, the Tetra Brik carton – which was introduced by the Swedes in 1963 – is hard to beat. It's usually in a rectangular shape, it's usually a litre in size, and its seal protects the wine, because it can exclude all air contact.

When I first saw a Tetra Brik line at work, there was just this great roll of flat plastic and cardboard that came out the other end of the filling machine as a really concise little block of wine that looked far smaller than a litre bottle, but clearly wasn't. The only problem really with these Briks was opening them without squirting wine all over yourself. Funny. When it's a milk carton, I don't spill milk all over myself.

Well, modern Tetra Briks – often called 'aseptic', meaning they keep the liquid fresh without needing refrigeration – do have decent opening systems, they tick all the eco-boxes, and are so simple to use. We now just have to put decent wine in them, and serve it unapologetically.

After all, I didn't think tin cans were much good until that Pinot Noir came along, followed by a string of super American craft beers, which showed that tin with a high-grade lining was absolutely fine as a package. So maybe, at last, this *is* a sight of the future.

A South African white in a Tetra Prisma carton, left, and right, a Californian red in a plastic-lined cardboard bottle.

1963
TORRES VIÑA SOL

I was on a wine trip to Spain some time in the 1990s, during which we kept a captain's log – the kind of log you'd keep if you were on a life raft after your ship had gone down. 'Seventeen days and still no sight of land... 25 days and still no sight of land... 40 days...' – you get the gist. Except what we wrote was 'five days and still no sight of Viña Sol... seven days and still no sight of Viña Sol...'

Day after day, winetasting after winetasting, all we craved was an ice-cold tumbler of crisp, lemony Torres Viña Sol. And we weren't getting any. It's not that there wasn't any to be had – it was probably in just about every bar in Spain by then – it's just that none of the wineries we visited were making white with the bright, snappy, thirst-quenching character that made us crave Viña Sol. They were trying, but the old original was winning hands down.

It's not really fair to call it 'the old original' – the first bottle had hit the market as recently as 1963 – but it *is* fair to call it 'the original'. The original modern dry white wine produced in Spain. Spain wasn't the home of white wine then, it was the home of yellow wine.

That's the way the Spaniards liked it. Catalonia was famous only for big, rich, yellow-to-brown Malvasias and Muscats. Yet Catalonia is where Miguel Torres came from. He'd gone to study winemaking and vineyards in France – Burgundy and Montpellier – and came back to his family company amazed at the possibilities he'd discovered, yet horrified at the tired old winemaking and vineyard practices he found back home. Interestingly, his father had introduced a brand called Viña Sol in 1956.

A 50th-anniversary label celebrating Viña Sol's half century. The fresh, snappy white is still the white wine of choice in most of Spain's bars.

And it gave young Miguel – all of 21 years old – the vehicle he needed. But Miguel's father was also an authoritarian – he wasn't going to have his smarty-pants young son coming in and turning the successful Torres winery upside down. So Miguel had to find somewhere he could experiment in secret, and he also had to find some grapes.

He found both in what's called 'Nordic Penedès' – the coldest, highest part of the Penedès wine region inland from the Catalan coast. The village of Pontons was about 20 kilometres away from the family winery, far enough away for a secret experiment, and it was 600 metres above sea level, with some chilly vineyards as high as 750 metres. He found some Parellada grapes – up until then thought of merely as an acid little number, useful for making sparkling wine – and he found a garage. Well, it *was* a secret experiment. He was trying to pick the freshest grapes he could find and ferment them as coolly and slowly as he could, so a garage in the coldest part of the region was not a bad start. Because he didn't have any cooling equipment, any stainless steel. The whole of Spain didn't have any.

The experiment worked. Miguel's father was persuaded to shell out for Spain's first stainless steel tanks and first temperature control equipment. And in 1963, the brand was launched. Along with its sibling, the red Sangre de Toro, it not only became the most successful brand in Spain, but it finally began to haul Spain into the 20th century. And when Spain needs leadership in the 21st century, Miguel Torres is still there to provide it. He's already growing grapes at 900 metres above sea level in the pre-Pyrenees. But he's bought Pyrenean land at 1500 metres. With climate change proceeding at such an alarming rate, he says that's where he'll be growing his Chardonnay, Riesling and Parellada in 10–20 years' time.

Torres Sangre de Toro is the red sibling of Viña Sol and is probably Spain's most widely available red.

1964
GALLO HEARTY BURGUNDY

I had my first taste of it in a smoky, noisy room in a snow-smothered Madison, Wisconsin. I was a student, and a lot of that smoke wasn't of the particularly legal kind. But the red wine was a revelation.

Gallo's Hearty Burgundy. In a big bottle, but costing almost nothing. Now, I was a bit of an expert on the kind of wines you got at student parties in England – I even managed to keep some of them down. But I'd never realised that cheap red plonk could actually taste good. No, that night it tasted delicious. Full, fruity, ripe, with a kind of plum and cherry jam flavour that wasn't all that dry, but nor was it harsh or sour or bitter. It was just an excellent drink. Made, as it happens, from grapes.

These weren't grapes from Burgundy, of course, they were from California. But cheap grapes from Burgundy would have made a *far* worse drink. I also guzzled some Chablis Blanc that night – or was it called 'Mountain Chablis'? That was pretty good, too. Cheap, fruity, not quite dry. Definitely not from Chablis. And did I then try some 'crackling pink Chablis'? Or was the passive smoking of all that whacky backy going to my head? Whatever. It doesn't matter, because I had made a monumental discovery. Cheap wine does *not* have to taste filthy. This was the 1970s. In Britain we'd been starved of fruit and freshness and ripeness in our basic wines for centuries. Well, forever. Within a decade this would all change in Europe, but the first people to make decent quality mass-market wines for the table were the Americans, and Gallo's Hearty Burgundy, which was launched in 1964, was the best of the lot.

This is what Hearty Burgundy looks like now. I wonder if it's as good as it was in those hazy student days.

Gallo made their first Hearty Burgundy in 1964. Obviously they weren't too worried about legally protected European place names – port, sherry, Burgundy and Sauterne (it should be spelled Sauternes) all appear in this ad, but the wines were certainly not from Portugal, Spain or France.

Over the years I haven't used the word 'best' about all that many Gallo wines. Volume has been their god. Domination of markets, pursuit of profit at all costs. Yet that's to forget that the passion and determination that made E & J Gallo the biggest winery in the world (they lost that title to the massive multi-national Constellation only in 2004) was based on improving vineyards and winemaking, not just on ruthless marketing – although they led the world in that. Gallo produced a 300-page manual on how to sell wine, down to the last detail. For example, '7 foot across is the widest the human eyes can take in at one go – so make all your Gallo bottle displays in a store 7 foot across'; 'Put highly advertised bottles at eye level, impulse purchases at waist level, biggest bottles to the right of smaller bottles' – oh, it goes on, and basically ends with something like: Just keep on filling up the fridges and shelves with Gallo until the competition caves in.

But back to the quality. Gallo was started by two brothers – Ernest and Julio – in 1933, just before Prohibition ended, to sell bulk wine. Within three years they'd built a winery with a 1.5 million-gallon capacity. They started bottling their wine in 1938, and by 1950 had the largest winery in America. But it wasn't until the 1960s that the winds of change swept through this vast industrial complex in California's Central Valley. Until then they'd mostly made stuff like Night Train Express and Thunderbird – oh, you know it? It's still the sign of a misspent youth.

But the Gallos could always sense a shift in the market, and there was a new generation growing up who were keen to drink table wines with their meals. Julio Gallo offered growers long-term contracts at fixed prices to plant better grape varieties. He brought in stainless steel tanks, started making amber-green 'flavour-guard' bottles (they had their own bottle factory) to guard against oxidation from sunlight, and began to refine their blending. They'd always bought a lot of grapes from Sonoma and Napa to improve the sun-scorched produce of the Central Valley. Now they had the chance to use them properly to produce a fresh, fruity, delightfully drinkable red Burgundy wine, which was largely based on Barbera and Petite Sirah fruit from those new contracts, and certainly not containing a single Burgundian Pinot Noir grape – and, frankly, all the better for it.

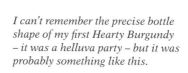

I can't remember the precise bottle shape of my first Hearty Burgundy – it was a helluva party – but it was probably something like this.

1965
BAG-IN-BOX

It must have been pretty bad, because I can still remember the taste of it. My first bag-in-a-box wine. It came from Bulgaria. And it tasted of geraniums. Geraniums in a garden. Nice. Geraniums in a glass of wine? Not nice at all.

I later discovered that this rather nauseating geranium taste came from lactic acid bacteria reacting with sorbic acid – a chemical used to combat the growth of fungus in the wine. All pretty distasteful? You got it. Those first bag-in-boxes took a real hammering from us wine critics. We compared their wine with supposedly the same wine coming out of bottles, and invariably the bag-in-box wines were inferior – fruitless, rough and usually just plain unclean. They would never catch on…

Well, they did. In some markets – Sweden is an example – they captured as much as 50 per cent of sales. And nowadays, the quality is invariably pretty good. For that – as in so many other facets of basic wine quality – we have to thank the Australians. The Aussies have always been sticklers for detail in wine – crucial, because wine is a living thing, and microbes, bacteria and fungi just love to create havoc in wine if you let them. The Bulgarian stuff was probably poorly grown, definitely made in a slovenly way, and packaged without due care. It was never going to taste better than rubbish. But the concept of bag-in-box was a good one.

You could pack a much bigger volume of wine into a smaller space than if it was in bottles. It weighed less, and it wasn't breakable. If you were a restaurant, you could use it to provide wine by the glass without being left with half-empty bottles every night. And at home, you could pop this compact container into the fridge – three litres taking up less space than four 750 ml bottles – and you would always have a glass of chilled white or rosé ready, day or night.

Thomas Angove, a winemaker from Renmark, South Australia, was the first guy to invent 'cask wine' packaging, patenting it on 20 April 1965. In 1967 Charles Malpas and Penfolds Wines patented a plastic, airtight tap welded to a metalised bladder-like bag, making storage more convenient, pouring easier and spillage less certain.

I suspect one of the reasons the Australians became the experts on bag-in-box was because they love to barbecue, to picnic, to head for the beach and the great outdoors. The box was perfect – or rather the innards of the box were, since they often ripped out the bag and threw the box away as they sloped off to Bondi Beach with their 'bladder pack'. Basically you have a collapsible laminated bag inside its box. The bag is usually made of polyester layers with a layer of aluminium between them. This keeps oxygen out. A tap fits into the bag and sticks out at the bottom of the box. This is where the greatest danger of wine spoilage occurs, trying to get an absolute impermeable seal between the tap and the bag. But it's perfectly possible. They reckon a really good sealing tap costs only a few pence more than a bad one, so there simply isn't any excuse for an inefficient seal.

The bag collapses as the wine is drawn out. Getting the last glass of wine out is not always easy. You can just cut the bag open and drain the dregs. But that means you won't be able to enjoy the bag to the full since, when it's empty, you can blow it full of air – and it becomes a very comfortable pillow.

Thinking outside the box. This paint can from McCann Vilnius is a very different take on the bag-in-box.

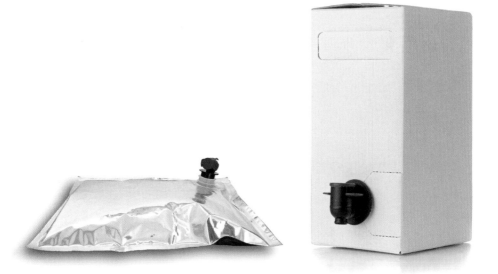

Here's your bladder pack. Just imagine that full of ice-cold white wine. You can squirt it into your mouth and when it's empty, blow up the bag to use as a pillow as you sleep it off on the beach at Bondi.

1966
MICHAEL BROADBENT
AT CHRISTIE'S

We were at Domaine de Chevalier in Bordeaux, and there was a gap between the 1971 white and the reds. Eyeing the Bösendorfer piano, Michael says, 'Oh God, I can't wait any longer, I'm going to play it.' And he does – a heartfelt Chopin prelude wafts out over the vines. The reds – even the 1961, which later made me want to dance on the table it was so deliciously good – the reds can wait.

Later on, at Château Figeac, the 1934, bottled in Belgium, holds us rapt and Michael can't resist the sight of another piano or the sight of Marie-France, our delightful hostess. Her husband plays waltzes on a pianola as Michael and I – much more him than me – trip the light fantastic with Marie-France while the frogs in the château pond noisily complain about the disturbance. And maybe, as dawn rises, just maybe, Michael is out there, with sketchpad and pen, catching the beauty of the vintage sunrise.

To see Michael Broadbent, who died in 2020, simply as one of the most important wine men of the 20th century is to miss much of his personality, because it was his charm, his persuasive manner, his artistic sensibility and his almost patrician air that allowed him to become such a success. Before he could become the consummate wine seller, he had to become a shrewd and relentless wine hunter, because he didn't just sell any old bottles, he sold the finest, the rarest, the most ancient.

There wasn't a market for ancient, rare bottles of wine before Broadbent became director of the newly launched Wine Auctions for Christie's in London.

Christie's had held occasional wine sales ever since the 1760s, but in 1966 they decided to take it more seriously and recruited Broadbent. An inspired appointment. He knew his wine well; he was fiercely ambitious, but he was also an artist at heart and used his suave and genteel manner to charm wine out of cellars where

A magnum of the celebrated 1864 Lafite, which Broadbent sold in 1967, about to meet its fate in 2004 at a gourmets' dinner in Tokyo. Its precious label is well-protected.

it had lain for 100 years, and then charm ever higher prices out of an increasingly American crowd from the auctioneer's podium. It's strange to say it, but fine wine had been rather out of fashion for most of the 20th century, and all over Britain, grand houses and castles had cobwebby cellars full of 19th-century treasures that no one in these grand families drank any more.

Broadbent had a nose for these. They weren't just bottles to him, they were 'living history'. Within months he'd inspected, catalogued and agreed to auction the dusty gems of the Marquess of Linlithgow's cellars; followed by the Earl of Rosebery's glorious 19th-century Bordeaux, many in giant bottles. By May 1967, Christie's ushered in a new era of wine appreciation and kickstarted a craze for collecting old and rare wines that enthusiasts simply hadn't known existed.

And it was the American collector who was the most avid, and who could pay. A magnum of Lafite 1864 from the Rosebery cellar sold for $225 in 1967, and for $10,000 in 1981. Broadbent even began going to the States to conduct tastings there, and prices soared. This amazing run of auctioning old wines lasted for the best part of 20 years – and continues in a more subdued mood to this day. But there are only so many old bottles you can find, and as the prices became crazy a darker side of counterfeiting and fraud began to surface. When Broadbent started out, provenance was simple to prove. As sources dry up, it's become much more complicated.

1966
ROBERT MONDAVI
& THE REBIRTH
OF NAPA

Punching your brother on the nose isn't the generally accepted way of ushering in a new era in the world of wine. But in November 1965, when Robert Mondavi biffed his brother Peter and stormed out of the Charles Krug winery, which the Mondavis ran, California wine was about to take a massive leap forward.

Within a year, Robert Mondavi had formed the first new winery to be established in the Napa Valley since Prohibition. That doesn't mean that Mondavi was the first to realise Napa's great potential; he wasn't the first to embrace single varietal wines (in particular Cabernet Sauvignon), he wasn't the first to use modern marketing ideas, or new oak barrels or stainless steel tanks. Yet, somehow, it seemed as though he was the first person to do all of these, all at once. The other improvers in the valley had been building on something already present. Mondavi seemed to be starting the whole shebang from scratch. In his image. In his way.

I met Robert Mondavi many times over the years, and I'm not sure I've ever been faced with anyone so completely convinced of himself, so utterly determined to get his viewpoint across. You could call it sublime self-confidence. Or you could call it an almost pathological desire to prove himself. Either way, it was exactly what California needed in 1966. Mondavi's family was tough. His father came west from the iron mines of Minnesota during Prohibition and managed to establish himself as a grape grower; he quickly parlayed that into winemaking as Prohibition ended. Robert Mondavi showed his mettle by getting into Stanford, California's leading university, but by 1936 he was back home, making wine in the Napa Valley. At the Charles Krug winery, which the family

The first Mondavi Cabernet Sauvignon blended Bordeaux methods with California ripeness – something he tried to achieve with every ensuing vintage.

bought in 1943, he planted the classic French grape varieties, taught himself about stainless steel, cold fermentation to retain fruit flavours, and ageing wine in oak barrels. But it was his first trip to Europe in 1962 that showed him how far he was from producing world-class wines. It also beckoned him towards the solution – the importance of vineyard sites, of the right varieties for those sites, of mature vines, of controlled yields and of using only the best French oak for ageing your wine. And the trip gave him a vision of flavour. If you were going to make great wines, you had to know what great wines tasted like.

After revelling in the star wines of Bordeaux, Burgundy and the Rhône, Mondavi knew what greatness tasted like, he had a vision of flavour, and he spent the rest of his life trying to achieve it in his wines.

You only had to taste the first Robert Mondavi Cabernet Sauvignon, the 1966, to realise that he had taken the French model and made a remarkable success of it. Its ripeness was more like a really ripe Bordeaux, and was completely different from the rich overripe style he'd been making at Charles Krug. He was convinced that the soils of Rutherford and Oakville in Napa Valley could be the California equivalent of Bordeaux's Pauillac and Saint-Julien. His goal was not to produce identical flavours in their fruit, but by applying Bordeaux winemaking methods and using the best French oak barrels that money could buy, he was certain he could produce Cabernet wines that deserved to be served on the same top tables as the French greats.

And to persuade the world of that, he'd need to do some marketing. Well, Robert Mondavi may be known as a great winemaker, but he should be known as a great marketeer. And a great salesman. In the 1960s, America's East Coast wouldn't touch expensive California wine. *Gourmet* magazine stated: 'Our readers don't drink domestic wines.' Mondavi won them over by fearlessly placing his wines next to top French ones at every opportunity. Thirty years on he was still doing it, to such an extent that I always knew when the Mondavis were in town because I'd get to taste Château Latour, Margaux, Domaine de la Romanée-Conti – all the top French stuff – just so long as I also tasted the Mondavi, and agreed, yes, it had indeed earned the right to be served at the same table.

1967
WASHINGTON STATE

If the only place in Washington State you've visited is Seattle, you could be forgiven for thinking, Hell, no one could ripen grapes in this fog. Pass the freshly brewed coffee.

True, Seattle is seriously foggy. In 1579, Sir Francis Drake tried to see what was going on in Seattle's Puget Sound, and was beaten back by 'the most vile, thick and stinking fogge.' Well, take out the 'stinking', and the rest holds true. But there are two Washington States. The western part, based in Seattle, where people go to the opera, win the Super Bowl and drink some of the world's best coffees and beers. And the eastern part. For that you need to clamber over the Cascade Mountains, and as you breast the ridge, the air clears, the sun blinds you with its brilliance, and the land of thick green forest and manicured suburbs is replaced by windswept sagebrush ranges, crouched like the great hunched backs of vast animals, and a barren moonscape, inhospitable, desolate, sun-bleached.

This is extreme country. And it is *very* dry. But it has one massive asset – the mighty Columbia River, America's fourth largest in volume of water. So surely some of that could be used to irrigate a vineyard or two? Of course it could. The Columbia River Basin covers 260,000 square miles. The potential for a vineyard based on irrigation and sunshine was massive. But someone had to make the first move. Well, there had been a few attempts in the 19th century, and irrigation schemes in the Yakima Valley (the Yakima River flows into the Columbia) from 1906 onwards brought vineyards, but most of the grapes were for juice or eating, not wine; locals said the delicate *vinifera* varieties could never survive the freezes. And they had quite a few of those – autumn and winter freezes in 1949, 1950 and 1955 destroyed thousands of acres of fledgling vineyards.

Riesling has always been a Washington strong point, ever since the triumph of Ste. Michelle Johannisberg Riesling in 1974 at a Los Angeles wine taste-off.

So who finally took the plunge? A couple of home winemakers, egged on by America's most famous wine writer of the time, Leon Adams. He tasted a Grenache rosé made by Lloyd Woodburne, a professor of psychology at the University of Washington, in 1966 and loved it. He persuaded California's most famous wine consultant, André Tchelistcheff, to come north and have a look. Again, a home winemaker (meteorologist Philip Church) produced the only wine that Tchelistcheff liked on his whole trip – a Gewürztraminer that he said was the best one he'd had in all of America.

This was 1967 and in the same year – inspired by Adams and Tchelistcheff – *two* now important wine producers made their first wines. One was Château Ste. Michelle, whose Ste. Michelle is now the most famous label in Washington State and one of the leading labels throughout America. The other was Associated Vintners, which grew out of the bunch of home winemakers, and in 1983 became Columbia Vintners, another important Washington label.

Which was first? Well, Associated Vintners had been dabbling in home winemaking since the 1950s. American Wine Growers had been going as a commercial concern since 1954, and even produced a Grenache-based rosé called Granada. But if I had to choose, I'd go for AWG's Château Ste. Michelle as the winery that got modern Washington moving. Tchelistcheff worked on Château Ste. Michelle's wines from 1967. In 1968, in a blind tasting of Semillons, the Ste. Michelle beat all the other American Semillons, and was marked just a tiny bit behind 'Y' – the dry wine of world- famous Château d'Yquem from Bordeaux. And in 1974 in Los Angeles, the 1972 Ste. Michelle Johannisberg Riesling beat all the German, Australian and other American Rieslings. Washington was on its way, thanks to Château Ste. Michelle.

1968
ITALY BREAKS
THE MOULD

It was 1977 when the revolution in Italian wine hit home for me. I was lying in bed one sunny springtime Saturday in a new flat. No furniture, just a bed. No wine. Well, there was one bottle, given to me by a friend who said, 'This is going to change the world of wine.'

It looked nice enough – a simple white label embossed with an eight-point blue-and-gold star and the title Sassicaia (Cabernet Sauvignon). Let's indulge. A tooth mug should do. And so I took my first mouthful of Sassicaia 1968. And suddenly I was out of bed, scrabbling for some paper and a pen. I'd never experienced a flavour of such thrilling purity, such piercingly beautiful blackcurrant fruit spreading across my palate. A year later Sassicaia was voted the world's top Cabernet Sauvignon. And to everyone's amazement, it came from Italy.

This wine was made by Mario Incisa della Rocchetta, uncle of Piero Antinori. Piero was the heir to Italy's oldest wine dynasty, based in Tuscany, and in the 1960s the future looked bleak, with Tuscan wines, and above all Chianti, at an all-time low in quality, price and critical appreciation. To be honest, there weren't really *any* Italians that could sit at the top table of world wine. That table was packed with Frenchmen, and Uncle Mario's Sassicaia showed young Piero the way to joining them. His father had previously planted a slope called Tignanello with Cabernet Sauvignon. Piero revived the vines and resolved to mix Cabernet with the local Sangiovese, to age the wine in small new oak barrels (just like in Bordeaux), do the malolactic fermentation to soften the wine (just like Bordeaux), and he wouldn't

The faded label of the original Sassicaia. The wine's flavour hasn't faded. I remember it as if it were yesterday.

Left: Piero Antinori used Bordeaux methods and Bordeaux's Cabernet grape to help create Tignanello, but with a majority of Sangiovese fruit, it never lost sight of its Tuscan roots. Right: When Angelo Gaja planted Cabernet on some of his best Nebbiolo land in Barbaresco, his father sighed 'Darmagi' – what a pity. So he called the wine Darmagi and it achieved instant notoriety.

even try to call it Chianti. Just basic 'Vino da Tavola' would do. In fact, he was following Mario's lead to make a 'Bordeaux' in Tuscany. Yet Antinori was a proud Tuscan and had great foresight. He needed to show he could create a wine of top international quality before he moved on to creating purely Tuscan styles. So he used Bordeaux as his template for Tignanello with phenomenal success; his 1985 Tignanello won the 1990 International Wine Challenge red trophy. At which point he turned back to Tuscany, to estate wines like Pèppoli and Badia a Passignano, sold as Chianti Classicos, without a Cabernet grape between them, but given the respect they deserved because of the 'international' success of Sassicaia and Tignanello.

At the same time, Angelo Gaja, in Piedmont, felt caught in the same bind. His family company had made Barolo and Barbaresco for just over a century, but as he tried to improve quality and price he was held back by complacency and mediocrity all round him. Angelo had studied at Montpellier in France and worked in Burgundy. He felt an immediate affinity with the tricky Pinot Noir grape and its need for very focused site selection to ripen properly. Above all, he saw that all the wines of the best Burgundy sites were sold under their own names – whereas in Barolo and Barbaresco everything was lumped together. And he discovered small, new 225-litre oak barrels for ageing his wines.

Like Antinori he realised that he'd have to raid France for ideas if he were to force the wider world to take his Barbaresco wines seriously, and he chose Burgundy as the best model for his Nebbiolo-based reds. But he also planted Chardonnay and Cabernet – right in the middle of some of his best Barbaresco land – because, like Antinori, he needed a tool to make people sit up and give respect to his part of Italy. Chardonnay and Cabernet could do that, before he settled back to making the best Piedmont wine a Piedmontese could make.

THE BURGUNDY EFFECT

People talk a lot about the Bordeaux effect on the world of wine. But what about the Burgundy effect? It's just as important, although perhaps a little less obvious in the global marketplace due to the amazing spread of Bordeaux's most famous grapes – Cabernet Sauvignon and Merlot. So what about Burgundy's most famous grapes?

Chardonnay. Is there a more famous white grape than that? Well, Chardonnay is a Burgundy grape – *the* grape for Chablis, Meursault, Pouilly-Fuissé, and every top white wine in between. There's even a village called Chardonnay in Burgundy. And the history of savoury yet rich, dry yet succulent, toasty, complex, oak barrel-influenced white wines around the world is the story of the Burgundy white wine effect.

The Burgundy red wine effect could be called the anti-Bordeaux red wine effect, the 'anything-but-Cabernet' movement, as an increasing number of winemakers rebelled against the worldwide onslaught of Cabernet. Predictably, the grape they chose to use was Burgundy's pride and joy – the fickle, demanding, over-sensitive, sulky, capricious, yet occasionally uplifting, sensual and memorable Pinot Noir.

In the days when taste in wine was dictated by the British – and, unbelievably, it wasn't that long ago – white wine basically meant something from Germany (Mosel or hock) and something from Burgundy. The British had no desire to look any further. But the Americans, later to be followed with equal enthusiasm by the Australians, were determined to. Starting with Hanzell winery in Sonoma County, California, just after the end of World War II, Americans who had travelled to Europe and tasted Burgundy's glorious whites set out to recreate them in their Golden West. They couldn't take the soil and the climate of Burgundy home with them, but they could learn or buy everything else.

Left: Josh Jensen was inspired by the limestone soils in Burgundy to seek out limestone in California. There isn't much – and it's very remote – but Calera uses it for highly successful Pinot Noir. Right: The white Burgundy effect began with Hanzell winery in Sonoma County, California, where James D Zellerbach, the retired US Ambassador to Italy, set out to make Burgundy-style wines. His were the first great California Chardonnays.

Above all, they could plant the Chardonnay. They could use the same barrels to ferment the juice, cultivate the same yeasts, install humidity and temperature systems to mimic Burgundy's cellar conditions. And as best they could, they made and matured the wine in the same way. In exactly the same way? The same as the timeless, generation-after-generation expertise and subconscious knowledge that marked out the greatest Burgundians? No. These earlier Californians – Hanzell, Heitz, Beaulieu, Stony Hill, Freemark Abbey – made fine wines, maybe great wines. They weren't Burgundy but they spurred on the rest of the world to try to imitate white Burgundy, and that movement has shown no signs of slowing down.

The red Burgundy effect was much less successful at first, and even now is less universal, partly because Burgundy is a very marginal, cool-climate area in France, where the Pinot Noir manages to creep slowly to ripeness only when nature is kind, whereas the New World tyros, almost without exception, were established in far warmer, sunnier conditions where the cool-seeking Pinot Noir quickly turned to jam on the vine, while Cabernet flourished. But, just as with Chardonnay, Americans had been to Europe and tasted the tantalising beauty of red Burgundy.

Two of them reckoned they'd found the answer in the high crags of the Gavilan mountains. Limestone is rare in California, but the crags that crumble into soil over the millennia in Burgundy are limestone, and Chalone and Calera made California's first Burgundy-ish Pinot Noirs off the pale mountain soils. Since then, first Carneros, on the San Francisco Bay, and then Santa Barbara and the foggy Sonoma Coast have waved the Pinot Noir flag. Very little of it tastes like Burgundy, but it's delicious in its own right because of the efforts to imitate Burgundy.

Oregon has also succeeded – a Burgundy ideal producing a Pacific Northwest original. Australia, with Tasmania and Victoria, has had some success, as has Chile, but if we are to look for a place where the Pinot Noir really does rival the best in Burgundy, it's New Zealand – cool, marginal, but sunny New Zealand. Their Pinots don't taste like Burgundy either, but they taste how they do because of the example Burgundy set.

1970s
RETSINA

It's a moment I look forward to every year at the International Wine Challenge. Sometime during the week, one of the tables will collapse into a wheezing heap of wine tasters hardly able to draw breath as they cough and splutter and inveigh to the heavens about the awfulness of it all and what have they done to deserve this, and blah blah blah. And I smile and think to myself, ooh, good, they've got the retsina class.

Of course the wines all get zero-rated, but the chairmen eagerly set the masked bottles out and taste them again. And the biggest decision for us to make is – can we find a gold medal in there? Retsina, a wine with a totally undeserved bad reputation. Partly because it is completely different from the normal run-of-the-mill wines we might get from France or Spain or Italy – or anywhere in the New World. And partly because for so many of us Europeans it was the first memorable wine we ever drank, the first one whose flavour we will never forget, the wine for which many of us have a secret, guilty fondness – not really because of how good or bad it was, but because of all the other wonderful, adolescent, fumbly, clumsy, never-to-be-forgotten pleasures that drinking it led to.

Of all the wines in the world, retsina is the ultimate wine to remind you of your Mediterranean summer holidays.

Even in a grimy Greek taverna in the depths of a rain-soaked dismal north European winter – perhaps, particularly then – the first ice-cold gulp of this resinated, pungent white wine mixing and matching with the taramasalata as both slip greasily down your throat, takes you right back to a better, warmer, happier place and time.

Ah, this brings it back – a chilled, crown-capped half litre plonked down on your table next to a mound of pitta bread and taramasalata, and the whole scented, sultry Mediterranean night stretching ahead of you.

Well, congratulate yourself, because it's the explosion of tourism to Greece after World War II that transformed what was a local wine from the plains near Athens to a national phenomenon. Due to tourism, every region of Greece was offering retsina by the 1970s. Not necessarily from locally grown grapes or from locally grown pine resin, but retsina became known as *the* taste of Greece, so every tourist taverna would have some bottles.

The Attican plains near Athens were the historical home of retsina because they also boast vast forests of Aleppo pines. But that doesn't completely explain why Greece should be the only country that still thinks it's a great idea to add lumps of pine resin to its wine, and has even managed to get a special dispensation from the EU. You can't go round throwing pine resin into your French wine without expecting a loud knock on the door from the *gendarmerie*.

Even so, adding resin to wine is a very ancient practice – the Chinese are supposed to have employed it even before the Greeks and Romans. The initial objective was to try to preserve wine in the clay pots or goatskins being used to transport the liquid and, later, in Roman times, in barrels. Resin had antiseptic and antioxidant properties, and if you smeared the inside of your vessel with resin, or coated the stopper with it, your wine lasted longer. But, of course, it also tasted of pine resin. Given the quality of a lot of old-time wine, that might not have been a bad thing, and the Greeks and Romans in particular took a liking to its tang, and especially to what is called its 'pseudo-cooling' effect – similar to the sensation that menthol gives of cooling your mouth. The bitter finish of a resinated wine gives the same kind of pleasure as the aftertaste of a well-hopped beer.

Retsina is now in decline, even in and around Athens, its traditional heartland. But at its best, fresh and

A modern export-quality brand of retsina, less resinous than before but still a reviving ice-cold mouthful.

A herringbone effect on an Aleppo pine tree as the resin is drained off, much as syrup is extracted from the maple tree.

cold, it's still a wonderfully evocative drink. Modern retsina doesn't need the resin for protective purposes, so lumps of resin are added to the grape juice before fermentation and the turmoil of the ferment extracts all the flavour. And it's a lot less flavour now. A hundred years ago they might add 7.5 kg of resin to every 100 litres of wine – enough to take the skin off your lips. By the 1950s you might still get 2.5–4 kg of resin added, but the commercial bottlers were decreasing the load bit by bit so that when the EU legislated on retsina, it allowed a mere 0.15–1 kg per 100 litres. No wonder people stopped drinking it if you couldn't taste the resin. But there are some wild men in California adding a bit more than that, so it might just make a comeback yet.

WINE BRANDS

Wine brands are created for a variety of reasons. Sometimes, as with Mouton Cadet in Bordeaux during the 1930s, they are a clever and desperate way to try to shift vats full of seemingly unsaleable wine by a brand new approach to labelling and design.

Sometimes, as with modern brands like Yellow Tail in Australia or Blossom Hill in the United States, they are simply profit-driven – create the image, market and advertise the image, then find the wine needed to fill the bottles. And there are times a brand emerges from what was a really high-class wine that just became too popular for its own good, or else attracted the beady eye of financiers and marketeers who were quite willing to sacrifice quality and character in the pursuit of profit and market share. Obvious examples of this are Harvey's Bristol Cream Sherry, Kanga Rouge and Rosemount Estate in Australia, and most famous – or infamous – of them all, Blue Nun Liebfraumilch.

I must be one of the few wine enthusiasts alive who has been thrilled by the quality of Blue Nun. But then, the Blue Nun I loved was from the 1921 vintage. It was labelled *Auslese* (i.e., really special, late-picked) and I drank it when it was 70 years old – golden, honeyed, scented with autumn richness and the mellowness of decay. What class. The Sichel company had created Blue Nun in 1921 as a high-quality product to defy the collapsing market in post–World War I Germany.

Originally, the two nuns at the front of the label wore brown habits, while the background nuns wore blue. By the 1970s, the nuns were all blue and by 1985 – when almost half the wines drunk in Britain were German, mostly Liebfraumilch in style – Blue Nun (the best-known Liebfraumilch) was selling two million cases a year worldwide, 1.25 million of them in the United States alone. And it wasn't the quality of the

The Australians are experts at de-snobbifying wine – this Kanga Rouge label was jokey in the extreme, but the grog was good. Coonawarra Shiraz is seriously tasty stuff.

A Blue Nun advertisement from the 1970s, when it was at the height of its fame, and before a massive explosion in sales caused it to lose the 'exclusive' appeal that this scenario suggests.

wine anymore, it was the marketing. It took a bit of a bashing in the 1990s when fictional British TV host Alan Partridge named Blue Nun as his favourite wine, erasing the cooler vibes of Jimi Hendrix swigging Blue Nun before going on stage at Woodstock, man.

Of those other quality brands, Harvey's Bristol Cream used to be a superb Old Bottled Cream Sherry before the marketing men transformed it into a blue-bottled source of little pleasure and some ridicule. Kanga Rouge is thought of as an early joke Australian brand, but I have a bottle of the 1978 here: it's a Coonawarra Shiraz – top stuff, before marketing took over. The Rosemount Estate was a fantastic single vineyard in the Hunter Valley near Sydney before marketing and money transformed it into discount fodder.

I'm almost happier to see brands that are total creations like Yellow Tail because, supposedly, brands are there to take away fear in choosing a wine; to provide reassurance in a confusing arena; consistency not personality; they are wines marketed on their name and image, not on their inherent qualities. One identity expert said, 'It's not so much what you can say for it. It's just that there's not much you can say against it.' And if that means reducing the tannin in red, the acid in white, and increasing the sugar in both – but thereby giving pleasure and introducing millions to wine – well, brands have done a remarkable job in the 20th century. And anyway, they provide the jumping-off point to something much better.

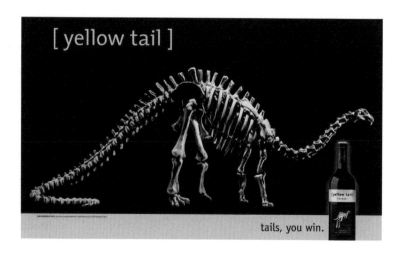

Brilliant advertising and marketing – not the wine's flavour – made Yellow Tail into one of the 21st century's most successful wine brands.

GERMAN WINE CLASSIFICATIONS

The new German Wine Laws of January 2021 re-focussed on geographical origins of area, regions, village and vineyard – much like wine laws in the rest of the European Union. But Germany has a parallel system measuring quality according to the amount of natural sugar in the grapes – and this method of measuring quality by ripeness has been going on since the 18th century.

In a northern clime like Germany's, sweetness of any kind has long been treasured, since nature provided few fruits with any luscious sweetness, and the occasional wine that turned rich and dense with sugary flavours was always lauded to the skies. However, because the German autumn could be cold, and the winter definitely was, many wines wouldn't finish their fermentation and so had *some* residual sugar left in them. The Germans were also among the first to rediscover the use of sulphur in winemaking – the Romans had used it, but the methods had been lost in the Dark Ages. The Germans actually regulated sulphur use as early as 1487. It was very useful for helping stave off oxidation and vinegariness in the light wines that Germany produced, but it was also crucial in arresting fermentation so that sweetness remained in the wine.

The establishment of Riesling as the dominant grape of the Rheingau region is important here, and began with the replanting of Schloss Johannisberg in 1720.

Initially only 15 per cent of the new vines was Riesling, but the owners quickly realised they were vastly superior to the other types and the Schloss was completely converted to Riesling – the first estate in Germany to be 100 per cent Riesling. This coincided nicely with the growing interest in *Naturwein* – unsugared, unmucked- about-with wine – around 1750, since Riesling could make delightful wine without any adjuncts. In 1775, the movement towards greater quality received a big fillip with the adoption of the concept of *Spätlese* – late harvesting as a desirable objective.

In 1787 Schloss Johannisberg went further and instituted *Auslese* harvesting – select picking of grapes affected by the sugar-intensifying noble rot fungus. And a year later, in 1788, the local government at Mainz issued a general edict exhorting the local growers not to pick before full ripeness at the very least, and, ideally, overripeness affected by 'noble rot'.

This obsession with ripeness ruled German wine for the next 200 years, although many of the best estates regularly produced dry – not sweet – Rieslings of full ripeness. Laws regulating wine started appearing in the 19th century – a national wine law came in 1892. It was revised in 1909. In 1930, a new wine law arrived and in 1971, the most controversial of all the wine laws turned up. And one thing stands out. Most wine laws are obsessed by boundaries, by the place a wine comes from. Yet the German wine laws have largely concentrated on ripeness levels, and, especially in the 1971 version, been very cavalier about well-established vineyards, and made no rules about what grape varieties are allowed. The law has been tinkered with since, and many leading estates have preferred to opt out of any kind of classification.

It's a very crude classification, but in a cold country like Germany, you can see why an obsession with ripeness dominated thinking. Global warming, as much as anything else, has rendered it largely irrelevant.

Even so, for the record, here are the bare bones. *Tafelwein* is basic table wine. A Qba wine has some quality pretensions, but can have sugar added. QmP wines have no sugar added, and the higher the natural-sugar level, supposedly the greater prestige and higher price a wine commands. *Kabinett* is the least ripe.

Spätlese means late-picked. *Auslese* means the bunches are selected, and may be infected with noble rot.

Beerenauslese means the grapes are picked berry by berry. *Trockenbeerenauslese* means they are picked berry by berry and must be infected with noble rot. And *Eiswein* is made from frozen grapes in which the sugars are concentrated. There are precise sugar levels for each category, but I think that's enough about German classifications for now.

Left: A traditional wine label from the Pfalz, showing vineyard, grape variety and ripeness level, but no longer the village name (in this case, Deidesheim). Right: This will be very basic stuff, and may have a completely made-up winery name. Sonnengarten – sun garden – sounds lovely. I wonder where it is? Nowhere, probably.

1974
BEAUJOLAIS NOUVEAU

If you weren't there, you'll never know how gloomy November used to be in times past. Global warming seems to have played havoc with any consistency in our weather, and nowadays November is as likely to bring balmy sunshine as snowy whiteouts.

But the baleful, drab greyness – the miserable, damp gloom that signalled the start of Britain's notoriously unenjoyable winters – always marked November as the low point of the year, when you wondered, would the sun *ever* shine again? Yes, it would. Metaphorically at least. Some time before dawn on the morning of 15 November, explosions of joy and silliness and inebriation would break out all over Britain. *'Le Beaujolais Nouveau est arrivé '* and until the hangover kicked in around lunchtime, Beaujolais provided one last joyous romp fuelled by the first wine of the vintage, purple and prickly and potent, wine that a mere six weeks before had been grapes upon a vine.

If you wanted to put a date on the beginning of the Nouveau phenomenon, 15 November 1974, would do pretty well. Allan Hall, who wrote the 'Atticus' column for the *Sunday Times*, thought up a wheeze, and devoted precisely 6.5 centimetres of copy to it. He said he'd be in the newspaper office on the morning of the 15th and were anyone inclined to turn up with a bottle of that year's new Beaujolais, he would swap it for a bottle of champagne. It was just a little jokey afterthought in the whole column. But it lit a flame.

It's about 500 miles from Beaujolais to London. A rabid crowd of eccentric Brits thronged the start line of what was suddenly a race – and less than three hours later, a bloke panted up the stairs to Hall's office to claim his bottle of bubbly. Hall hadn't even had time to chill

I still get a buzz – even though it's a pretty small buzz nowadays – from seeing the first bottles of Beaujolais Nouveau arrive on the shelves.

The hairstyles give away the era – the 1970s. (Good gracious, could one of them be me?) But no one seems to be having much fun yet, so perhaps they're still on the first bottle.

it. The winner was a guy who'd started a dating agency, and he'd flown his Beaujolais over in a private plane.

Which was not at all in the spirit of things. You were supposed to drive it – in whatever vehicle you could commandeer; the more eccentric, the better – helter-skelter along the roads of northern France and southern England, scattering all before you. And that's exactly what happened for the first three years, until the police turned up and said Hall and his cronies were encouraging drivers to race upon Her Majesty's Highways. Desist or be jailed. They didn't fancy jail.

But the phenomenon of the Nouveau wouldn't stop. It completely took over the mindset of most of Beaujolais. In an area that had suffered more than its share of poverty since World War II, here was prosperity. What became a worldwide thirst for Nouveau – the first wine of the year's crop – meant you could pick, make, bottle and get paid for your wine in a couple of months. And quality didn't matter too much – it was the razzmatazz, the frivolity that mattered, the sizzle not the steak. By the end of the 1980s, over 60 per cent of Beaujolais production was sold in November as Nouveau to fan the party embers.

The craze has faded now. Southern hemisphere wineries can give us far better 'new vintage' wine to cheer our Novembers. But the real heart of the Beaujolais Nouveau phenomenon still beats. In 2022 I went to a Beaujolais Nouveau launch on a rainy morning in Edinburgh. Only a couple of people turned up, but we still had a party. It *is* a thrill to taste the first wine of a harvest whose vines have scarcely dropped their leaves by the time you slurp back this joyous youthful brew. In the city of Lyons, this is how Beaujolais has been drunk since time immemorial. In Parisian bistros in the 1950s and 1960s, these fresh young wines brought delight and happiness with no brouhaha, no inflated prices and madcap PR stunts. And that's exactly what they're doing again today.

EYRIE VINEYARDS' PINOT NOIR

David Lett wasn't the first person to plant grapes in Oregon. He wasn't even the first person to plant Pinot Noir. But in his curmudgeonly, irascible, single-minded way he defines the birth of modern Oregon wine.

And he achieved this by being determinedly, unashamedly anti-Californian. That's why he chose the Pinot Noir grape – the exact opposite of the big brawny Cabernets, Merlots and Zinfandels that California crowed over. That's why he chose Oregon – in its rainy, foggy, muddy unpredictability, the exact opposite of sunny, consistent California.

The settlers from the first Oregon Trail wagon trains established some vines in southern Oregon's Umpqua Valley in 1843. The first wine grapes in Willamette Valley – now the heartland of Oregon wine – went in as early as 1847. During the late 1800s a trickle of guys – mostly German – headed north from California looking for cooler conditions more like home, and planted Riesling vines. California provided the next trickle of immigrants too, several generations later. But this time it wasn't Germans dreaming of Willamette Valley becoming America's 'Rhineland', but a more world-wise and world-weary crew, bearing Pinot Noir vines and dreaming of Oregon becoming America's Burgundy.

Pinot Noir does strange things to people, perhaps because it seems to be so capricious a vine and seems so difficult to transplant from its Burgundy homeland. Perhaps because even in Burgundy it requires talent, commitment, the right sliver of soil – and luck – to make a success of it. Perhaps because in the 1960s, when these California exiles began to arrive, great bottles of red Burgundy were rare indeed, but revered for their delicacy and scent and filigree textures, while the world as led by Cabernet and Merlot was making wines of more tub-thumping density every year. Whatever. That overused phrase 'the Holy Grail' was adopted by these newcomers: Oregon would provide 'the Holy Grail' – at last, another patch of land in the world where Pinot Noir just might create wines indistinguishable from red Burgundy.

And at the head of this tiny band was David Lett of the Eyrie Vineyards. He'd nearly become a dentist, but changed his mind and studied viticulture (not winemaking) at the University of California, Davis – the state's wine hothouse. He learned his winemaking in the marginal climate of Switzerland and France's Alsace and Burgundy. Coming back to California, the Davis boffins told him nowhere in California was cool enough to grow Pinot Noir, but that Oregon was too cold and wet to grow anything; ripening would be six weeks later than California, though he might just squeeze out a light *white* wine from Pinot Noir. And anyway, one of the profs joked, 'You'll be frosted out in spring and fall, rained on all summer, and you'll get athlete's foot up to your knees.' Lett realised it was the risk factor of growing great grapes that was putting them all off – the risk of insufficient summer sun, of harvest-time rain.

Yet it was just such risks that provided the tantalisingly quasi-Burgundian possibilities he needed to explore.

He made a splash of 1969 Pinot in a 'diaper pail', a bit more in 1970, and then gradually he got the hang of it – so much so that when, in 1979, the French food and wine magazine *Gault-Millau* held a wine Olympiad in Paris, Lett's 1975 South Block Reserve Pinot Noir came in third out of 330 wines. The French couldn't believe it. They beefed up their Burgundies in particular, and re-ran the competition. Eyrie came second, ahead of a Chambertin 1961, and one-fifth of a point behind a Drouhin Chambolle-Musigny 1959. With that single flourish, David Lett and his 1975 Eyrie Pinot Noir proved that Oregon could make wines to match Burgundy. Oregon's considerable reputation nowadays as making the most Burgundian of all America's Pinots can be traced back to a small batch of wine made by a determined old grump in a mucky turkey shed down by the railway tracks.

David Lett had it tough starting out. Those barrels didn't look very new, that wall doesn't look very clean, and he looks cold in his woolly hat. But Lett was rebelling against the warmth and the razzmatazz of California to the south of Oregon, and I suspect he was just as happy as he would ever be.

David Lett was the opposite of a self-promoter. He didn't even have a properly printed label for his South Block Reserve Pinot Noir, which triumphed in the Paris Gault-Millau tasting of 1979.

1975
WHITE ZINFANDEL

It certainly wasn't what I was expecting. I'd been to a big tasting of Mondavi wines in London – really serious reds and whites – and you presume the hosts will pull out a few stops at lunch. Some older Reserve Cabernets always go down well, single-vineyard Chardonnays likewise. But Mondavi offered us pink wine for lunch. Well, only just pink, sort of 'blushing white'. And it was quite sweet. What was going on?

This was the early 1990s, and what they called 'White Zinfandel' or 'Blush' wine had been the wine-marketing phenomenon of the 1980s. Wineries had made tons of money out of it, and smart outfits like Mondavi and Beringer couldn't resist getting involved in something that was cheap to make and quick to sell. And their examples were actually very good – far more flavour than a typical off-dry rosé – peaches and cream, grapes and a whiff of rather fine Virginia tobacco. Even so, not quite the thing at a smart West End lunch.

Ah, there's the wine snob talking. Why not? It's a helluva good drink, isn't it? Well, yes, it could be – from Beringer or Mondavi. They're very smart wineries.

But White Zin didn't start smart. It didn't even start on purpose. Like so many wine innovations, it just sort of happened. Zinfandel is the archetypal Californian red grape variety. So it's pretty likely people had thought of making pink wine from it. Records show it being made in the 1860s; Robert Louis Stevenson liked it when he visited in 1880. And more recently the great Paul Draper had released a Ridge White Zinfandel in 1970. But these were probably all serious dry rosés. That's not why White Zin became the most popular wine in North America in the 1980s.

Pale pink, sweetish White Zin is one of the great marketing successes of 20th-century wine, and Sutter Home led the way with their first cautious offering in 1975.

This could just be where it all started – the 1975 vintage of Sutter Home, labelled in the French way, 'Oeil de Perdrix' (Partridge Eye), meaning a very pale pink colour. Within a short time you didn't need any of the French la-di-da – White Zin had arrived.

Bob Trinchero ran a small winery called Sutter Home in the Napa Valley. It wasn't thriving, but Bob had discovered a source of 120-year-old Zinfandel vines in Amador County – gold rush country further inland up in the Sierra Nevadas. The grapes were being bulked off for blending. He took the whole 1968 crop, made some serious red, and for the first time was getting glowing reviews for his wines. Before this, Sutter Home had made up to 52 different sorts of wine – every year. After this, Sutter Home became a Zinfandel-only winery. That was pretty brave. Zinfandel was becoming thought of as a bit old hat. Growers were ripping out their old Zin vines to plant the newly fashionable Cabernet Sauvignon and Chardonnay.

And it's here the story gets a little fuzzy. Some say Trinchero told a Sacramento expert he wanted to make a white wine, and the guy said Zinfandel will make a great pale rosé. Some say his red was a bit thin one year, so he added the skins from another vat to deepen the colour and he was left with some pink wine he needed to sell. But these were dry rosés. He certainly made a couple of hundred cases of dry rosé in 1972, and he struggled to shift it. So did he decide to make the wine crisper, fruitier, sweeter?

Or did the fermentation stick in 1975, leaving some residual sugar in a pale pink, crisp, fruity Zinfandel, which the consumers loved?

A few hundred cases in 1975 became 47,000 cases in 1980, and three million cases in 1987. White Zin. Blush wine was the generic term. It was the marketing triumph of the 1980s and its influence is still felt today. Big brands still make it and sell shed loads of it. I suspect it got a lot of non-wine-drinkers into wine, and they've stayed there. And it reversed the decline of Zinfandel in California. Thousands of acres of new Zinfandel vineyards were planted – just to make Blush wine. High-yielding vines, flat, fertile land, easy to mechanise, nothing fancy. They're just for Blush. But, more importantly, no one is ripping out those 120-year-old vines in the gold rush Amador Hills any more.

1976

BARBOURSVILLE CABERNET SAUVIGNON

You can't say they didn't try. The English pitched camp at Jamestown, Virginia, in 1607 and one of the first things they set out to do was to plant the grape vines they'd brought from Europe.

That's easier said than done if you set up your tents in a swamp and the natives aren't friendly. They weren't. Starvation was a more common condition than inebriation. Still, the settlers tried again. A fresh crew of sturdy souls arrived in 1619, determined to... well, to make a profit, really.

The Virginia Company, like all the other trading companies, was after profit, and thought this could be achieved by supplying to the English merchants what the continental European wars were denying them – silk, olive oil and wine. 'Acte Twelve' of the Jamestown Assembly in 1619 – this was the first elected assembly in the New World – stipulated that the head of every household had to plant 20 of the imported European vines on his land.

Which is all very well. But how do you make the grapes grow? Raccoons, bears, birds and deer tucked into this new fruit like it was Christmas. All kinds of fungi were delighted to welcome new prey. And the settlers quickly discovered that there was a native crop called tobacco that grew like a weed and rapidly generated all the profit you could want. And there was something else. A secret enemy, invisible, relentless, implacably bent on destroying this vine interloper from Europe – *Phylloxera vastatrix:* the Destroyer, the aphid of Destruction.

This is the very first Barboursville wine, one of just over 300 bottles of 1978 Cabernet Sauvignons made. It sparked the overdue revival, or, you could say, long-delayed birth of modern Virginia wine.

What no one knew was that this lethal aphid was native to America's Northeast, and local vine species – America has loads, all different from the wine vine or *Vitis vinifera* that produces Europe's wines – were able to coexist with it. But the European *vinifera* vine couldn't; the aphid ate its roots and the vines died. They died right through the 17th century. Virginians tried again in the 18th century – Founding Father Thomas Jefferson at Monticello attempted to grow European vines for 36 years and never made a bottle of wine; first President George Washington tried for 11 years at Mount Vernon before giving up and turning to apple brandy. They went on trying in the 19th century and winemakers had some success, but only with native vines, not *vinifera*.

And so the 20th century arrived, along with Prohibition, the Great Depression, World Wars, Coca-Cola and milkshakes.... How much more discouragement did you need? But by now, growers understood how to combat the phylloxera aphid – you graft European *vinifera* like Chardonnay or Cabernet onto native American rootstocks. All it needed was someone inspired enough – or mad enough – to give the *vinifera* one more chance in Virginia.

That man was Gianni Zonin, boss of Italy's biggest family-owned wine company. He fell in love with Virginia on a visit in the springtime – difficult not to – and thought what a wonderful place for a vineyard. History said 'uh huh' – they've been trying without success since 1607. The local officials offered Zonin cigars, saying: 'The future of Virginia is tobacco, not wine.' But they were wrong. Zonin bought the Barboursville Estate, along with the ruins of a mansion designed by Thomas Jefferson. On 13 April 1976, he broke the soil, and, in 1978, produced 300 or so bottles of Cabernet Sauvignon. Since then Virginia has paradoxically gained a worldwide reputation for growing the grapes other places find really difficult – Viognier, Petit Manseng, Petit Verdot, Nebbiolo – and making sensational wines from them. But it all began – at last – with the Barboursville Cabernet Sauvignon 1978.

Gianni Zonin, on the left, planting his first Virginia vineyard – some 370 years after the first attempt.

Thomas Jefferson seemed to enjoy designing homes for his friends – where did he find the time? – and the Barboursville mansion borrowed much of the Palladian style he employed at his own home, Monticello. It burned down on Christmas Day, 1884 – I've always thought setting light to the Christmas pudding after having one too many was a trifle risky.

1976
JUDGMENT OF PARIS

Springtime in Paris, tra la la, tra la la. What a lovely time for a wine tasting. Especially one full of good humour and celebration. And so it seemed on 24 May 1976, as a group of exceedingly distinguished French wine experts turned up at the Intercontinental Hotel in Paris to taste a bunch of American wines. Well, that's what they thought.

The year 1976 was the bicentenary of the American Declaration of Independence. This tasting was seen as a demonstration of Franco-American historical ties, mutual respect, long-term friendship – and, of course, the French had been very helpful to the fledgling Americans in their fight against the British 200 years ago. And so now they made wines. Quite good, so they'd heard. Well, let's go along and give them a bit of encouragement.

If that's what the French experts thought, Steven Spurrier, a young Englishman who ran one of Paris's best wine shops, as well as an Académie du Vin, had something slightly more ambitious in mind. He knew French wines inside out, and knew all the leading personalities in the French wine world. But he was also a radical, perhaps even something of a revolutionary. Much as he loved France, he was well aware of the amazing progress the wines of such places as California and Australia were making. And the bicentenary seemed like too good a chance to miss for shaking up the complacent French wine establishment a bit. It was he who organised this Paris tasting. But it wasn't just California wines. He had chosen a tip-top range of French wines, too. He would mix them up, they would be tasted blind, marked, and winners would be announced.

Steven knew the French well enough to know that if he told them it was a competitive France versus California tasting, they wouldn't turn up. There was a lot of pride and reputation at stake. The man in charge of judging wines for the National Institute of Appellation Contrôlée was a taster. The Secretary of the Grands Crus Classés in Bordeaux, the co-owner of Burgundy's greatest estate, the editors

This is the red wine that shocked the world by beating Bordeaux superstars Mouton-Rothschild and Haut-Brion. These French vineyards had been producing grapes for hundreds of years. The 1973 Stag's Leap was made from their first crop of grapes!

For a short while in 1976, the most famous – or infamous – white wine in the world: the upstart Californian Chardonnay, which beat the cream of Burgundy.

of France's two leading wine magazines, two three-star Michelin restaurateurs, were tasting – people who had made careers out of their ability to discern and define flavours and quality through their sense of smell and taste. So he told them he'd added some French wines only as they arrived at the tasting. Some might have refused to participate. None did. Probably because they were completely convinced that anything decent on the table would be French, and ridiculously easy to identify.

Spurrier certainly didn't load the dice in California's favour. He included some of the most famous white Burgundies from Meursault and Puligny-Montrachet. And he included two First Growth and two top Second Growth Bordeaux. The French thought that France was sure to win, so every wine the judges really liked, they put down as French. And when the wrappings were removed from the wines, these 'French' favourites turned out to be Californian – Château Montelena Chardonnay 1973 beat Roulot's Meursault and Leflaive's Puligny-Montrachet, while Stag's Leap Wine Cellars' 1973 Cabernet Sauvignon beat Mouton Rothschild and Haut-Brion.

The French judges did not react well. One tried to change the marks of the French wines – upwards. Others refused to give Spurrier their notes. Another protested he'd been tricked into taking part in a 'traitorous' activity. The French press who had attended seemed to slink away and no stories appeared. But one journalist didn't slink away. By chance, George Taber of *Time* magazine was there. He couldn't believe what he saw unfolding. And he wrote the story for *Time*, headlining it 'Judgment of Paris'. The French tried to dismiss it. But it was a moment of enormous importance. The young pretenders from California had beaten the cream of the French wine elite. There was no more god-given right to produce the world's greatest wines solely on the sites hallowed by time. California had modelled its wines on France's best and now it had taken on and vanquished its idols.

1978

PARKER POINTS

I didn't go to Robert Parker's Gala Hedonist's Dinner in 2015. I wasn't invited. And the idea of paying £1800 for a good dinner and a taste of eight top wines didn't give me any warm feelings. Indeed, the whole event rather disturbed me. This was part of a 'Grand World Tour' being undertaken by Parker, a kind of imperial long last farewell tour, a grand parade of the world's most expensive wines being drunk in the company of the world's richest wine lovers. But this wasn't how Parker started out. And this wasn't what Parker's stated purpose was in the world of wine.

When Robert Parker began writing about wine in the late 1970s he saw himself as a Ralph Nader figure, taking on the establishment, exposing mediocre and poor wine, questioning overpriced wines, as well as seeking out the 'values' – the five- and ten-dollar wines that tasted like something that cost two or three times as much.

His aim, he said, was to democratise wine, give good unbiased opinions in a world where most wine criticism was far too cosy with the hand that fed it – the wine trade. And to best achieve this, he adopted the 100-point scale of marking that Americans are used to from school. It's easy. The higher the mark, the better the wine, starting at 50 – that's how they do it in America – and ending at 100. Simple, isn't it? Pick the level you want, or can afford. Buy the wine. Though Parker wrote rather enjoyable, dense and frequently very informative prose, hardly anyone read it. They read the scores. And this was the great strength and great weakness of the mighty communicator. Parker wanted you to read his opinions, not just check out the mark. But that's not the world we live in, and this new world has definitely been created in part by Parker.

He shot to fame with his unalloyed approval of the 1982 vintage in Bordeaux. Parker's enthusiastic reviews were picked up and quoted by the merchants, whose sales rocketed. But above all, they picked up the marks. They realised this simple method of endorsing a wine was a marketing tool beyond worth. Parker's power grew rapidly during the 1980s because wine retailers, importers, distributors

*Here's the portrait of a happy wine taster. Petrus 1990 in the palm of his hand, 2000
Cheval Blanc ready to back it up, and a bottle of luminously golden 1948 Doisy-Daëne
Sauternes to finish off with. The world's greatest wine critic at play.*

and collectors all began to take note of his marks and opinions. The producers followed, and soon the whole professional world of wine – well, by now it was fine wine, not your basic stuff – was somewhere between keen and desperate to know what he thought.

Particularly in Bordeaux and California, his views could make or break reputations and wines were increasingly made to please his palate. In other parts of the world – Spain, Italy, Australia – Parker became the only palate the producers at the top end were desperate to please, because a 95 score made a difference of millions of dollars. Parker *did* change the way wine is made – riper, fleshier, richer – but isn't that an improvement on the thin old things that abounded before he came along? Less encouragingly, his attempt to democratise has actually created an elite; his marking system offers certainty where no certainty exists, substituting blithe reassurance for hard-earned personal opinion. And it stifles disagreement where cordial disagreement is the lifeblood of the wonderful, subjective, unpredictable world of wine.

As Parker withdraws from the scene, and an array of bloggers, tweeters and critics begin to find the confidence to offer up a thousand different views, he can rest assured he changed the world of wine more than any other writer has. And for better or worse? That's subjective.

1979

OPUS ONE

Baron Philippe de Rothschild reckoned he did 90 per cent of his business in his bedroom. In his bed, in fact. Now, now, no misunderstandings. Well, maybe; because Baron Philippe had led an outrageously 'colourful' life by the time he conducted a meeting with Robert Mondavi from California in August 1978.

But if you want to show who's boss, it's not a bad idea to be lying decadently among a pile of pillows on a vast bedstead while your meeting partner seems almost like a supplicant craving indulgence. Such thoughts might have been going through Robert Mondavi's head, too: the New World pretender at the court of Old World royalty. But he was here on a mission. A mission to gain the legitimacy he craved for his California wines by entering into a joint venture with the owner of the famous Bordeaux First Growth Château Mouton Rothschild.

If Robert Mondavi needed the Baron to help him lead his crusade to have Napa Valley wines accepted as the equal of the great wines of France, Baron Philippe didn't *need* Mondavi. But he wanted him. He had always been a restless, ambitious, relentlessly dynamic man. He'd fought for 50 years to have his Château, Mouton Rothschild, reclassified as a First Growth in Bordeaux in 1973. He was now 76 years old. One more challenge. Why not California? He'd been a Hollywood film producer briefly before World War II; he'd often holidayed in Santa Barbara, and at the end of the 1970s, the political situation in France was increasingly unsettled. He'd already tentatively mentioned his interest in a California Cabernet Sauvignon wine to Robert Mondavi, way back in 1970. Now he was going to do it.

The meeting to establish the joint venture was remarkably easy, because both parties were so eager.

The famous 1979 Opus One. The giant egos are perfectly offset in this label –
two proud profiles, and two powerful signatures to balance them.

The ultra-modern Opus One winery. It takes up a fair bit of land, so you can be sure it's not situated on any of Robert Mondavi's best vineyard sites.

The only hiccup came when Rothschild suggested Mondavi might sell some of his vineyard land to the joint venture. 'Would you sell yours?' asked Mondavi. Of course not. No. Neither would Mondavi. They would start out buying grapes and making the wine at Mondavi's winery. They would look for land to buy for a vineyard, and then they'd build a winery. The winemaking would be jointly done by Mondavi's and Rothschild's winemakers. Oh, and they needed a name. And a label.

This wasn't so easy. Two big egos. Two equal partners. Various names came and went; names like Alliance, Duet, Gemini – which Rothschild liked but Mondavi told him was the name of San Francisco's leading gay newspaper – and finally Opus: as with great composers, as with the great writers and their magnum opus. And this would be Opus One. The first creation of a master. The label design process took over two years to create a Janus-like image of the two heads – with Rothschild's profile just that bit higher, but Mondavi's signature first, so honours were even.

But before the naming and label design, the wine had to be made. The French team favoured finesse, the Californian team more power, in their Cabernet Sauvignon (the wine was initially 100 per cent Cabernet Sauvignon, though now it is merely Cabernet dominant). But it was basically made in as Mouton Rothschild a way as possible because Mondavi, despite his immense self-confidence, knew that this relationship with one of Bordeaux's greatest wine properties would lift his winery's reputation to an entirely new level, and, anyway, if the Opus One team could make a Napa Valley Cabernet taste like a Bordeaux First Growth, that would be a massive coup.

In the end the coup was more one of marketing. They managed to pre-sell the first case of the unnamed and unbottled 1979 wine – called Napa Médoc at that stage – at a charity auction for $24,000; $2000 a bottle.When Opus One was finally released in 1984, at $50 a bottle, it was still the most expensive release of any Napa Valley wine. With the help of the maverick genius of Baron Philippe de Rothschild, Mondavi and his winery had arrived on the world stage. And so had the whole of Napa Valley.

VARIETAL LABELLING

The first varietal wine I drank was Lutomer Riesling from Yugoslavia. Well, that's not quite true. I drank several stiff gulps of 'my mum's' damson wine when I was three, but not much of it stayed down. No. It was a mouthful or two, at Christmas years later, of Lutomer Riesling (quite nice). And then what happened?

I went out into the great wide world of being a student and beyond, and, unless you were a bit of a wine geek like me, the labels on any half-decent wines were incomprehensible. Why were there so many syllables and umlauts in German wine names? Why did French labels befuddle you with place names and classifications and whether the winemaker had a moustache or not? Wasn't anyone going to tell me what the wine might taste like before I bought it?

Well, the most utterly, completely fundamental contributor to a wine's flavour is the grape variety the wine is made from. In the old days, everything got muddled up in the vineyard, but in our era everyone knows what grape varieties are grown in their vineyards. Why don't they tell us? One grape variety is as different from another as one apple is from another. Blindfold any of us and give us three apples – let's say, a Cox's Orange Pippin, a Granny Smith and a Golden Delicious – and I guarantee you, anyone without a lead palate can tell the difference between them. It's the same with grape varieties.

In fact, they're even more different. A Chardonnay, a Sauvignon, a Riesling, a Gewürztraminer in the white corner. A Merlot, a Cabernet Sauvignon, a Pinot Noir, a Sangiovese in the red corner. They're so different.

Why weren't their names being put on the label? Well, in the States, a wine writer called Frank Schoonmaker in the 1930s had begun to shame local producers to use the grape name on the label, but in Europe it took a lot longer – I'd say until the 1980s. And then – smash, bang, wallop – the Aussies arrived. They saw how convoluted and unfriendly European wine-labelling regulations were and decided: OK, I'll tell the consumer what my name is, what country I live in, and what grape variety I make my wine from. So simple.

Why hadn't anyone done it before?

It struck home to me as I tasted a range of rather boring French wines – oh, Beaujolais, Muscadet, something like that – at a London wine show. This hairy, khaki-clad, not entirely fragrant character sidled up to me and said in a broad Aussie accent, 'What flavours do you guys like in your wines?' Almost to clear the air and stamp on an unwanted conversation, I spluttered, 'We'd love it if our whites tasted of peaches and our reds of blackcurrants, and they cost £3.99.' A year later, at the same show, this same uncouth character shuffled up and said, 'Here, taste this.' It was a glass of white. 'Wow,' I said, 'it tastes of peaches.' 'That's what you said you liked.' 'How much is it?' '£3.99. That's what you said you wanted to pay.' 'And what's it called?' 'Chardonnay.' He did the same with the red. Blackcurrants, £3.99 – and called Cabernet. So simple to understand. So delicious to drink. My varietal epiphany.

The three most important wines, wines that transformed the British wine-drinking culture, were Lindeman's Bin 65 Chardonnay, Penfolds Bin 28 Shiraz (both from Australia) and Montana Sauvignon Blanc from New Zealand. These three wines changed British and, I suspect, northern European wine-drinking for ever. Labelled by grape variety. So easy to understand. So full of flavour and unmistakable Aussie or Kiwi personality. And they simplified life for all of us.

There are now Cabernets, Shirazes, Chardonnays or Sauvignons for over a hundred pounds or less than a tenner. If a new country – Turkey, say, or Croatia – wants to export its wines, it labels them by grape variety, sometimes using the international varieties for familiarity, but increasingly using the local varieties for intriguing *un*familiarity. And when I go into my supermarket and gaze at the wine racks, with the bottles labelled by grape variety, I finally know what I'm getting.

Three wines that changed Britain's wine culture. All tasted excellent, all tasted very distinct, and none of them were that cheap: you quickly made up your mind it was worth paying a bit more for a guaranteed flavour.

THE 1982 VINTAGE IN BORDEAUX

If there is a day on which the new age of Bordeaux was born for me, it was in the spring of 1983, when I had my first – and pretty nearly only – mouthful of Petrus 1982.

I still have the yellowing tasting notes. 'Amazingly...' Amazingly good? It doesn't say, just 'Amazingly...' 'It hasn't even...' – another sentence unfinished. I finally manage 'It's like a sweet dry syrup, an essence...' Of what? Tell us! Well, actually, I can still vividly remember the astonishing flavours and texture of that wine, so shockingly good that I simply couldn't get words down on to my pad. And there's no doubt that this wonderfully rich but bountiful vintage ushered in a new era. The idea of top quality allied to abundant quantity was something totally new – classic vintages in the past had almost all been small. Yet here we had leading properties making 50 to 100 per cent more wine than usual – and it was delicious, lush, rich, sensual and ridiculously easy to drink at a young age. Again, breaking the rules. Red Bordeaux is supposed to be really difficult to taste when it's young – that's if it's going to age well. But the 1982s were so easy you could drink them by the jugful straight from the barrel, and yet, I'm delighted to say, they're still tasting wonderful at 41 years – the ones under my stairs anyway.

The 1982 vintage created the reputation of Robert Parker, the most influential wine critic of all time, and by doing so, indirectly changed the wine styles of areas all round the world as they fought to please the ultimate arbiter of price and fame. Also, indirectly, 1982 provided the breeding ground for a new species of international wine consultant, epitomised by Michel Rolland, who became supremely influential not only in Bordeaux, but also globally. Perfect timing. The continuing, almost helter-skelter improvement in vineyard techniques and winery practices during the 1980s gave them the tools to, literally, create the required flavours in any part of the world they set foot in.

Left: Petrus is not one of the 1982s I have under my stairs for when the vicar calls, and I can only guess at how it now tastes. So I think I'll stick with the epiphany that was Petrus 1982, lying in its barrel, less than a year old. Middle: Le Pin 1982 is just about the rarest of all the Bordeaux 1982s, and the most 'cultish'. Right: Harlan is one of the most successful cult wines in California's Napa Valley – the result of investment and hype, but also passion and quality.

The 1982 vintage also significantly upset the balance of power in Bordeaux. Previously, the wines of the so-called 'Left Bank', led by the group of châteaux called the 1855 Classed Growths, had always been thought of as superior, with their dark Cabernet-dominated wines. Yet in 1982, the tiny area of Pomerol, on the Right Bank, garnered most of the superlatives with irresistible, hedonistic, exotic fruit bombs based on the juicy Merlot grape. Perfect for the new American market. But there was a problem. Availability.

Most of the properties were small. Some were minute. Château Le Pin was only a few acres. Just enough to make stunning wine no one could get hold of. There were other tiny properties, little parcels of top quality soil, that over the next decade or so started selling their precious bottles under their own label. To great critical acclaim. For higher and higher prices. Cult wines. The age of the 'cult' wine began in 1982. Wines made from these top patches of soil have managed to remain crazily sought-after, yet respected.

The 'Garagiste' movement brought a similar 'cult' mentality to less good patches of soil, and has peaked. But around the world, the 'cult' movement is still alive – Pingus in Spain, La Turque in the Rhône Valley, Harlan and Screaming Eagle and others in California are among the leaders of the movement. All too often when a billionaire decides to buy or create a vineyard and winery, he believes that money spent, publicity bought and a stratospheric price charged will bring instant icon status. These guys should check the dictionary. Icon status needs to be earned, not bought. Even so, the good pieces of vineyard will survive and flourish. The ones based solely on hype and manipulating supply and demand will crash in flames.

1983
MONTANA MARLBOROUGH SAUVIGNON BLANC

My wine world changed on 1 February 1984. At eleven in the morning. On the 17th floor of New Zealand House in London. Just inside the door on the left. Third wine along. That's the first time I tasted a Sauvignon Blanc from Marlborough in New Zealand's South Island. Montana 1983.

My wine world would never be the same again. No one's wine world would ever be the same again.

Because that Montana Sauvignon had a flavour, a personality, unlike that of any wine ever made before. The Sauvignon Blanc grape had been around in France for centuries, and had made some attractively sharp-edged, leafy wines in Bordeaux and the Loire Valley. But nothing like this – the sweet-sour greenness of cooked gooseberries, the crisp earthy greenness of a fresh-cut pepper, the greenness of blackcurrant leaf, of apple peel, of lime zest scratched with your fingertips, of new-season asparagus. All of this, and more, in just one mouthful of wine. From a brand new vineyard in a brand new wine country – the South Island of New Zealand.

In reality, one of the main reasons Montana had gone there was because land was cheap. Dirt cheap. The Montana wine company (now Brancott Estate) was looking to expand in the early 1970s. Land around Auckland was too expensive. Land at Hawkes Bay on the North Island was pretty expensive too. But Marlborough in the South Island was cheap as chips with its hardscrabble stony soils peopled by stray sheep and peppered with garlic. So in 1973 they bought 1600

An old Montana Sauvignon from 1981. The bottle may not look revolutionary, but the snappy, mouthwatering white wine inside revolutionised the world of wine.

hectares – they didn't muck about – and on 24 August 1973 planted the first vine. It was a Cabernet Sauvignon.

But because of the massive nature of the undertaking, Montana's boss Frank Yukich had put the word out: I need vines – any vines – to plant in Marlborough. And one of the job lots that came through was Sauvignon Blanc. The stony soil, the sunny but cool conditions, the lack of autumn rain and also the open-mindedness that came from a complete lack of preconception down here – where the local officials said, you might try apples, but it's too cold for grapes – all these conspired to produce the shocking, exhilarating wine that is now the world-famous Marlborough Sauvignon Blanc. They didn't make the first example until 1979, and it wasn't until the 1983 vintage that the rest of the world realised something as new and thrilling in its own way as the draining of the marshes in Bordeaux's Médoc, or the first scaling of the slaty slopes of Germany's Mosel Valley was happening on the last scrap of land before the Antarctic.

And one more thing. Montana's land was cheap. There was some even cheaper land – too stony and bony to plant, they said. Even the sheep starve on it. An Australian named David Hohnen bought that. In 1985 he made the first Cloudy Bay from its struggling vines. In 1986 that Cloudy Bay was voted best Sauvignon Blanc in the world.

If you think it looks pretty rudimentary, it was! The locals turned up at this great slab of virgin land and planted 700,000 vines – all by hand. Did they know what they were doing? Some didn't. A lot of the vines were planted upside down.

1985
MOST EXPENSIVE BOTTLE

If you've ever bid at an auction, you'll know that you can go slightly crazy. As the price rushes up towards the limit you'd set yourself, you feel as though you're being sucked into a mighty whirlpool. The price reaches your limit and you convince yourself to make just one more bid, because every other bidder is sure to drop out.

And they don't. And you break out in sweat, and feel faint, and desperate, and out of control.

And still you bid, often against just one other adversary, until, for one of you, the madness passes, the bidding ends, and, if you're lucky, the other person has paid an insane price, not you. And all this might take a mere couple of minutes. On 5 December 1985, at Christie's sale rooms in London, a battle between two men over a bottle of wine took just 1 minute, 39 seconds. Ninety-nine seconds. After which there was a new record for the most expensive wine in the world; the first ever wine to sell for £100,000.

In fact, it was £105,000 ($131,250), and, luckily, the guy who could afford it bought it – Christopher Forbes, son of Malcolm Forbes, one of the richest men in America. He'd flown over in a private jet from New York to buy this bottle – not bid for it, buy it. Very rich people don't expect to be outbid. The plane was waiting on the tarmac at Heathrow to fly the bottle straight back to New York. And this bottle had not merely smashed the world record, it had vapourised it. The previous record had been for a bottle of Château Lafite 1822, sold for $31,000 (about £24,730) in 1980. This new bottle was also a Lafite, but much more special. It came from the 1787 vintage – the oldest authenticated red wine ever to be sold at Christie's. And the bottle was engraved with the letters 'Th. J.'. These are the initials of Thomas Jefferson, author of America's Declaration of Independence, and her third President. This wasn't wine Forbes was bidding for. It was history.

No one doubts history happened. But a lot of people have very different views about exactly *what* happened in history. And the appearance of this 1787 Jefferson bottle didn't go unchallenged. Jefferson was a meticulous record-keeper. He had kept all the letters he'd ever received – 40,000 – as well as duplications of every letter he'd ever sent, yet the Jefferson experts at Monticello in Virginia could find no record of its purchase. And it had supposedly been found in, well, let's say, fortuitous circumstances, in Paris. A German wine collector called Hardy Rodenstock said it had been found by workers knocking down an old house, who discovered a cache of ancient wines behind a false wall in the cellar. So where was this house? Rodenstock seemed strangely unwilling to give details, merely saying that the cellar was virtually hermetically sealed, at a constant temperature, which would explain the wonderful condition the bottles seemed to be in. Some less friendly experts suggested this might be part of a hidden Nazi hoard. The Nazis filched an awful lot of top wine. When the Allies liberated Hitler's Eagle's Nest hideout in the Alps, they found half a million bottles – including old Lafite.

Well, the cynics had a point. The great Jefferson 1787 Lafite was proved to be a fake. But by then I'm not sure it mattered. The Forbes family gave the bottle pride of place at a Jefferson exhibition they were hosting at Forbes Galleries. The bottle basked in the heat of publicity, and of a highly efficient spotlight. For a few months. And then the cork fell in.

It looks real enough to me, but what do I know?
The unmasking of this bottle as a fake led to the exposure of a
whole slew of supposedly noble and ancient bottles that turned out
to be fake. The World of Fine Old Wine is still awash with them.

1987

CENTRAL OTAGO – FURTHEST SOUTH

There are lots of things I like about Central Otago, right at the bottom of New Zealand's South Island, not least the fact that when the first vineyards were planted there back in the 1980s the nearest set of traffic lights were 200 kilometres away.

It suggests an environment just about as pollution-free as you can get in our modern world. And it also gives me a sense of the people. After all, there are towns there – Queenstown is quite big – but a traffic light would be an imposition on the freedom of spirit that has created this weird but wonderful vineyard area, which is the most southerly proper wine region in the world. There are a few vines further south in Chile, at Aysen and at Lake Puelo and there is a vineyard in Argentine Patagonia, which, at 30 kilometres further south, would like to nab this record. I've got cousins in southern Argentina. They're Welsh. They emigrated because it's like Wales down there: cold, windy, wet, lots of sheep. Will this vineyard flourish? Central Otago is different – it's quite ridiculously sunny. In fact, it's a desert, New Zealand's one and only desert. Even so, it's not an immediately obvious place to start a vineyard – in the most isolated part of the most isolated country in the civilised world.

The thing you have to remember about New Zealand's South Island is that people always said it couldn't be done when it came to vinegrowing. Always too cold, always too windy; plant apples, run sheep. They said that about Marlborough and Nelson, they said that about Canterbury and Waipara, and they sure as hell said it about Central Otago. But it had been done once before. In 1864, a Frenchman called Feraud planted vines near Clyde, at the

Gibbston Valley 1987 was Central Otago's first commercial release of Pinot Noir. The winery still produces excellent Pinot.

The Elms Vineyard at Bannockburn, after harvest. This is Felton Road's original vineyard, planted in 1992, and source of some of New Zealand's greatest Pinot Noir, Chardonnay and Riesling.

southern end of Central Otago – not necessarily, I admit, because it was a suitable site, but because gold had been discovered and there was money to be made. Slaking the miners' thirst was a far surer way to a fortune than panning the river beds. Over 100 years later, the pioneers were back.

Numerous varieties were planted near Alexandra, near Queenstown, and further north at Lake Wanaka, but it soon became clear that Central Otago could do what almost no other New World area could do – ripen Pinot Noir, and make wines from the variety of a depth, flavour and structure that were as good as Burgundy but completely different.

Is Central Otago similar to Burgundy? Well, they're both continental, not maritime, but whereas Burgundy seems to nestle cosily in a bucolic French world, Central Otago's beauty is gaunt, scarred and forbidding. The ruins of those goldmines taint the landscape wherever you look, vineyards often being the only sign of green in a tumbled vista of rubble and cliffs, relieved only by the banks of purple thyme that blanket the hills.

We're at 45° south here and between 200 and 450 metres above sea level, crowded into deep valleys topped by snowcapped mountains. New Zealand's hottest and coldest temperatures have been recorded at Alexandra in the south, and the difference between maximum and minimum temperatures every day is quite extreme – I've seen it go from 33°C to 3°C in one 24-hour period. This is great for acidity and colour in the grapes. Mostly, the air is bone dry, the temperature peaks at 31–32°C, and the sun shines and shines, well into the autumn. Usually. When it doesn't, frost comes down like a clawhammer, and at the beginning and end of the ripening season you can lose your crop.

But since Alan Brady at Gibbston Valley released the first commercial Pinot Noir in 1987, wine lovers have flocked to Central Otago, the world's southernmost full-scale vineyard region, to pay homage to the risk-takers who create such wonderful wines.

1987
FLYING WINEMAKERS

The term 'flying winemakers' was coined by Tony Laithwaite, the genius behind Britain's biggest direct wine-selling operation – aptly called Direct Wines.

He'd been to Bordeaux as an archaeology student, then begun a wine business – literally a van full of Bordeaux wine in a small railway arch just below the Castle at Windsor. But he saw immense potential in France – if only someone would teach them how to make wine. In particular, France was awash with decent vineyards whose fruit was unenthusiastically carted off to the local co-op, where they had not the slightest idea how to turn it into decent grog. Laithwaite reasoned that the Australians were making a name for themselves by meticulous attention to detail and relentless insistence on modern machinery and almost aseptic conditions in the winery. And by their willingness to work all the hours God gave – including the then obligatory mid-morning *casse- crôute*, the long lunch, the long weekend, the endless fag breaks; all the things that produced sloppy, dirty wines from grapes that could have made something bright and fresh. Oh, and one more thing. Australia's in the southern hemisphere. They do their vintage in Europe's winter and spring. By the time the French vintage came along in September, the Aussie winemakers had got time on their hands. So in 1987 he brought a bunch of young Aussies, headed by Nigel Sneyd, down to work in a group of French co-operatives and dubbed them 'flying winemakers'.

They weren't actually the first. Two of the people now regarded as Australian giants had already been there: Martin Shaw of Shaw & Smith, and Brian Croser, virtual doyen of Australian winemakers. They'd been in Bordeaux, teaching the locals about cleanliness, cultured yeasts, enzyme settling, acid adjustments and the use of new oak – all the tools of the New Wave winemaker. But Laithwaite's move caused a surge that was most evident in the vast swathes of under-performing vineyards and wineries in southern France. Many areas of the Languedoc had been famous in the 19th century, but since the ravages of phylloxera most of these reputations had sunk without trace. The Flying Winemakers took one look at the broad, hot hectares and thought: Australia. Rip out the rubbish grapes, plant Cabernet, Merlot, Shiraz, Chardonnay – you know, Aussie stuff – and begin pumping out good grog at low prices.

During the 1990s, Australian-accented French exhorting the locals to try harder came to be heard all over southern France. But not just there. Non-Australians – like the English Hugh Ryman and Angela Muir, or the French Jacques Lurton – took these New World ideas of hard work, cleanliness, attention to detail and, increasingly, a vision of the flavour of the wine they wanted to create, to other parts of Europe. Eastern Europe benefited enormously but so did Italy, Spain and Portugal. In time, Flying Winemakers like Lurton were turning up in places like Chile and Argentina – after all, their vintage was just when everyone in the *north* had time on their hands.

Touché. People criticise the flying winemakers for homogenising wine. I don't agree. They introduced the future to places stuck in the past. They kickstarted an international wine trade in places where there was none. And they provided the cheap, cheerful, tasty wines that allowed supermarkets in places like Britain to lead a revolution in wine-drinking habits.

Tony Laithwaite (far right) and a bunch of likely lads sampling the wares – probably direct from the barrels of Château Grand Tertre that they're perched on. Was this a bottling party? Laithwaite established his empire from this railway arch in Windsor.

Brian Croser taking time off from being a Flying Winemaker to establish his Tiers Vineyard in South Australia's Adelaide Hills.

1980s-1990s
INTERNATIONAL CONSULTANTS

It seems a bit petty in the 21st century to complain about globalisation. In the last 20 years or so our whole lives have been knit closer and closer together by globalisation, and we revel in it. But not, so it seems, when it comes to what we eat and drink.

We want our wines to taste of their place, of their special climate and soil, of their traditions. But what if those traditions never produced any interesting wine? What if those unique soils and climates were being squandered? What then? Or what if an estate was starting from scratch, or was being taken over by a new generation much more worldly-wise than the last, who were desperate to excel? You've got to call someone in. And that someone is likely to be one of a relatively small bunch of international wine consultants, led by the affable and indomitable Michel Rolland.

The consultant is a bit different from the 'Flying Winemaker', who knuckles under and actually makes the wine, more often than not. A consultant might have 100 clients – either wineries, in the case of people like Rolland, or vineyards in the case of someone like Dr Richard Smart. And they really do have an effect. Even if the hard yards are being done by resident wine staff, these globetrotting experts have become successful primarily because of the power of the vision they possess. Smart genuinely believes he can transform how wine tastes and what it costs by his revolutionary methods in the vineyard, especially concerning trellising, pruning, irrigation, and choice of clones and rootstocks. Rolland and others like him normally base their ideas very strongly on their home turf, and their advice, right around the world, is tinged by that core experience and belief.

But that's not to say that a consultant's wines will taste the same wherever they are made. Men like Rolland or his fellow Bordelais Stéphane Derenoncourt start their consultancy work by trying to understand a wine's vineyard. When Rolland says, 'I am a man of the soil', that's exactly what he is. I've spent days with him among the vines and never seen him happier – though nowadays he spends so much time in airport departure lounges that he probably pines for his muddy acres back in Fronsac near Saint-Émilion.

One of the clichés about wine consultants or consultant oenologists is that they are there to fix broken wines. Nothing could be further from the truth for the top players. They are often employed to improve an estate's performance, and in particular to try to garner 90-plus or 95-plus marks from the übercritics like American Robert Parker – so to do that they may fine-tune what already exists, or, especially in the case of the super-wealthy who buy up wineries and expect immediate success, they may have to, literally, create or invent a totally new wine.

There's no doubt that there is a kind of recipe for success they can apply in almost any circumstance for this, but in most cases, a good consultant will start from scratch in the vineyard. They know they have to get the grapes right; otherwise, by the time they have advised about what barrels to buy, what yeasts to employ, how long to macerate the skins and the juice, whether to micro-oxygenate or do the malolactic fermentation in barrel, to filter or not – had enough? – they know that if the grapes aren't right, the wine will be hollow. And at the moment of truth, when all the samples of all the different pickings from all the separate parcels of vines – all fermented in different batches – when all these samples are arrayed on the tables to make the final blend, it won't work, unless they got the vineyard right at the start of the process.

1990s
CABERNET CONQUERS THE WORLD

What brought it home to me this year was studying the statistics about where each grape variety is grown around the world. By a country mile, Cabernet Sauvignon is now the most widely planted grape in the world.

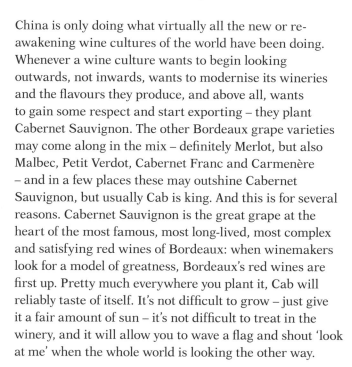

Pretty much everywhere you look, Cabernet is on the increase – and then you look at China. Well, no one has been able to pin down the precise figures for Chinese grapegrowing. You ask 10 different authorities, you get 10 different answers, but one thing is clear – China is in love with Cabernet Sauvignon. China may be growing as much Cabernet as the whole of France. Or perhaps twice as much. Some figures show about three times as much land in China growing Cabernet Sauvignon as in France.

China is only doing what virtually all the new or re-awakening wine cultures of the world have been doing. Whenever a wine culture wants to begin looking outwards, not inwards, wants to modernise its wineries and the flavours they produce, and above all, wants to gain some respect and start exporting – they plant Cabernet Sauvignon. The other Bordeaux grape varieties may come along in the mix – definitely Merlot, but also Malbec, Petit Verdot, Cabernet Franc and Carmenère – and in a few places these may outshine Cabernet Sauvignon, but usually Cab is king. And this is for several reasons. Cabernet Sauvignon is the great grape at the heart of the most famous, most long-lived, most complex and satisfying red wines of Bordeaux: when winemakers look for a model of greatness, Bordeaux's red wines are first up. Pretty much everywhere you plant it, Cab will reliably taste of itself. It's not difficult to grow – just give it a fair amount of sun – it's not difficult to treat in the winery, and it will allow you to wave a flag and shout 'look at me' when the whole world is looking the other way.

A Cabernet-based blend from Ningxia which has rapidly established itself as China's leading and most ambitious area for Cabernet. By some reckonings China now has the largest expanse of Cabernet vineyards in the world.

Left: This wine single-handedly put Lebanon on the wine map. Created by Serge Hochar, who trained in Bordeaux with Château Léoville-Barton, the wine brilliantly blends some Bordeaux rectitude with an unmistakeably exotic, almost Casbah-like personality unlike any other red. Cabernet is blended here with Carignan and Cinsault from Bekaa Valley vines planted in the 1930s. Middle: On a label entirely in your own language (this is Slovenian) putting Cabernet Sauvignon in big gold letters at least gives you a chance in the export market. Right: Superb, intense, brilliantly focused Cabernet from Henschke. Cabernet revels in the relatively high vineyards of the Eden Valley in South Australia.

So Cabernet Sauvignon has had a truly important role to play in improving the world of wine. It has been so successful that it now has as many detractors as supporters. But its critics should look at the good it has done before getting on their high horse and mouthing off about the destruction of local flavours and so on. For a start, before Cabernet Sauvignon arrived, there often weren't any local flavours that anyone but the most local consumer would want to drink, and Cabernet's arrival fuelled the vineyard and winery revolution that is now allowing all kinds of local initiatives to flourish.

Sometimes Cabernet Sauvignon put down permanent roots – the Napa Valley in California, Margaret River and Coonawarra in Australia, Hawkes Bay in New Zealand, Stellenbosch in South Africa, Maipo in Chile. But just as often Cabernet was a phase that gave the confidence to the locals to return to their indigenous grapes. Tuscany was dragged into the modern era by Cab, yet now is almost overly determined to concentrate on its local varieties like Sangiovese. Spain used Cabernet Sauvignon to kickstart the wines of Rioja, as the base for Vega Sicilia, and as a 100 per cent varietal in Miguel Torres' Black Label, which won a prestigious tasting organised by *Gault-Millau* magazine in France and caused the manager of Bordeaux's Cabernet citadel, Château Latour, to pronounce, 'It may be alright for a bawdy night out, but hardly for an elegant luncheon.' Pity that the Black Label had just beaten his Château Latour on the tasting table. Now Spain is in the grip of maximising the potential of its local grapes, but Cabernet provided the spur. Just as it did in southern France as it struggled to throw off its reputation for making cheap gut rot, as it did in Bulgaria, in Croatia, Greece and Lebanon.

In all these places it's still there, but taking more of a backseat to other more local varieties, and all I can say is – well done, Cabernet Sauvignon, thank you, Cabernet Sauvignon.

1990
ROYAL TOKAJI

There are many potent symbols of the crumbling of the Soviet Union and the collapse of Communist rule. For me, as a young member of Solidarnosc, the Polish resistance group – yes, honestly, I was the London Actors' representative – Lech Walesa and the Gdansk shipyards are the most potent memories.

For others it might be the jaw-dropping public execution of Ceausescu in Romania, or the fall of the Berlin Wall. But the most potent symbol in the world of wine was the rebirth of one of Europe's greatest wines, after generations of political suppression – the rebirth of Hungary's Tokaji, the wine of princes and popes and potentates from centuries gone by.

The Tokaji that was legendary 300 or 400 years ago, when no one had heard of the great châteaux of Bordeaux or the wines of Champagne, was barely a wine at all. It was an impossibly sweet viscous syrup called Essenzia. Bunches of nobly rotted grapes would be piled on top of each other in a tub with a perforated bottom and left. They wouldn't be pressed. Over the days or weeks, drops of this dense nectar would plop from the mush, squeezed out by the weight of the grapes alone. The sugar content of this thick syrup was so high it was barely able to ferment; typically it would be at least 500 grams of sugar per litre, though in 2000, the Disznók estate produced an essence at 914 grams per litre – quite possibly the sweetest wine ever made.

And it was this unthinkably sweet syrup, probably just barely affected by fermentation, that had tsars and kings desperate for a sip whenever they felt their libido declining, or on their deathbed with the hand of the grim reaper on their collar. When the 'Essenzia' had dripped out there was still loads of intensely sweet juice clinging to the grapes and this was then trodden and fermented with a little

The famous Mézes Mály grapes are at last being bottled under their own vineyard name, to exciting effect.

normally ripe grape juice to create the still unbelievably sweet Imperial Tokaji – one that you could just about drink at table, not at deathbed.

I'm not joking about its reputation. Berry Brothers & Rudd, London wine merchants, regularly listed Tokaji at over a century old, along with testimonials. One listing read: 'Send immediately one case of the wine that removes the screws from the coffin lid.' I'm not sure if it was the gentleman himself or his grieving wife who sent the order. Another read: 'Your Tokay has given me good nights. I have a wine glass nearly full, then the masseuse sister comes and rubs my back with a special liniment and I curl up like a contented pussy and go to sleep.' Yours sincerely, the Archbishop of Canterbury. No, just kidding. And the wine lasted forever. In 1939 the wine merchant Fukier in Warsaw had every vintage going back to 1606 (326 bottles of that), thousands of the 1668, the 1682 and so on, until the Nazi occupation – when in one heartbreaking drunken riot the world's remaining store of this wine from the 17th century was all pissed away.

Well, this is the grand notoriety that so attracted British wine writer Hugh Johnson and his Danish partner Peter Vinding-Diers in 1989. Hungary became the first Eastern Bloc country to open its borders. With the gay abandon and fervour of dreamers rather than businessmen, Johnson and Vinding-Diers set up the Royal Tokaji Wine Company as a joint venture in September 1990. They'd guessed right. Soon afterward, the Hungarian government announced a privatisation programme. Royal Tokaji was first in the queue, though big money quickly arrived as AXA Insurance bought the Disznók estate; Spain's fabled Vega Sicilia bought the great Oremus vineyard; and Grands Millésimes de France, partly owned by Suntory, bought the slopes of Hétsz l.

But Johnson and his partners might have the last laugh. The vineyard of Mézes Mály was historically Tokaji's greatest vineyard. It was at Mézes Mály in 1571 that the process of separating shrivelled and nobly rotted grapes from the rest of the crop was first documented. How fitting that it should be Johnson's Royal Tokaji that now makes Mézes Mály wine.

Hungarian winemaker István Szepsy (left), with Hugh Johnson (centre) and Peter Vinding-Diers in 1990. This grainy-looking snap is the only photograph of founders Johnson and Vinding-Diers at Royal Tokaji in Mád in the year their company was established.

The leaves are beginning to fall in the vineyards sloping down to the town of Mád. When conditions are right – warm sunshine alternating with river mists – noble rot forms on the Furmint grapes, creating the unique blend of high acid and honeyed richness that has made Tokaji world famous for centuries.

1991
RISE OF THE GARAGISTES

I still remember my first visit to a 'garagiste' winery, although this was in the 1980s and 'garagiste' really didn't become currency until the 1990s.

I'm not sure Monsieur Thienpont didn't have to move a grimy old Deux Chevaux and chase out a few chickens as he showed me the handful of barrels sitting in the garage under the house at Le Pin. But as I tasted the dark, sensuous young Le Pin I knew this was something rare and special. What I didn't know was that Le Pin was about to start a new trend in red Bordeaux wine.

The reason that the Thienpont family bought this tiny two-hectare patch of land, now known as Château Le Pin, was because they knew it to be really special dirt; they owned the neighbouring estate of Vieux Château Certan, they knew every inch of local land, and this minute plot was five-star stuff. It might have made sense to simply incorporate Le Pin into Vieux Château Certan, but Jacques Thienpont saw it as offering a chance to break out from the traditional austere but excellent wines the family had been making at Vieux Château Certan since the 1920s. He says he wanted to make a wine of 'great richness and majesty'. He might have added 'and in tiny quantities, and sell it for tons of money' – but he didn't need to. Le Pin's success set off the 'garagiste' movement, whose objective was to make – you got it – tiny quantities of rich, majestic wine and sell it for tons of money. The trouble was Le Pin was a rare jewel of outstanding unexploited vineyard. The other 'garagistes' were going to have to start without any of Le Pin's advantages.

Absolutely. 'Bad Boy' for trying to shake up the cosy world of Bordeaux. And for Jean-Luc Thunevin for using humour on his label. Where's the respect?

The master in his 'garage'. Jean-Luc Thunevin with his 1998 vintage of Valandraud. He didn't need a big cellar then, but he does now. Valandraud is currently made in a proper château on the east of the Saint-Émilion plateau.

On the whole, low-lying vines on the banks of a stream and next to the communal vegetable allotments don't produce special wine. But this little patch is all Jean-Luc Thunevin could afford and it gave the fruit for his first 'garage' wine – Valandraud.

The most famous 'garagiste' is Jean-Luc Thunevin with his Château Valandraud. He started with just 0.6 hectare of pretty poor vineyard land in Saint-Émilion, down next to the communal vegetable allotments. And he *did* make the wine in his garage, releasing his first vintage in 1991.

But it wasn't just money or fame that fired up Thunevin – though he has achieved both – but a revolutionary fervour, a rebellion against the glitz and glamour and snobbery that dominated so much of Bordeaux. Even if you don't have the money to buy decent land or smart equipment, you can have the passion. Scrape together some vines; reduce their yields by half; care for the grapes one by one if necessary; pick them, if necessary, berry by berry, as ripe as you dare and then maybe even riper; take them back to your tiny winery; buy the best barrels you can afford; maybe do the second malolactic fermentation in barrels rather than tanks to gain a richer, more succulent texture; never cut corners; relentlessly remove any portions that you don't totally believe in; don't fine the wine, don't filter – and then triumphantly place tiny amounts of this heady brew on the market for an exorbitant price, which the consumer pays. Simples.

There are now many 'garagistes' – often from wealthy backgrounds rather than the original revolutionaries – promoting 'microcrus' on their properties, and the movement has run its course. Valandraud is now based on excellent vineyard soil and is positively mainstream. But Thunevin and his brethren showed that the old order can be broken, a new meritocracy can take its place. And, as he says, the revolution had to come from the little people because they had nothing to lose.

1991
CANADIAN ICEWINE

It was the smallest present of wine that I'd ever been given. A friend of mine came back from Canada and proudly presented me with a 50 ml bottle of Canadian Icewine. I mean, it felt like my friend was slipping me a miniature of vodka he'd nicked from the flight attendant's trolley on the way home. 50 ml. Really!

Smallest present of wine? I'm not an earrings and cufflinks kind of bloke. I reckon it could have been the smallest present of any kind I'd ever been given. And then my sister turned up. She's Canadian. (No, don't ask. It's too complicated.) And she brought me a 200 ml bottle of Canadian Icewine. I gave her an old-fashioned look. 'It's very expensive,' she said. 'It's rare.' Well, I sort of knew this already, but I had never been face to face with the phenomenon. The 375-ml bottle of wine is about as small as I can take seriously. In which case I might have had to pay $5000 for that little half-bottle indulgence. That's the highest price I can find so far for a half-bottle of Canadian Icewine. Hang on. Canada? Since when did Canadian wine get so special?

Well, probably in 1991. Vinexpo was arguably the world's most important wine exhibition. It took place every two years in France (and now on occasion in North America and Asia). The world's wines are on show, but you can feel in your bones that Vinexpo holds to the belief that French is best; at a pinch, Europe is best; at another pinch – no, there is no 'other pinch'. So, Canada won't figure, then. Sacré Bleu, polar bears, Mounties and snowmobiles – *non, absolument, non!* Pity then that out of 4100 wines entered for the Vinexpo International Challenge, just 19 won the Grand Prix d'Honneur – one of which was Canadian Inniskillin Icewine 1989, made from the Vidal grape, which isn't even allowed to grow in France. The French may have hated it, but overnight, Canadian wine, from nowhere, was famous.

This 50 ml bottle of Inniskillin Icewine bears a disturbing similarity to something off the in-flight drinks trolley. Even so, it's an excellent mouthful.

Canada had been growing good cool-climate reds and whites for a while – some very impressive Chardonnays, some good Merlots and even Cabernets. But they hadn't stacked up against the rest of the New World – Californian Cabernet, Australian Chardonnay, which one would you have chosen? A new country needs a unique calling card. And when you think about it, Canada and Icewine are made for each other.

So what is Icewine? (One thing – it's Icewine in Canada, ice wine elsewhere.) Basically, it's wine made from frozen grapes. Germany and Austria had periodically produced a little ice wine – or *Eiswein*, as they call it – but as a high-acid, high-sugar oddity. You need to leave healthy grapes on the vine way into November, December and, if necessary, January, February, March – I've discovered one wine picked in April – until they freeze on the vine. Not just freeze a bit: -8°C is the starting point. Every degree colder gets you more concentrated wine. How?

OK. Grape juice is sugar and water, the water diluting the sugar. When the grapes freeze, the water freezes at about 0°C, but the sugar doesn't. It concentrates. At below -8°C the separation is reasonably complete; thick, sugar syrup and shards of ice. So, usually at night, a bunch of intrepid pickers collect the frozen grapes. They need to be at least -8°C because the press has to coax out the syrup without melting the ice. This could take a day, maybe more, and the press is often outdoors to keep everything as cold as possible. Finally, this gloopy syrup is left to ferment. If you add special yeasts, it may get off to a reasonable start. If you leave it to its own devices, it may be six months before it begins to ferment. I've heard of one ice wine still fermenting 10 years after the harvest.

And the result? An amazingly rich wine, especially when Vidal grapes are used rather than Riesling – but always with a piercing acidity to hold it together. Not always easy to drink a lot of, so maybe the 200 ml bottle isn't such a bad idea.

It won't have been much fun picking these grapes under the gloomy Canadian winter sky, but you have to wait until it's -8°C for the water in the grape juice to freeze completely, leaving behind a thick, intensely sweet syrup.

1993
SYNTHETIC CORKS

If natural cork were a completely reliable substance, and if every bottle with a natural cork stopper turned out to be a beauty, there might not be much of a market for synthetic corks. But life's never that simple.

During the 1990s, we all became increasingly aware that a lot of our wines were tasting musty and dirty; at their worst, they reminded you of an old football shirt left unwashed in a kitbag through a long hot summer. I *know* that smell. I do *not* want it in my wine.

The smell is caused by a chemical that can occur in natural cork called 2, 4, 6 Trichloroanisole – TCA for short – and we describe a bottle as 'corked', or affected by cork taint, when this nasty chemical surfaces. It's pretty rare, but the trouble is, during the 1990s TCA seemed to be surfacing more often, and several companies saw the need for a bottle stopper that eliminated risk. So they turned to plastic.

The first plastic corks were frankly pretty poor. They were usually vaguely cork coloured, but they wouldn't fool anybody – they were shiny, slippery to touch and hard as bullets. You needed a jackhammer to get them out of the bottle – and a pile driver to get them back in. And they devoured corkscrews like a flesh-eating tropical plant. Many times I actually snapped a corkscrew as I desperately tried to open some hapless bottle.

Well, most of the early bottles *were* hapless. These joyless bungs were used only on cheap bottles, so TCA remained rife. Until 1993, when a US company called Supremecorq came up with a slightly more malleable plastic closure – you could get it out of the bottle for a start – and they came in a great variety of colours and designs. Suddenly a plastic cork could be fun. Lots of decent wineries tried them out, and during the feverish birth of the Digital Age, they were pretty cool. Probably the best plastic corks are now made by a company called Nomacorc (what's with these guys and their spelling?), who've invented a closure with a sort of spongy core wrapped in a plastic coating that does give a fair imitation of a real cork.

But are they any good? Well, they don't have any TCA taint, that's for sure, though there are feelings that plastic might flatten the flavour of wine over time. The best modern ones are good for keeping air out of the wine, the worst ones seem to lose whatever seal they had after about 18 months. I have just opened a 15-year old Chilean Cabernet with a shiny black plastic cork and the wine was excellent. They're certainly cheaper than a decent natural cork, and they don't threaten the existence of Portugal's cork forests, which are anyway doing just fine. But they're not biodegradable, even though they are recyclable. So it's up to you. They say that 30 of the largest 40 wine companies use them. And of the 20 billion or so bottles of wine that are produced each year, about two billion of them have plastic corks. And screw caps? That's another story.

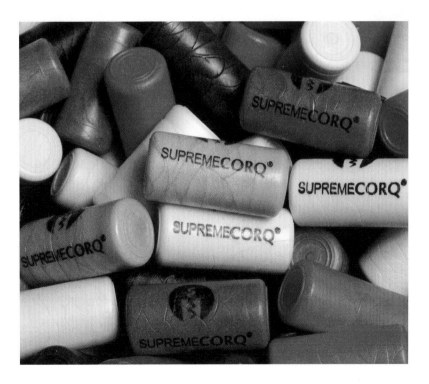

Party time around the turn of the century. Adventurous wineries used to print all kinds of stuff on these garishly coloured closures. The winemaker could have printed his phone number if he'd wanted to.

1994
CATENA MALBEC

**A country hoping to flee a featureless past is lucky if it has a
signature grape variety ready to lead the charge.**

New Zealand had none, but had the amazing luck of
Sauvignon Blanc landing on its doorstep desperate to
shine. Australia had Shiraz, but had despised it for so long
that it took some resolute shock and awe to persuade the
Australians themselves that it was a world beater. And
Argentina had Malbec. The grape had arrived during the
1850s – they say from southwest France, where it was the
principal grape in Cahors, but it's equally possible that it
slipped over the Andes from Chile – and for more than a
century was regarded as Argentina's best grape.

But how would you know? The Argentines drank it
voraciously and uncritically, with hardly a bottle
escaping to the outside world. It wouldn't much
have mattered if it had; Argentina drank all the
Malbec it made. Sides of beef suited the rough,
raw charm of the local red. As the 1980s dawned,
and the rest of the world began to wake up to the
astonishing possibilities that modern grapegrowing
and winemaking techniques had in store, Argentina
stumbled on in ignorance – not helped by military
dictatorships and hyperinflation.

But one man thought that not only could Argentina
do better, it was doomed if it didn't. Nicolás Catena
was a third-generation wine guy with an economics
PhD, and a successful family winery selling bulk
wines. But that market was shrinking as Argentines
turned away from wine – hardly surprising since
most of their wines, white or red, tasted like sherry
or Madeira.

Nicolás Catena was recognised by Decanter *magazine as its Man of the
Year in 2009, for his pioneering work in modernising Argentine wine.*

Catena Zapata's Adrianna vineyard at 1450 metres. The higher you march up the Uco Valley into the Andean foothills, the cooler it gets and the more thrilling your wine will be, red or white. These high vineyards now produce the grapes for many of Argentina's best wines.

Nicolas Catena and his daughter Laura relaxing in their vineyards. The Catena family have led the charge towards quality and innovation in Argentina.

While Catena was away teaching at the University of California in 1982, he visited Robert Mondavi in the Napa Valley and heard his story of starting from scratch in 1966 and succeeding by imitating the reds of Bordeaux and the whites of Burgundy, regardless of the totally different conditions in California. Catena decided to do the same back in Argentina. His father told him, 'It won't work, you don't have the terroir, you don't have the grapes. Don't get too big for your boots. Work with what you've got.'

His father was right. Catena didn't have Cabernet, but he did have Malbec. He still applied the Mondavi style of ripeness and loads of new oak, and some of those early wines tasted as much like Napa Cabernet as anything. But not quite. The oak couldn't subdue the beautiful damson and sweet plum fruit, the scent of violets tinged with aniseed. This wasn't Napa Cabernet.

It wasn't Bordeaux either. It was new, it was different. And it set a reactionary Argentina on a triumphant road forward. Catena used his scientific mind to figure out that what would work best was old vines in cool climates – and that, in Argentina, meant high altitudes. Most of Argentina's vines were clustered in cosy self-importance on the flattish land around Mendoza. But the Andes reared up just behind the city. Side valleys into the mountains were what Catena needed, and he found them in the Uco Valley and its upper reaches of Tupungato and Gualtallary.

When I first visited them with Catena's vineyard manager, all he could talk about was the lack of water and the risk of frost. Head up there now and all the smartest, most talented of Mendoza's winemakers are brushing aside the frosts and the lack of water and making a series of sensuous, scented, plump yet muscular reds that have brought Argentina, from an unpromising start, to its position as creator of one of the world's most irresistible reds.

1998
NYETIMBER

It took almost 2000 years before the world finally woke up to the fact that England can produce smashing wines. It took from the Romans to 1998 for anyone to take any notice. And then a wine called Nyetimber won the trophy for best sparkling wine in the world.

That's sparkling wine, including champagne. In the International Wine & Spirit Competition, the Nyetimber Classic Cuvée 1993 beat all comers for the top gong. And this was only the second vintage that Nyetimber had made. OK – get this. The year before, their first *ever* vintage – 1992 – had won best English wine, but, more importantly, had been chosen by the Queen for her 50th wedding anniversary bash. How could the dear old English go from joke to world beater in just a couple of years?

Well, we have to thank the Yanks. A couple of plucky Chicagoans – Sandy and Stuart Moss – got the idea that England could produce champagne-quality fizz. Really? When they bought the Nyetimber estate in 1986, they bought one of the most lovely manor house and garden combos I've ever seen. And it was on greensand soil – the soil that underlies chalk. Some of the best Champagne vineyards are on greensand, most of the rest are on chalk. Maybe the Mosses were onto something. They didn't muck about. Everybody told them they should plant apples – bureaucrats always say that; we'd have no Marlborough Sauvignon from New Zealand, no Oregon Pinot Noir, if the true believers believed *them*. The Mosses simply employed a champagne expert and told him to plant Chardonnay, Pinot Noir and Pinot Meunier as if he were planting vines back home. Then they told him they wanted to buy all the best champagne equipment. And then they told him they'd like him to show them how to make sparkling wine just like he did at home in Champagne. They planted their vines in 1988. In 1998 they won their award for best fizz in the world.

Maybe it's typical of the English that it took a couple of gutsy Chicagoans to prove that England is as good a place to make sparkling wine as Champagne – which is only 90 miles further south than Nyetimber, a couple of hours' drive from Calais. And their greatest gift was that they gave the English the confidence to believe they really could make great sparkling wine. The North and South Downs, which spread across Kent, Sussex, Surrey, Hampshire and Dorset are part of a ring of chalk and limestone called the Paris Basin. With global warming, southern England actually has warmer Septembers than Champagne does, even if our summer is cooler. But that's a good thing. As the world warms up, the champagne producers are very worried about plummeting acid levels in their grapes – good acidity is crucial for making fresh sparkling wine. But you have to be able to ripen your grapes. Since the 1970s, the sugar level in English grapes has virtually doubled. No wonder that in the 2010s, when I visited English vineyards, everywhere I went I heard that people from Champagne had just left. What were they doing? Admiring the view?

Nyetimber Manor once belonged to Anne of Cleves, the fourth wife of Henry VIII, and is one of the most tranquil wine estates I have visited anywhere in the world.

You've arrived in the fizz world when you create – and sell – a Prestige Cuvée which costs a lot of money. This one is named after the foundation date of the Nyetimber estate. Nyetimber has expanded its vineyards so that it now has over 350 hectares. Most are on Sussex greensand, but the latest plantings are on Hampshire and Kent chalk and are largely devoted to Chardonnay.

Leventhorpe wine from this northerly vineyard within the Leeds City Council limits used to be unremittingly gritty and raw. Not any more. Climate change means Leventhorpe whites are now delightfully scented and fresh.

The Olkiluoto nuclear power station in Finland, where they've been making wine since 2005. Tasting sample welcome.

2000s
MOST NORTHERLY VINEYARDS

Where will it all end? When I first discovered Yorkshire wine and marvelled at its gritty terroir, I thought no one will go further north than this to plant a vineyard.

Soon other vines started cropping up in Yorkshire, further north in Yorkshire, and then I found myself sitting in the evening sunshine, gazing out over the sands of Morecambe Bay and drinking a wine called Mount Pleasant. And I was sitting in the vineyard! But not Scotland, surely. Madness that way lies. Well, I suspect madness that way does lie for virtually everybody who gets involved in extreme vineyards. Why would you do it? What's wrong with a nice gaff in the South of France? The first guy who planted 48 vines on the Scottish mountain region of Tayside was South African, and, understandably, seems to have made himself scarce with no surviving tasting notes. But there's a tiny research vineyard of 0.09 hectares in Aberdeenshire. And a chap called Christopher Trotter in Fife hoped global warming would help his attempt to make fine wine there in 2014. He blithely said that his main problem was not lack of sunshine or the strong winds, but deer. I wonder if they said that in the Outer Hebrides, where someone has planted vines on the Isle of Lewis.

But these British Isles grape growers, intrepid though they may be, aren't even starters in the quest to make the world's most northerly wine. Germany thought it held the title for a while with vines on the island of Sylt, off Denmark. That's 55° North. But Denmark responded with a burgeoning vineyard culture of its own and over 100 vineyards. Latvia then claimed the most northerly title with a vineyard at 57° North. It grows an interesting array of grapes – Alpha, Zilga, Jubilejnaja Novgoroda and the tasty-sounding Skujins-675. I've checked with the world's greatest grape expert Dr José Vouillamoz. He knows every grape in the world. But not these. Actually, I have tried a couple of them – or were they Estonian? Filthy, anyway. And that was in Sweden, which has a thriving

50-plus vineyards in the south as well as claiming bragging rights with the Blaxsta vineyard west of Stockholm at 59° North. Is that enough?

Not quite. Norway squeezes in the Lerkekåsa vineyard in Telemark at 59°23'15" North. This is an area famous for apples and sour cherries. No winetasting notes, but you can rent a 'bed in a barrel' in the vineyard. Weird. Which leaves us Finland. I'm not joking. At 61°14'13" North, on Olkiluoto Island in the Gulf of Bothnia, they have a 0.1-hectare vineyard that gives a crop of 850 kilograms of Zilga grapes. It helps that it's next to the local nuclear power station and is kept warm by waste water coursing through the vines. But what a noble endeavour. And if there is a power cut in the Finns' long Arctic night, at least you won't lose your wine. It'll be the bottle glowing in the corner.

The Blaxsta vineyard west of Stockholm grows not only typically cold-climate grapes such as Vidal (shown here) but also the distinctly warmer-climate stars of Chardonnay and Merlot.

2000
SCREW CAPS

A lot of people may have one corked wine too many and say: That's it, I'm fed up with wasting my money, I'm going to start drinking wine with screw caps.

But we had 100 wines too many. I was judging wines in the Clare Valley in South Australia in 2000, and I began to think: Is it me or are there an awful lot of faulty wines here? I wasn't alone. The other judges were getting increasingly agitated. We were sending back 30 per cent of some wine styles because they were tainted by cork. When a wine is 'corked' it means that there's an impurity in the cork, often fungal in nature, that makes the wine taste flat at best and mouldy at worst. This affects some grape varieties more than others – particularly varieties that don't use oak-ageing to create extra flavours in the wine. Clare Valley's pride and joy was Riesling. It was being wrecked. And the winemakers, led by the incomparable Jeffrey Grosset, who had just been acclaimed 'Australian Winemaker of the Year', decided they would switch to screw cap. By 2001 they weren't alone. I was judging down in New Zealand. We were sending a ridiculous amount of Sauvignon, Semillon and Riesling back for cork taint. And the New Zealanders said the same: We've had enough, we're converting to screw cap.

Nowadays screw cap is not only completely accepted on most white and some red wines, it's positively looked for in wines like New World Sauvignon Blanc and Riesling.

But back then there was a sense that screw cap meant 'cheap'. It wasn't a new technology. It had been invented in England in 1889 – a guy called Dan Rylands patented it in Barnsley, Yorkshire. Presumably not for wine.

In 2004, Corbett Canyon, one of the largest US wine brands, converted all of its bottles to Stelvin screw-top closures.

A Swiss company called Hammel began using screw caps in 1972 because their delicate Chasselas wines were being destroyed by bad corks. South Africa and Australia were experimenting with screw caps during the 1970s – I've had 10-year-old South African examples in 330 ml bottles that were good, and Rieslings from Yalumba and Peter Lehmann in South Australia that were excellent at 20 years old.

But the experiments folded because the public still thought screw cap meant cheap. The declarations by the Australians, and then the New Zealanders in 2001, were perfectly timed. The New World was in the ascendant.

Fresh, bright wines were preferred over the indistinct, earthy wines of much of the Old World. New Zealand Sauvignon was a new superstar. If those guys said, 'We're switching to screw cap', an awful lot of the wine-drinking world was prepared to switch with them. The battle isn't won – many countries still prefer cork, both in Europe and the Americas. And some wines, particularly big reds, may well be better with good corks. But with those ice-bucket-chilled Sauvignons and Rieslings and Pinot Gris and Semillons – give me a screw cap any time.

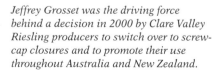

Jeffrey Grosset was the driving force behind a decision in 2000 by Clare Valley Riesling producers to switch over to screw-cap closures and to promote their use throughout Australia and New Zealand.

2001
ZINFANDEL

To hear some Californians talk about Zinfandel, you'd think that the grape was indigenous to California. Oh, isn't it? Didn't it make the original California wine? Didn't it slake the thirst of the 'forty-niners' in the Great Gold Rush? It's as Californian as the Golden Gate Bridge or the Hollywood sign. Except it isn't.

California doesn't have any indigenous wine grape varieties. Zin wasn't even the first grape variety to reach California – that was the Mission grape brought by Catholic missionaries during the 18th century. And actually, no one knows when Zinfandel got to California, or, to be honest, how it got to California. In fact, until recently no one actually knew what Zinfandel was.

But now we do know. California was a world centre for research into wine and vines throughout the second half of the 20th century. Massive amounts were learned about Cabernet and Chardonnay, Merlot and Pinot Noir. But there was always this gaping hole. People talk of Zinfandel as California's very own grape. But what is it? It didn't seem to be related to anything else in California, nor in France, where most of the Californian grapes emanated from. Spain? Italy? Ah, at last. A glimmer.

An American plant scientist – not a winemaker – tasted some wines from the Primitivo grape in Puglia, Italy's heel, during the 1960s, and thought they were just like California Zinfandel. He asked to see the Primitivo vines and thought they looked pretty similar too. So he arranged for cuttings to be sent to California and then planted next to Zinfandel. And by 1975, it was confirmed, Zinfandel is Primitivo.

Phew! Except the Primitivo wasn't actually an Italian grape. It had come from somewhere else; Primitivo was just a local name.

The Italians suggested that Primitivo had crossed the Adriatic from Dalmatia in southern Croatia and that it was the same as Plavac Mali. But it wasn't. They were related but they weren't the

Left: Ridge is California's most famous red Zinfandel winery, and Lytton Springs in Dry Creek is a famous old vineyard. Interestingly, in this vintage only 79 per cent of the wine is Zinfandel – 11 per cent being Petite Sirah and 10 per cent Carignane. This is the traditional 'field blend' of classic old California reds. Right: Sutter Home has always been a Zinfandel expert, helped by having access to some of California's oldest Zinfandel vines in Amador County in the Sierra Nevada Mountains. Nowadays they make a lot of other wines too, even including a sweet wine infused with blueberry and watermelon.

Crljenak Kaštelanski isn't quite as snappy a name as Zinfandel, but this is the real Zin, from the Dalmatian coast of Croatia – donkey and all.

same. Eventually it took an indefatigable bloodhound of a scientist named Carole Meredith, from the University of California, Davis, who, with some Croatian colleagues, combed Dalmatia's vineyards high and low, until in 2001 they found 10 old vines near Split that proved to be identical to Primitivo and Zinfandel. They were called Crljenak Kaštelanski. No wonder there were only 10 left. And then they found a couple of even older vines in another garden – yes, garden, not vineyard – near Split. They were also the same as Zinfandel. But called Pribidrag or Tribidrag, depending on whether the ancient owner had her false teeth in or not. So Zin is Primitivo, is Crljenak Kaštelanski, is Tribidrag … OK. Enough! But how did it get to California?

Well, we don't *know*, for sure. But what about this: Croatia used to be part of the Austro-Hungarian Empire. There was an Imperial Nursery collection in Vienna of all the varieties grown in the empire. Tribidrag would have been there. So would Zierfandler, a pink variety grown just south of Vienna. A nurseryman called George Gibbs brought a selection of vines from this collection to Long Island, New York, where he propagated them. A lot of them had long names, and I doubt if all the tags had stayed on during the voyage. 'Zierfandel', 'Zinfardel', 'Zinfindal', 'Zinfendal' – whatever. No one was going to be too bothered. Certainly not the Boston nurseryman selling black 'Zinfendal' grapes in 1832.

Certainly not the Californian Frederick Macondray or J W Osborne, who seem to have brought 'Zinfindal' to the West Coast of America from New England, nor William Boggs, the Sonoma grape grower who planted it, and sold cuttings. Ah. Did *they* bring Zinfandel to California?

Well, it might have been Antoine Delmas in Santa Clara County, because he brought some in from New England too. Or perhaps it was A P Smith from Sacramento – he'd got some nice 'Zeinfindal' growing. And Jacob Schram in Napa enthused about his 'Zenfenthal'. Who brought it in to California we're not sure, but it would have been one of those guys buying vines from the East Coast that originally came from Vienna's Imperial Nursery. And as to who finally decided to spell it 'Zinfandel' – well, it *may* have been a vinegrower called John Fisk Allen. But then…

2004
THE BERLIN TASTING

There comes a moment in every wine nation's development when it starts craving respect, craving recognition, craving an acceptance that its wines can be judged alongside the top wines of the world.

Usually it is poor old Bordeaux that is once again put up to be shot down, because her red wines are the most famous in the world, and they are based on grape varieties like Cabernet Sauvignon, Cabernet Franc and Merlot, which most new countries have a very reasonable chance of growing well. So a blind tasting is set up pitting Bordeaux's best against the young pretenders. And, of course, you need someone with the determination, the ego and the self-belief, firstly to strive to make wines at the absolute top level of quality, and secondly to place them in the public eye – as public as possible – and have them judged against the icons of the traditional wine world. California had Robert Mondavi. Australia had Len Evans. And Chile had Eduardo Chadwick of Viña Errázuriz.

Chile's need for vindication was slightly different from that of California or Australia. No one had accused these two of being dull – 'rustic', 'primitive', 'unsubtle', 'bumptious', 'brash' were the kinds of comments they had had to deal with, but not 'dull'. Yet Chile had somehow got branded as dull. A British writer had described Chile as the 'Volvo of the wine world' – by which he meant dependable, reliable, unexciting. Hey, I don't know what car he was driving, but a Volvo would have done me. It was a passing remark, but somehow it stuck. I thought it was unfair, because I wasn't having any difficulty uncovering amazing Chilean wines, but I think Chile did face a tougher battle to prove itself than California or Australia did. So Eduardo Chadwick planned a

Viñedo Chadwick comes from a classic gravelly vineyard in the area of Alto Maipo – long renowned as Chile's best Cabernet Sauvignon (and polo) region.

campaign. Not a single one-off tasting like the 1976 'Judgment of Paris', when Californian wines beat the cream of Bordeaux and Burgundy. He would take his wines around the world, relentlessly putting them up against the classics of Bordeaux, with the added spice of a super-Tuscan like Solaia or Sassicaia; as he became more confident, he'd go up against an occasional Californian interloper like Opus One, the joint venture between Robert Mondavi and Philippe de Rothschild of Mouton Rothschild.

And he put up his young pretenders for the first time in Berlin on 23 January 2004. He didn't stint on the opposition. Lafite, Margaux and Latour 2000, Margaux and Latour 2001. But the winning wine was Viñedo Chadwick 2000, from the Maipo Valley in Chile. Wine number two was Seña 2001, also Chilean, followed by Lafite 2000 and Margaux 2001. Buoyed by this frankly remarkable result, Chadwick set off round the world (to all his key target markets, admittedly). There weren't any tastings in San Francisco, or Sydney, Cape Town or Paris, for instance, but over the next nine years he held 21 tastings in places like São Paulo, Tokyo, Toronto, Beijing, Hong Kong, New York, Moscow and Stockholm – places where opinions needed changing and reputations could be made.

Invariably his wines did well, usually best. I was at the London tasting on 5 May 2009, and his wines did less well here than anywhere else; 2005s from Margaux, Lafite and Solaia took the top three places. I have to say, I felt there was still a bit of 'Volvo residual' sentiment in the room; London has an awful lot of Bordeaux freaks. But me? I put my top wine as Viñedo Chadwick 2006, despite being a massive fan of Bordeaux 2005. Some of the assembled judges told me rather sniffily that it couldn't be that good since it came from a re-planted polo field.

That's exactly the attitude that Eduardo Chadwick was striving to overcome by taking his Berlin tasting all round the world. I checked the soil profile of the old polo field. It's a classic stony alluvial terrace – a sort of South American version of Bordeaux's Médoc. It's just that in the 1940s, when Eduardo's father was captain of the Chilean National Polo Team, polo was more important than wine. The vineyard took over from polo in 1992. And in 2004, its wine changed the world's opinion of Chile's potential for good.

The Viñedo Chadwick vineyards are situated on the southeast border of Santiago, in the foothills of the Andes.

Just a couple of polo goalposts are left to show this was once a top-level polo field. Well, it's now a top-level Cabernet Sauvignon vineyard – the Viñedo Chadwick – and that soil profile of a stony alluvial terrace looks just about perfect to me for encouraging Bordeaux varieties to thrive.

2006
HIGHEST VINEYARD

I'd like to say I've tasted the wine from the highest vineyard in the world, but you never know with this 'highest' business.

Everyone was sure that the highest vineyard was in Bolivia. They do have vineyards at up to 2850 metres, so that wasn't a bad guess. Then rumours started to seep out about vineyards slowly clambering up the Himalayas – Bhutan seems to have one at about 2300 metres, and Nepal goes one better at 2750 metres. Then Tibet comes out with one at 3563 metres. Really?! Anyone tasted the wine? While I wait for a sample, I'll return to the Andes and Argentina, where Colomé has its main vineyard at 2300 metres, four or five hours on a dirt road high into the Andes near the Bolivian border. Its neighbour at Tacuil went higher. So Donald Hess, owner of Colomé, upped his game – first to El Arenal at 2500 metres and finally, another two hours' drive into the high wilderness to Rio Blanco, and Altura Máxima, the 'maximum height', a beautiful, isolated, 35-hectare vineyard, planted in 2006. And this remote patch of Malbec, Pinot Noir, and Sauvignon Blanc is at 3111 metres. And *this* is the wine I've tried – the Malbec, tasting like very ripe but sweet-sour wild cherries strewn with violets. If the Chileans have their way, they'll overtake Altura Máxima – their leading vines specialist Pedro Parra is trying to establish a vineyard in the Valley of the Moon at 3410 metres – but for now, I'm saying this is the highest whose wine I've verified, in any case!

In hot countries like Argentina, with very little respite from the powerful sun, and few vineyards anywhere near the cooling sea coast, going up the mountains is the only answer if you want cooler conditions. Australia is increasingly forced to do the same, and South Africa and Chile choose to because they see great quality possibilities. There's no doubt about that,

Colomé's Estate Malbec is already from some of the world's highest vineyards, between 2300 and 2500 metres, but this is bottle Number One from the 'Highest Vineyard' at 3111 metres.

Colomé's Altura Máxima vineyard, at 3111 metres, is the highest wine-producing vineyard in the world. 2011 was the first year they didn't get a spring frost – so they held a 'no frost' party. And yet aren't those cacti in the background?

but the exercise is fraught with danger. Frost is clearly the major risk. Frost at the end of winter, well into spring, possibly even in summer. And frost at the end of the season before the grapes have ripened. If you're not above the cloud line, you'll also risk cloud and rainfall when you crave open skies and sun.

But the positives, especially in a warming world, outweigh the negatives. In Argentina's Mendoza region, for instance, the heat means it's impossible to create scented, mouthwatering wines unless you go up the Andes. Every 100 metres you rise, it gets 0.6°C colder, and during the growing season, this heat loss may be as much as 1°C per 100 metres. Global warming has not only increased temperature, it has also increased the amount of carbon dioxide at higher altitudes, which makes it much easier for the vine to respire and photosynthesise in balance. Especially at lower latitudes – and Colomé is near the Tropic of Capricorn at 24° South – increased ultraviolet penetration aids photosynthesis, stimulates the aromatic precursors in the grapes, and thickens the skins with ripe polymerised tannins and really intense colours. This is helped by a massive difference of up to 20°C between day and night temperatures.

It's not just the New World that seeks altitude in its vineyards. Valley floors are usually fertile with very rich soil – great for cereals, no good for fine wine. So slopes have always been valued by quality-conscious growers. It depends how high you are brave enough to go. Already there are tales of vines at 2740 metres in Colorado, where they'd probably like a dip at the world record, and I've tasted some exciting, finely focused, high-altitude Colorado wines already. For a long time, Europe's highest vines were thought to be at Visperterminen, just below the Matterhorn in Switzerland. But these, it transpires, are at only 1100 metres. Sicily's Etna matches that, and Aosta in northern Italy does better at 1300 metres, but can't match the Troodos mountain vineyards of Cyprus at 1500 metres and maybe more (it's pretty wild up there) or what currently holds the European crown – Abona in the Canary Islands' Tenerife, flexing its muscles at 1600 metres.

2010
EXTREME ATACAMA

I woke up in the middle of the night. I couldn't breathe. My nostrils were stuck tight shut, my throat rattled as I tried to draw breath. I lunged for some water, and managed to moisten my throat just as the grim reaper crooked his finger in my direction. And I thought: How could anyone live here? How could anyone put in an eight-hour shift? Why would anyone live here?

More to the point: Why, and how, would anyone plant a vineyard here? Well, it was because of a vineyard that I was here, up on the edge of the Atacama Desert in northern Chile.

The wines didn't even have a name. But, wow, they had a flavour. A Sauvignon Blanc was as nervy and taut as a white wine could be, pithy, leathery, squirted with grapefruit zest, streaked with graphite. Extreme. A Syrah had an amazingly intense flavour of damson, lime, blackberry and leather, liquorice and Vicks VapoRub. And the alcohols were 12.5 per cent. Could I buy them? I doubt it. They'd made only 80 bottles of each.

These were the first experimental wines made in 2010 from Huasco, up on the fringes of the Atacama Desert. It hadn't rained there for 50 years. It probably wouldn't for another 50. The Atacama Desert was the driest place in the world. So why plant a vineyard there?

From my point of view – it was because the wines would have remarkable, unique flavours. There is a slightly more mundane reason. The owner of the vineyard was a bit of a baron – he owned 70,000 hectares of Huasco land, on a small proportion of which he'd planted olives. Olives and wine? Sounds good. Except, remember, this is the Atacama. It hasn't rained for 50 years. Your only chance of water comes from the Huasco River, the last dependable river before the desert devours the other snowmelt trails from the Andes. And the government won't issue any water rights in Huasco. Unless you're already there. This guy had previously bought 70,000 hectares of land just to get enough water rights to plant some olive groves. But he was prepared to give up a little of the water to help a single hectare of vines, then another five, and finally a vineyard of 13 hectares in an arid land that is all wind, sun, pale rubble and dust, vast open skies – and salt. Ah yes, salt. They literally have salt mountains here, thrown up from the salt-pan landscape. But salt and vines don't go, surely. No, they don't, unless you're prepared to embrace the extreme.

Not only is the land salty, but the water from the Huasco River is packed with minerals and unmistakably salty. But that's the only water there is to irrigate with. You have to use it. And paradoxically, you have to use as much of it as you can. Small frequent irrigation doses simply coat the vine roots in salt and the vine withers.

Long, intense irrigation sessions every two weeks wash all the encrusted salt off the roots, but of course add minerals and salt to the soil in a never-ending carousel. They tried using salt-resistant rootstocks – they proved to be the worst vines on the estate. No. This is an extreme area. The whole point is to make limited amounts of extreme wines. Otherwise, why not plant your vines somewhere easier? The Huasco vines are planted on their own roots, and the ones that survive this challenging environment are the ones that will express the soul of this place. For now, the Sauvignon, Chardonnay, Pinot Noir and Syrah have viscous textures; piercing acid, funky fruit flavours; a real insistent streak of minerals; and the lick of salt.

Oh, and the alcohols from this desert are only just over 12.5 per cent. With the help of sea fogs and cold nights, and maximum ripening period temperatures of 24–25°C, the fruit is balanced and ripe at 12.5–13 per cent. In a desert. Where it hasn't rained for 50 years and the irrigation water is halfway to brine. You should be growing raisins. But you're growing some of South America's most fascinating – if extreme – wines.

The first commercial releases from Tara Atacama. Note the no-nonsense names: White Wine 1, Red Wine 1, Red Wine 2. All three were produced and bottled by hand, hence the low yield. Only 409 bottles were released of the first white and only 487 of the first red.

2011
CHINA

I got to know a bit about Chinese wine rather earlier than my friends because I had a reputation as an intrepid, blind wine taster, willing to tackle any liquid of any form from anywhere. And in the 1980s there were few more exotic wines than those from China.

Actually, only two Chinese wines got to Britain – Great Wall and Dynasty – and it was usually Great Wall that was lurking in the brown paper bag as wild-eyed wine-lovers leapt from the shadows and cried, 'What's this?'. I always got it right. Not because I could taste the grape variety, the terroir, all that. But there was no wine that had such a lethal pong of my maiden aunt's mothballs. Naphtha. Those bottles could last 100 years, and maybe some will, because surely no one drank them.

But I also saw a different side of Chinese wine in the 1980s. I went there filming – mostly food stuff with some railways thrown in – and by nosing around I found some very attractive, bright, fresh Riesling and Chardonnay, grown in Shandong, south of Beijing, and some promising Cabernet Franc from the same area. This, I thought, should be the future, since these wines went beautifully with the various eastern Chinese cuisines. Yes, that may still be the future, but it isn't the present. Since my first visits, China has changed beyond all recognition, and one of the numerous signs of this progress has been the attitude to wine – both imported and home-grown. Imported wine has made more headlines as, for a few heady years, prices of top French wines – mostly red Bordeaux – went wild on the back of China's new-found passion for anything that could be construed as a symbol of wealth, elegance and success. A bottle of a leading Bordeaux – above all, Château Lafite, or any property connected with it – became a potent status symbol. Red is the colour of luck, red wine

I was as surprised as anyone when Jia Beilan won the Decanter Trophy for red Bordeaux varietals over £10. But it's good stuff, and bodes well for the future.

is good for your heart, and somehow that name Lafite just struck home. With current anti-corruption drives, Covid and general anxiety, the frenzy has cooled, but my Chinese friends expect Bordeaux to hold its place against Burgundy, Italy and others.

Home-grown wines changed dramatically with the liberalisation of the Chinese economy. I have to admit, on my trips to China I used to look in vain for many locals enjoying a glass, but the expansion of vineyards has been startling. China may already have the world's biggest plantings of Cabernet Sauvignon, as well as serious amounts of Merlot, Carmenère and Marselan. And it has some vast vineyards – one outfit in the northwest province of Xinjiang has a 10,000-hectare vineyard, and wineries to match. It's in the Turpan Depression, 80 metres below sea level, with hot dry summers and winters so cold the vines need to be buried to survive.

Vines need the same protection in Ningxia, south of Mongolia, where some of the best wines have originated. High-altitude vineyards are sprouting in Yunnan in the far south. But the most commercial activity is near Beijing, in Hebei and Shandong, where Château Lafite have a joint venture. And the giant is stirring. In

2011, Jia Beilan, a wine from Ningxia, won the Decanter Trophy for Red Bordeaux varietals over £10. In 2012, Château Reifeng-Auzias, a wine from Shandong, won the Trophy for Red Bordeaux varietals *under* £10. This one was based on Cabernet Franc.

And this was just the start.

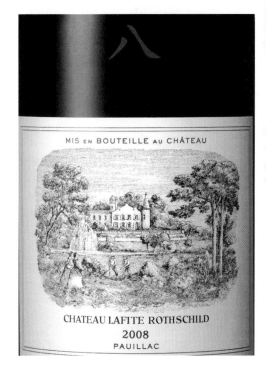

MIS ᴇɴ BOUTEILLE ᴀᴜ CHÂTEAU

CHATEAU LAFITE ROTHSCHILD
2008
PAUILLAC

Château Lafite Rothschild is the most sought-after Bordeaux wine in China. They didn't do themselves any harm by including the Chinese symbol for eight on the bottle of the 2008 vintage, since eight is lucky in China. Ostensibly it was to celebrate the establishment of a joint venture vineyard and winery in China; any beneficial effect on the Lafite price would be purely coincidental.

2014
FRAUD - RUDY KURNIAWAN

It's when they start finding fake bottles of Jacob's Creek, with words like Australia and Chardonnay misspelled, that the issue of fraud hits home for most of us. But sadly people have been counterfeiting and adulterating wine for as long as it has been bought and sold.

The Persians, the Greeks, the Romans – they were all at it. The Romans were adding gypsum and marble dust and lead and goodness knows what. The French were still at it 1500 years later. In Britain, a form of fraud was still legal until the country joined the European Union in 1973. There was an outfit in Ipswich that used to fill up a great vat with cheap gut rot red from the South of France and then sell it off – legally – as Beaujolais, Châteauneuf-du-Pape or Nuits-Saint-Georges; different labels, different prices charged, but the wine was all the same gut rot and it had nothing to do with Beaujolais, Châteauneuf-du-Pape or Nuits-Saint-Georges. And why? The same reason as ever. There was money to be made.

Wine laws have made it more difficult to cheat with the everyday stuff. But at the top end of the market it's a different matter. Trendy labels and those in short supply have an inflated value. At least with a knock-off Rolex watch or Louis Vuitton bag an expert can immediately tell the real from the fraud. But a large number of wine frauds are of old, rare bottles. Who really knows what these are supposed to taste like? The number of experts with such experience is extremely limited, but a large number of these trophy bottles are bought for reasons of ego and prestige by very wealthy people with little or no wine knowledge – often in places like Russia and China, where loss of face is no laughing matter. If they've been sold an expensive fake, they might prefer to keep quiet about it. And it is such markets that have been the breeding ground for fraud worth millions, worth tens of millions – worth hundreds of millions of dollars. We just don't know how much money is involved.

This double magnum of Château Petrus's fabled 1947 vintage looks genuine enough – but it isn't. It's a very good fake that was produced as evidence of fraud in Rudy Kurniawan's trial.

Certainly, if we take the two highest profile cases of the 21st century as examples, the money involved is probably hundreds of millions – especially if Hardy Rodenstock, a German who supplied the famous, but not genuine, Jefferson £105,000 bottle, and a talented counterfeiter named Rudy Kurniawan, who was convicted of wine fraud worth tens of millions in 2014, are anything to go by. Was Kurniawan really working as a lone wolf? Is there a whole network of counterfeiters coining big money from gullible millionaires round the world? Kurniawan was ordered to pay $28.4 million in compensation and made to forfeit $20 million in assets – this is just one guy! The feeling is that he produced many times more fakes than have been discovered and that they may be floating around for decades, and who will know? Kurniawan was really good at faking bottles, labels and corks. As for the flavours – I've had a few of the Rodenstock bottles from the 19th century and thought they tasted rather good, if on the young side.

Top properties like Château Petrus or Domaine de la Romanée-Conti now use secret antifraud processes on their bottles and labels. Restaurants are requested to smash empty bottles after the wine is drunk. But that won't stop magnums and double magnums of fabled vintages surfacing – and being bought – and, probably, being enjoyed.

The toolbox of the wine fraudster. Labels of old vintages of famous wines – which look a bit new but can be scuffed up – along with old corks and capsules ready to be reused, though altered where necessary.

NATURAL WINES

I love the disagreements that tasting wine entails. I love the discussions, the new insights, the alternative views and above all, perhaps, I love the way the wine bottle empties quicker when spurred by enthusiasm and debate. And at the end of it I always learn something from the other person's point of view.

Which is why the 'natural wine' movement used to trouble me. Now, if this is a movement, i.e., a groundswell of opinion, a surge wanting to do something in a manner different to the mainstream – I'm all for that. Bring on the discussions. But if it's an ideology, a dogma – I'm not so keen, not so keen at all.

So what is natural wine? Well, potentially, some of the best and most interesting wine on the planet, but also some of the least drinkable because nature will turn wine to vinegar if you let it. In simple terms, it usually involves organic or biodynamic grapes, and in the winery, a vinification with as little human or scientific intervention as possible. Indigenous vineyard yeasts, no enzymes, no sugaring or acid additions (sometimes in a really cold year, a little sugar may be needed to help the fermentation), no addition of cultured malolactic bacteria, and no preservatives – though sometimes a touch of sulphur dioxide may be used if there's a risk of the wine oxidising or turning to vinegar. And ideally no fining or filtration. All noble aims in a world where wineries can contain more and more reverse-osmosis machines, spinning cones, vacuum concentrators.... Sounds a bit industrial? It is. But an awful lot of top-notch wineries contain these machines. Supposedly they make the wine better.

Well, you can't fault its lack of old school seriousness. This is what they call a pet nat, a sparkling wine with almost no human intervention. Crown cap, flip it off, pour a frothy, probably cloudy, brew and whop it back. Feel ever so slightly intoxicated, but ever so slightly virtuous, too.

And here's the nub. What is better? All these machines can increase or decrease alcohol levels, deepen colours, massage textures and tannins – but don't they also denature wine? Well, yes, I think they do. But some people, including many of the most powerful wine critics and merchants, like the results. And we have to let them have their say. I might think that if the opposite approach, the natural way, can produce wines that are wild and challenging and unpredictable, that have different colours and textures and harbour flavours I'd never considered to be possible in a glass of wine – surely that's a better way. For some people, yes. But for many, no. Natural wine should not be a religion, it should be an aspiration that some talented winemakers can realise. Maybe the trouble is that 'natural' wine is too good a title. It claims all the moral high ground.

Now, natural wine certainly didn't start in the 2010s, but it was in the 2010s that more and more of us began to take them seriously, and stopped dismissing them as some radical lunatic fringe. That's because they got a whole lot better. And we became a whole lot more open-minded.

Frankly, there shouldn't have been such a fuss about 'natural' wines – people have been writing since Roman times about abuses in the creation of wine, and moaning about how difficult it is to find the real thing. 'Real' Falernian in Roman times was pretty rare. In the late 17th century the term 'natural' wine crops up, when compared to the various methods English vintners used to 'sophisticate' their wines (the English were notorious for this, right up until joining the European Common Market in 1973). In 1731 a famous dictionary defines 'natural' wine as 'such as it comes from the grape without any mixture or sophistication'.

Well, to be honest, all kinds of pretty terrifying additives and methods were used on wine until fairly recently, by no means all good for your health. The 19th century additives to sherry or red Bordeaux would put you off the stuff for life – if you survived that long. But the current fascination with 'natural' wine is more recent, and a reaction to far less deadly forces. After World War II it became possible to use chemicals to control weeds, insects and fungus in your vineyards. It also became possible to use

Natural activity in the vineyard is just as important as in the winery, and there is nothing more timeless than the sight of a vigneron and his horse quietly ploughing their vineyard rows. Even so, some of the natural wine proponents reckon that even ploughing interferes with the soil too much.

Vigno is an association set up to save the last remnants of old, dry farmed Carignan grapes in Maule, Chile. It's been a resounding success and these wines are some of Chile's most original.

cultured, industrially produced yeasts to give you a guaranteed result in your fermentation. Before then, weeds, insects and fungus were a recurrent nightmare for grape growers, and fermentations that wouldn't start, or wouldn't finish, or ended up with a liquid tasting like vinegar or cider were an annual nightmare for winemakers.

For most winemakers, the arrival of science and technology was a godsend. Suddenly your basic grapes could be made into decent wine. Cheap wine, in particular, became tasty and refreshing. But didn't it all start tasting the same? Well, to some extent, yes – it tasted clean and balanced and non-vinegary. That was a massive step forward for most of us.

But in the fields of the Loire Valley during the 1950s and in Beaujolais during the 1960s and '70s a resentment built up against this easy-come, easy-go type of wine. Particularly in Beaujolais where the industrially created 'happy juice' Beaujolais Nouveau completely took over from artisanal production. There was a famous 'Group of Four' I used to visit in Morgon who were probably the genesis of a modern 'natural' wine movement, and whose wines were intense and rich and ever-changing as they coursed down my throat. I loved them. But I also loved Beaujolais Nouveau. And I loved delving into the muddy fields of Anjou and tasting some frankly pretty bracing 'natural' stuff, but I also revelled in

The 'cool' side of natural. A rapper, a winemaker and one of Paris's leading wine merchants head off into the Auvergne hills, blend naturally made Gamay and Chardonnay together and label it as A La Natural Rouge.

the easy joys of Muscadet and Sancerre. It seemed to me the two different philosophies were completely compatible, doing entirely different jobs. And I still think they are. But in 2001 a ferocious article appeared in the *New York Times* excoriating the toxicity of most of the wines we drank. The writer was quickly joined by others sharing her pretty radical views. And by the 2010s there was a healthy ding-dong going on between those who swore by 'natural' wine and thus demonised the vast majority of wine drinkers, and those who said, 'Hey, hey, ease up. Why can't the two co-exist?'

To be frank, there was a reason to start shouting about the state of wine at the beginning of the 20th century. Most of it was becoming richer, softer, thicker in texture and losing any particular sense of place – even expensive wines. And people began putting the blame on chemical habits in the vineyard, numerous interventions in the winery, and manipulation of the style toward the lush and easy-going. Well, that's what people liked to drink!

The natural wine movement said that wasn't the point. Their grape growers respected the soil, often used horse- and hand-ploughing, never used chemicals on their vines, encouraged biodiversity and as far as possible let their grape juice ferment into wine pretty much all on its own. Well, this is fine, in small doses. But you don't make millions of bottles of Australian Chardonnay or Californian Cab or New Zealand Sauvignon, which will make millions of wine drinkers happy, like this.

And there's something else. An awful lot of natural wines, made with almost no human intervention, didn't taste good. They tasted sour and dirty. Being lectured as to how this was the way wine should taste, when I knew perfectly well that wasn't true, didn't go down well with me – or with many others for that matter. The 2010s were the decade when everything became less shrill, when each side started listening to the other, and when conventional grape-growing realised the importance of sustainability and conventional winemaking realised a lot of interventions *were* unnecessary. And natural wines became an awful lot better to drink. Suddenly an argument has become a discussion, preferably over a couple of bottles of wine, one 'natural' and one 'conventional'.

THE COLOUR
IS ORANGE

'Orange' wines, now made on every continent, from dozens of different grape varieties, and fermented in cement, oak, stainless steel and sometimes clay pots, are now sufficiently mainstream that I can order one at my local theatre bar.

Well, 6 January 2023 was the landmark day for me. I actually ordered an orange wine in preference to anything else on the list. I've tasted dozen upon dozen of orange wines, but faced with a list of Sauvignon and Assyrtiko, Chardonnay and Chenin and Chablis, I've never plumped for the orange one. Until 6 January, at the Old Vic Theatre in London, I put down my money for a Naranjo Moscatel, Torrontel and País blend from Maule in Chile. And this hazy, pale russet mouthful was exactly what I wanted.

I wasn't in the mood for Sauvignon. Red was a bit much for me. Rosé wasn't enough. I needed something different and that's what orange wine has been offering brilliantly for the last decade or so. Offering wines which have flavours and scents outside the normal repertoire – this one smelled of tamarind and tangerine peel, apricot skins and faded, damp blossom – but, above all, offering a texture quite different to white, pink or red wines. In particular, a chewiness, a bitterness, sometimes a dustiness a bit like a burr caught on your tongue out on a country walk, sometimes a muscularity that reminds me of the tarpaulin over our garden shed when I was a kid. You see what I mean about 'different'?

Why are they so different? Well, the simplest way of describing it is to say that orange wines are from white wine grapes but are made more like red wines than white wines. With white wines you might leave

Even England is getting in on the orange act. This is a delicious wine from Denbies in Surrey, a big operation who are always prepared to push the envelope.

the skins and the juice macerating together for a few hours, but mostly you press the grapes and straight away remove the juice from the remaining pulp and skins. You're usually very keen to avoid any bitterness from skins, pips or stems.

With red wines, it's the opposite. All the colour is in the grape skins, so is most of the aroma, and so are those bitter tannins which make your mouth water and your mind think feverishly of fresh-grilled beef ribs. Without tannins red wine doesn't work. So, you crush the grapes and then leave all the juice, skins, pips and, sometimes, stems to slosh about together, sometimes for days, and then you ferment them – all together. That's how you draw all the character, the colour and the bitterness out of the grapes.

Now the idea of orange wine is to use white, or maybe slightly pink varieties like Pinot Gris, and either macerate the juice and the skins together for a few days, or a few more days, a month or two, several months… By this time, the juice and the skins, and the pips and maybe the stems, will have fermented together, too. Just like red wines do. You will have drawn out quite different flavours from your white grapes, flavours and textures which most conventional winemakers really don't want. But orange wine isn't supposed to be conventional – though this was how they made wines, red or white, 8000 years ago, and they still do every year in Georgia, in earthenware pots called *quevri*.

The name of orange wine was actually coined by an innovative Edinburgh wine merchant in Scotland. He had discovered these curiously arresting, challenging, bitter sour skin contact wines being made in Georgia and also along the Adriatic region, mostly in Slovenia and Italy's Friuli region. They weren't white. They weren't pink. The skins and pips and oxidation had coloured them. They were a sort of amber-orangeish colour and since wines were classified by colour, he chose 'orange'.

Santorini is one of the most isolated and fascinating wine regions in Europe – on the island site of an old volcano. The Assyrtiko grape takes easily to the 'orange' treatment.

This is a great way to serve orange wine. The most 'natural' of them will be unfiltered and contain sediment. If you want to gaze at a brilliant golden wine like this Slovenian Ribolla, decant it and sit back for a moment as the rich liquid glints in the sunshine.

Nowadays, a more accurate description is 'skin contact', to describe the days, weeks, months where first the juice and then the wine from these white grapes stays in contact with the skins. Interestingly, Sauvignon Blanc, perhaps the best known of all our white wine grapes, makes a really exciting 'orange' style, and it lets you see the massive difference between the zesty, bright, citrous conventional Sauvignon wine, and the chewy, challenging, raw yet rich, scented yet sullen style of the 'orange' version.

So how has 'orange' wine managed to move from radical niche to a sort of hip mainstream? Maybe it's a generational thing. In the 2010s we had the millennials and more recently Generation Z saying, 'We're bored with the old mainstream styles of wine, we want something different, something we can "own"'.

'Natural' wines, with their whiff of authenticity and 'back to the future' anti-establishment aura, provided one source. And 'orange' wines, so different that most of us bred in the conventional world of whites, took years to finally appreciate them, were another perfect vehicle.

ORANGE
NATURAL WINE

VEGAN WINE - NO ADDED SUGARS
NO ADDED YEASTS - NO ADDED SULPHUR

MADE NATURALLY

You can't order this wine by mistake. It says 'Orange' in large letters on the label. It's natural, with no added anything.

HOW FAR CAN
THE UK GO?

Is 2018 when it really all began? Is 2018 the year when English and Welsh wines stepped up from being hopeful curiosities to the real deal? I think it probably was. For UK winemakers, climate change has transformed grape-growing for the better in many ways, but that transformation is not without its challenges.

2018 was the year when the summer never stopped. Golden July and August into golden September and balmy October. It was only halfway through November that we went from late summer to winter in a matter of days. Was this another false dawn, or were we really warming up at last?

We had been here before – 15 years earlier in 2003, and 27 years before that in 1976. Those are very long gaps to keep your optimism bubbling. Well, we needn't have worried. We thought 2018 was hot? 2019 was even hotter. It was Europe's hottest ever year. July 2019 was the world's hottest ever month. And Britain had its hottest ever day, 38.7°C in Cambridge, beating 38.5°C in Faversham in 2003.

But it wasn't all plain sailing. British grape-growing had been kept going all this century by reliably warm and fairly dry autumns. Yet in 2019, after a second scorching summer in a row, the heavens opened and we had one of the wettest ever harvests.

Never mind. 2020 came along. More records broken for heat, for dryness, for sunshine hours – if this was the new normal – three great summers in a row – there weren't many complaints. Three heatwaves and grapes coming in at never-before-experienced ripeness. One vineyard in Essex managed to produce a Pinot Noir red at 14.7% alcohol.

Danbury Ridge in Essex has become famous for producing probably the ripest Pinot Noir in Britain, and using them to make deep, rich, quite 'un-English' reds.

This is Ryedale in north Yorkshire. A generation ago you wouldn't have had many sunny days like this. But now the sun shines more often than not, and the grapes ripen more often than not.

Conwy Vineyard in north Wales uses sheep fleeces to deter pests, nourish the soil and reflect sunlight onto the vines. It's a brilliant idea and seems to work superbly. And north Wales does have a lot of spare sheep. There's been interest from New Zealand, too.

Unheard of. Three in a row. Can we make four? No. The year 2021 brought an old-fashioned, misery guts of an English summer – but September and October were warm enough to bring in a crop. And 2022? Well, you thought 2018 was good? 2022 was *too* good. Europe's worst drought for 500 years meant that vines in eastern and southern England suffered from lack of moisture. In England! It was so hot and dry that many of newly planted vines died. July only had 8% of the usual rainfall – the driest ever. And temperature records weren't merely bettered, they were battered. 2019's record UK temperature of 38.7°C was shoved aside by the first ever 40°C+ – 40.3°C. And that 38.7°C mark was officially beaten in 30 other UK sites. Unofficially? A vineyard in Essex recorded 42.2°C between the rows. Now. Does this look like the real deal. It sure does.

And clearly the Brits think so. The 2018 crop was the biggest – definitely – and the best – maybe – yet. Momentum kicked in – three million new vines were planted in 2019, between one and two million in 2020 and 2021, and another couple of million in 2022. The increase in planted vineyard land from 2010 to 2023 is approaching 400 per cent. So far, the majority of this has been in the well-established counties of Kent, Sussex and Hampshire with a late surge from Essex. But a report by Professor Alistair Nesbitt – and one of the great experts on British vineyards – reckons that we haven't even scratched the surface yet. We have 4000 hectares of vines so far and rising. Professor Nesbitt reckons that Britain has over 30,000 hectares of prime vineyard land, almost none of it so far developed.

And he goes further in another report published in 2022. He has been doing a lot of climate modelling, and he reckons that typical British temperatures during the growing season went up by 1°C in the 40 years to 2018. He predicts they will rise by a further 1.4°C in less than 20 years, to 2040. This means that vintages like 2018, greeted with disbelief at the time, will become normal. Great swathes of England and parts of Wales will have 2018 conditions – hot and dry – in up to 70 per cent of the next 20 years. And at the same time rainfall will decline in the East, the South and the West, though not in the South-East. East Anglia will explode in importance – it already has; England's ripest Pinot Noirs and Chardonnays are already coming from here, and new plantings are feverish. But there are numerous other areas he picks out which are so far largely undeveloped but full of promise. Suffolk, Cambridgeshire, Lincolnshire, the south Midlands, north-east and coastal south Wales, the Severn Valley, north Somerset and the coastal South-West. All of these will experience '2018' conditions again and again.

Of course, it won't be as simple as that. Climate change is causing events to occur in extreme ways that can knock the best plans sideways. And if we really are facing a 1.4°C rise in temperature before 2040, we should take heed of another respected academic, Professor Selley of Imperial College, London. He shows well-documented climate predictions that put the growing season temperatures rising by as much as 5°C by 2080 in the South-East. This would render the Thames Valley and considerable coastal areas from Norfolk right down to Cornwall, and up along the Severn Valley too hot for wine grapes. Only suitable for raisins, he says. That may be a bit extreme but it's entirely possible that we will be facing localised temperatures of this sort. Luckily Professor Selley is a geologist and is able to show that brilliantly suitable cretaceous chalk and Jurassic limestone soils (the same as those in Champagne and Chablis) sweep through England, right from the south coast to the north of Yorkshire. The dales and moors of Yorkshire and Derbyshire may be too high and cold now, but they won't be in 20 years' time.

And Scotland may at last have its day in the sun. Aberdeenshire is already surprisingly dry and has a vineyard, Dalrossach – not a big one, at 0.09 hectares, but it's there and experimenting with a host of varieties, many East European in origin. Yet the most intriguing idea is that the south-facing north shores of the great lochs will be coated with vines, just like the steep slopes of Germany's Mosel Valley are today.

Pommery is a famous brand of champagne. And now they have taken a dive into England and established a vineyard and winery in Hampshire. Taittinger have done the same in Kent. And they won't be the last.

2020
'CAN DU VIN' ANYBODY?

Wine no longer has to be in a bottle. Wine in Tetra Brik cartons and bag-in-boxes has been around since the 1960s but modern technology means that the quality has vastly improved. Wine in cans, pouches and even paper bottles is a 'must-try', and obviously appeals to the sustainability lobby.

Sir David Attenborough is one of many people who talk about the need for change. We go through climate change conventions pretty much every year now, and sometimes, not always, they come out with a bit more than just hot air and vague good intentions to show for their efforts. But when Sir David pronounces, we do listen. And in 2020, he thundered, 'The moment of crisis has come. We can no longer prevaricate.' And all over the country people began to recycle more, to check how much single-use plastic they were buying, to consciously cut down on their car use.

But we still almost always choose glass bottles for our wine. And they are still almost always green glass, which is recyclable, but which there is too much of in any case, so most of it goes into the hardcore base of new roads.

Why don't we want to change the containers we buy our wine in? Nearly every other beverage has embraced alternatives to glass bottles. When was the last time you bought fruit juice or milk in a glass bottle? But we stubbornly stick to the glass bottle for wine. Now, this may make sense for a wine which is intended for long ageing – no one has yet found a better medium and wine connoisseurs enthuse about wines from glass bottles in wonderful condition at a century old.

But hardly any wine is made for long ageing. And hardly any of us ever buy such wine. Most of us buy wines to drink within 24 hours which are contained in a glass bottle which lasts for years. The use of screwcap closures which are a virtually hermetic

New brands of canned wine are tumbling over themselves to attract our attention. Some of them are fresh, fruity crowdpleasers and others are more serious mouthfuls – all served up in bright, attractive, easy-to-carry, easy-to-open, easy-to-drink cans. The future beckons.

seal means that even a cheap bottle of wine can stay good for an unfeasibly long time. Are we still victims of an insidious wine snobbery? Would we accept our regular wine being served from a keg or a bag-in-box, or paper bottle? Or maybe a plastic bottle made out of all the discarded rubbish which is the curse of oceans worldwide?

Or maybe, if we still feel the urge for glass, we could reuse the bottle, we could refill it. In the old days, that's what the brewers used to do with their beer bottles. And Barton Family Wines, who make some of France's longest-lived wines at Château Léoville-Barton in Bordeaux, have launched a wine brand from their extremely high-quality neighbouring property, Château Mauvezin Barton, called 225 which is sold as a refillable bottle. They say the bottle can be reused 30 times before being recycled. The trouble is – will we, the wine consumers, support the idea? So far, only 20 per cent of people who buy the 225 brand return the bottle to be refilled.

And almost every attempt to create an environmentally friendly package is still running into our stubborn fondness for old-style glass bottles. Take heavy bottles. Some bottles weigh more when they are empty than a typical bottle full of wine. I've got two bottles in front of me: the full bottle of Chilean Sauvignon weighs 1.177 kilograms, the empty bottle of Spanish red wine weighs 1.286 kilograms. Madness, surely. Yet there are consumers who absolutely refuse to accept lighter bottles. To them, heaviness equals quality. Even in a country like Britain, we are nervous about light glass bottles. We pick them up and our immediate response is, there's less wine in the bottle. And I do sympathise. A typical 750ml bottle of wine made of less and lighter glass feels more like a 500ml bottle of wine. We think we are getting less wine.

This is exactly the same shape as a bottle, but a fraction of the weight of a glass one, and gives the chance to print your marketing and brand image over the entire surface.

Well, we are going to have to deal with this. It would help if all the well-established wine brands would champion alternative packaging, but they stick resolutely to what they know works. Until the consumer is prepared to change, big business won't do it for us with their profitable brands. But *new* brands – that's different. The recent change in attitude toward general sustainability has been nothing short of remarkable, and you could call it a silver lining in the black clouds of Covid-19 and Putin's war. New brands, launching now, would have to be more sustainable, surely? Why would you use glass, which can be up to 70 per cent of the carbon footprint of a bottle of wine?

And there are alternatives. Cans, for a start. Anyone lucky enough to be flying First Class Virgin Atlantic is in for a shock. They serve 'The Uncommon' English wines in cans. What? In First Class? But cans aren't serious. Exactly. Most of the times we want a glass of wine aren't serious events either. Hey, a *glass* of wine? With a can you don't need a glass. Slurp it from the can, in the park, on the train – or in Virgin First Class, just as you would a Beavertown Neck Oil Beer or a ready mixed G& T. And cans are 100% recyclable. Again and again. Eighty per cent less carbon footprint than glass. If Glastonbury can ban glass at its Festival, surely we can all give cans a go. The supermarket Waitrose obviously thinks so. On 15 January 2023, they replaced their small glass bottles of wine with cans.

What about paper bottles? A bottle that's exactly the same shape as a glass bottle, but is made of paper. My first experience of them a couple of years ago wasn't great. The screwcap was tight and I twisted off the whole neck. But that was then. Now the screwcap isn't so tight, the entire paper bottle is printed out with whatever message the producer wants, and the whole process emits one-sixth of the carbon used in creating and transporting a glass bottle.

And I've got a Zoom tasting New Zealand wines coming up next week. The wines will be delivered to me in light, laminated pouches. They'll be as fresh as from a glass bottle and their carbon footprint will be barely noticeable.

2022
FIRE AND SMOKE

From Chile to the Cape, from the heart of Napa and Sonoma in California, to historic wine regions in Australia, vineyards all over the world are being devastated by wildfires. Removing the effect of smoke taint on grapes is a serious problem for winemakers affected by these fires.

It hit home in 2023 when my neighbour said, 'Oh, we could barely breathe when we opened the windows, the air was so acrid.' I'd only asked her how she'd enjoyed her trip home to Vancouver in late 2022. Well, she was telling me. And 'not much' was her answer. The reason? Smoke. I know Vancouver, out on Canada's West Coast and have always thought of it as a magical city, ideally placed between the mountains and the Pacific Ocean – and definitely blessed with pure, breathable air.

Not any more. My neighbour said that her eyes watered all day, her clothes smelled of ash and wood smoke when she returned to London, and sometimes the smoke was thick enough she wanted to choke when she drew breath. What is going on?

Well, it's our 'old' – or should I say 'new' – friend climate change at work again, causing an annual scourge of wildfires and bush fires worldwide. And while it's making ordinary citizens' lives pretty miserable along much of the West Coast of America, it's now having an increasingly serious and regular effect on the flavours of the wines, not just in North and South America, but also in South Africa, Australia and even Europe.

And you only have to keep the most casual eye on the news to know that these fires are becoming more frequent and are spreading far wider, often at alarming speeds, whipped into a frenzy by powerful winds that turn a manageable forest fire into a vicious beast which destroys everything in its path. And that includes vineyards. Until 2017 I had heard tales of vineyards suffering from wildfires but I didn't know these vineyards. It's different now in 2023, I *do* know these vineyards and wineries, in prime positions in the USA, in

A shocking image of the Glass Fire raging in the hills above Saint Helena in California's Napa Valley in September 2020. Famous wineries like Newton were burnt to a cinder as the flames roared through. The fire raged for three weeks and did massive damage as well as the billowing smoke affecting areas far away from the actual inferno. Terrifying, and it will happen again.

Chile, in South Africa, in Australia and even in France. The fires are now reaching into the very heart of Napa and Sonoma in California (the Glass Fire of 2020 destroyed over 27,000 hectares of land, including famous wineries like Newton). It's the same in the states of Victoria, New South Wales and South Australia, and in the winelands of the Cape.

When these furious fires hit your estate or winery, its land and undergrowth having been dried into tinder by severe droughts which are now some of the worst for 500 years, you can expect to lose your vines and your stock of wines, and if you don't move fast, your life.

But the effects of the billowing blankets of smoke spread much further. If you were upwind of the fires, your grapes could be sweet and clean almost next door. But if you were downwind, that's a different matter. One of the challenges of modern wild fires is that they are being fanned by unprecedented winds. So their smoke may be shoved hundreds of miles away from the actual fires. My friend in Vancouver was probably suffering the effects of fires way south in the US states of Washington and Oregon, and maybe even California because the mountain ranges on the West Coast run south–north and the air currents suck the smoke northwards as if in wind tunnel.

When Tolpuddle, Tasmania's leading Pinot Noir winery, didn't release a 2019, it was because smoke from fires over 100 kilometres away had been blown into their vineyards. The winemaker was heartbroken when he tasted his ferments and said, 'Dammit, there's smoke taint. We can't release the wine.' And they didn't.

Now, 'smoky' is a term I've often used in wine judging. Some varieties like Shiraz often seem to taste a bit smoky – and all the better for it. If you use oak barrels that have been heavily toasted on the inside to create a chocolaty richness, I'll often describe the wine as 'smoky'. Whiskies and brandies are often 'smoky'. And smoking foods such as fish and meat has a long, illustrious history of providing us with delicious delicacies to eat. So is smokiness in wine such a bad thing?

Well, there is smokiness and smoke taint. I don't think I'm an expert on smoke taint yet, but increasingly judges at wine shows are questioning whether a wine is 'smoke tainted'. I thought fermentation should get rid of smoke taint on the grape – it gets rid of a lot of other unwanted flavours – but it seems that smoke from wood fires contains volatile phenols that can penetrate the grape skins. The Australians say it make take as little as half an hour of exposure to taint the grapes. Their juice may taste fine, but the fermentation and the maturing process can release flavours you hadn't spotted at the point of picking them. Suddenly, from nowhere, your wine is tainted.

There are various scientific methods like reverse osmosis which claim to be able to separate out the smoke flavour. But so far most winemakers admit these methods also remove far too much of the wine's actual character. Some tainted wine might get poured down the drain – but not much. There are now millions of litres of smoke-tainted wine being blended away each year. We've probably all had some. It didn't kill us, and maybe we even liked it. Maybe smoke is just one more example of nature putting its thumbprint on this human invention of ours called 'wine'.

GLOBAL WARMING – HOW WARM IS WARM?

Olivier Bernard is the thoughtful owner of Domaine de Chevalier, one of Bordeaux's best wine properties. In the middle of 2022, he pronounced 'Global warming has been good for Bordeaux'!

Olivier Bernard also said, 'In the last century it was always the rare "warm" years that had achieved great vintages.' But in the last seven years, he went on to say, Bordeaux had achieved five great vintages – 2015, 2016, 2018, 2019 and 2020. If he had held on for another couple of months, he could have added another – 2022. Six great vintages in eight years. 'I have never', he said 'seen that in all the history of Bordeaux.' But then he added, 'The worst is in front of us.'

Monsieur Bernard was putting into words what a lot of us have felt in northern Europe and maybe parts of northern America, too – that global warming has been pretty good for us so far. But should we stop glibly using that term 'global warming'? As we in northern Europe look up into bright blue skies and endless sunny days we need to rethink our terminology. 'Climate Change' – of course. But that sounds almost pedestrian, easy to control, easy to corral into the right direction. Why don't we call it 'Climate Chaos'? Yes, that might shift us out of our complacency.

So what has Climate Chaos been up to in 2022? One-third of Pakistan was submerged by flood water, displacing millions and killing thousands. That's global warming. That's climate chaos. Hurricane Ian was one of the most relentless and destructive hurricanes ever to hit North America's East Coast. It caused $65 billion worth of damage in Florida alone. It may not feel like it as you stand shivering in the washed-out ruins of your home, but that's global warming for you. That's climate chaos.

Now let's go back to the vines. In 2017 Europe was battered by springtime frosts so severe that France declared 2017 its most

A Bordeaux vineyard stricken by spring frosts. Ironically, global warming makes these frosts more likely, since a warm start to spring means the vines bud too early.

damaged vintage since World War II. Hey, just wait. In 2021 the March temperatures in France were the hottest since 1947. So the vines budded like mad, and then springtime frosts arrived again, and reached south to Italy and Spain, and devastated regions which hadn't seen frost for more than a century. Crops were decimated, livelihoods destroyed by the vicious freeze. Then it rained. In buckets. And mildew arrived. Rampant. There's your global warming at work again. The worst icy frost in a generation, the rain, the mildew, the hail – that's global warming.

And if you think conditions eased up in 2022 – no, they didn't. Places like Chablis still got clobbered by frosts, but most peoples' problems were different to this. In 2022, Europe was suffering its worst drought for 500 years. Burgundy has records going back to 1354, and the climate is now the hottest and the driest it has ever been (though they admit that 1540 and 1473 were pretty hot and dry). The River Po, a massive river, dried up in Italy, as did the Loire, another massive river, in France. The Rhine in Germany became so low that boats and barges ran aground.

Oh, and how did France get on with 2022? Well, drought from January, so soils were critically short of moisture. April, as usual – frost – frankly nowadays, with warm winters and dry soils leading to early budburst on the vines – some areas are frosted more often than not. May? Well, there's still no rain, so the crops are dehydrating on the vine, and then in June hailstorms with hail as large as golf balls, sweep across the country – not little showers but big, angry fronts of hail, miles wide. Then the drought returned, with heatwaves lasting between seven and 10 days as against the more usual two to three. Then more hail.

Isn't there any good news here? Well, yes there is. 2022 has turned out to be a smashing vintage in France and in much of Europe. Not an easy one. There were challenges all the way, the kind of challenges that used to come once a generation are now coming thick and fast more years than not. But not only are grape vines showing that they can adapt to heat, but grape growers and winemakers are falling over themselves to make changes in the vineyards and in the wineries. Old grape varieties from around the Mediterranean basin often abandoned for being too difficult to ripen are now enthusiastically rediscovered. Classic regions are questioning whether they will have to change their permitted grape varieties to more heat- and disease-resistant ones. Bordeaux started looking at 52 possible new varieties as long ago as 2009, and has recently agreed to allow six heat-resistant varieties – including Touriga Nacional from Portugal's blindingly hot Douro Valley. Champagne has just validated a grape called Voltis because of its extreme resistance to fungus and mildew. The Champagne house Charles Heidsieck is already planting it.

And if you really want a good news story, look further north, to Belgium. The Aldeneyk winery whose vineyards straddle the river Meuse along the border of Belgium and the Netherlands says its conditions are now drier than those in Piedmont, in north Italy. Denmark now has 20 wineries and over 100 vineyards. Sweden has more than 50 vineyards – and the wines are good. I have a bottle of Vittsjö white on my tasting bench right now. And Norway? Predictions were that Norway would get its first vineyard in 2050. Well, it's got 15 vineyards already and has even started producing Riesling wine.

Hawkes Bay, on New Zealand's North Island East Coast, is well used to rain at vintage time. But not like this. Cyclone Gabrielle arrived in March 2023 in ferocious mood. Rivers cascaded over their banks, roads were washed away, rail tracks ripped from the track bed and vineyards completely submerged in soupy, brown, muddy floodwater. And vintage was just about to start. Hawkes Bay has coped with extreme weather often enough, but this was far more destructive. Will it happen again? Almost certainly.

INDEX

Page numbers in *italic* refer to illustrations.

ACKNOWLEDGEMENTS

We are committed to respecting the intellectual right of others. We have therefore taken all reasonable efforts to ensure that the reproduction of all contents on these pages is done with the full consent of the copyright owners. If you are aware of unintentional omissions, please contact the company directly so that any necessary corrections may be made for future editions.

The publisher wishes to thank the following for kindly supplying the images that appear in this book:

Adrian Webster: 251 (below). Alamy: 41, 72, 91. Amfora: 245 (middle). Barboursville Vineyards: 215 (above). Bassermann-Jordan: 203 (left). Beaulieu Vineyard: 146. Bell'agio: 69. Blaxsta Vingård: 266. BNPS: 151. Bodega Catena Zapata: 258, 259 (both). Bodega Colomé: 274, 275. Brancott Estate: 227 (middle). Buena Vista Winery: 110. Bürgerspital Würzburg: 40. Calera Wine Company: 193 (left). Canned Wine Company: 301 (above left). Casa Vinicola Zonin S.p.A.: 213. Castillo de Perelada: 167. Les Caves de Pyrène: 287. Celi Wine, Cantina Goccia: 302. Cephas Picture Library: 55, 71, 101 (both), 114, 150, 158, 161, 251 (above), 264 (above), 294. Château La Conseillante: 164 (right). Château Duplessis: 155 (below). Chateau Haut-Batailley 86. Château Haut-Brion: 104. Château Lafite Rothschild: 105 (far left), 283. Château Latour: 105 (second from right), 153 (left), 164 (left). Château Léoville Barton: 107 (right). Château Margaux: 105 (second from left), 106. Château de Marsanny: 36. Château Montelena Winery: 217 (below). Château Mouton Rothschild: 105 (far right), 135, 136. Chateau Musar 245 (left). Château Pichon Longueville: 107 (middle). Château Pichon Longueville Comtesse de Lalande: 107 (left). Château Le Pin: 229 (middle). Château Ste. Michelle: 187. Château Talbot: 39. Château Valandraud: 250. Concha y Toro: 165 (left). Corbett Canyon Vineyards: 267. Corbis: 127 (above), 147, 183, 220, 257. Corena Hodgson: 311. Danbury Ridge: 296. Denbies Wine Estate: 292. Dom Pérignon: 66. Domaine la Croix Chaptal: 90. Domaine de la Romanée Conti: 153 (right). Dr Konstantin Frank Vinifera Wine Cellars: 171. Du Toitskloof Wines: 173 (left). Duckhorn Winery 165 (right). E. & J. Gallo Winery: 176, 177, 178.

Gai'a Wines: 293. Gaja: 190 (right). Getty Images: 2, 8, 21 (above), 27, 31, 54, 64, 113, 127 (below), 205, 235, 285, 286, 305. Gibbston Valley Wines: 236. Greek Wine Cellars: 196. Grosset Wines: 268. Gwinllan Conwy: 297 (below). Hanzell Vineyards: 193 (right). Harlan Estate: 229 (right). Harveys: 47 (left). Henschke 245 (right). Herederos del Marqués de Riscal: 116, 117 (right). Hugh Johnson: 249 (above). Inniskillin: 253, 255. iStock: 309. Jamsheed Wines: 16. Jia Beilan: 282. Joachim Flick: 98. Justino's, Madeira Wines, SA: 57. Kanaan Winery: 244. Klein Constantia: 61, 63 (both). Laithwaites Wine: 52, 241 (above), 295. Lea & Sandeman: 96. Le Dome: 108. The Liberator: 301 (above middle). Lindeman's: 93 (left), 94, 227 (left). Louis Jadot: 87 (left). Louis Roederer: 144 (left). Malamatina: 195. Marchese di Barolo: 95. Marchesi Antinori Srl: 190 (left). Marks & Spencer: 204. Marqués de Murrieta: 117 (left). Mas de Daumas Gassac: 154. McCann Vilnius: 181 (above). Metropolitan Museum of Art: 21 (below), 22, 34, 77. Miss Vicky Wine: 301 (above right). Mucha Trust: 169. Musée d'Orsay, Paris: 120. Nice Drinks: 301 (below right). Nyetimber Vineyard: 262, 263. NZWines: 232. Opus One Winery: 222, 223. Orange County Archives: 133. Oz Clarke: 141 (both), 142, 198. Paperboy Winery: 173 (right). Penfolds: 93 (right), 159 (both), 227 (right). Pernod Ricard Winemakers: 231. Perrier- Jouët 143. Petrus: 229 (left). Piper-Heidsieck: 144 (right). Pol Roger: 126. Pure Wines: 290. Quinta do Noval: 139. Ridge Vineyards: 270 (left). Robert Mondavi Winery: 185. Royal Tokaji Wine Company: 247. Ryedale Vineyards: 297 (above). Schloss Johannisberg: 83. Sichel: 199. Shutterstock: 45, 59, 85, 181 (below right). Small Things: 301 (below middle). Sogrape Vinhos, S.A.: 149. Stag's Leap Wine Cellars: 217 (above). Sutter Home Winery: 210, 211, 270 (right). Tapanappa Wines: 241 (below). Tenuta San Guido: 189. Tom Ballard & Eyrie Vineyards: 209 (above). Torres: 174, 175. The Uncommon: 301 (below left). V&A Images: 79. Vega Sicilia: 129. Viña Ventisquero: 281. Vignadores de Carignan, Vigno: 289 (below). Viñedo Chadwick: 273, 275 (both). Vranken Pommery: 299. Weingut Prager: 87 (right). Wellcome Images: 121. Williams & Humbert: 47 (right). Willamette Valley Archival Photos – Eyrie Vineyards, Jason Lett: 209 (below). Yellow Tail: 200.

ABOUT THE AUTHOR

Oz is one of the world's leading wine experts, known for his phenomenal palate, irreverent style, accurate predictions, and enthusiasm for life in general and wine in particular. He is the author of many award-winning books on wine.

Before wine took over his life in 1984, Oz was a full-time actor and singer, appearing in West End hit shows and touring with the Royal Shakespeare Company.

Alongside his entertaining television and radio broadcasts, including *Food and Drink*, *Oz and James* with James May and *James Martin's Saturday Morning*, he presents a series of concerts, Drink to Music! with the acclaimed Armonico Consort. Oz is also sports mad. He was awarded an OBE in 2020.